THE
NYORO STATE

Mukama seated on royal stool: *c.* 1936

THE
NYORO STATE

BY

JOHN BEATTIE

WITHDRAWN

The Catholic
Theological Union
LIBRARY
Chicago, Ill.

OXFORD
AT THE CLARENDON PRESS
1971

Oxford University Press, Ely House, London W. 1

GLASGOW NEW YORK TORONTO MELBOURNE WELLINGTON
CAPE TOWN SALISBURY IBADAN NAIROBI DAR ES SALAAM LUSAKA ADDIS ABABA
BOMBAY CALCUTTA MADRAS KARACHI LAHORE DACCA
KUALA LUMPUR SINGAPORE HONG KONG TOKYO

© OXFORD UNIVERSITY PRESS 1971

The Catholic
Theological Union
LIBRARY
Chicago, Ill.

PRINTED IN GREAT BRITAIN
AT THE UNIVERSITY PRESS, OXFORD
BY VIVIAN RIDLER
PRINTER TO THE UNIVERSITY

Habw'Abantu ba Bunyoro–Kitara

PREFACE

I CARRIED out my field study in Bunyoro for about twenty-two months during 1951–3 and 1955, mainly with the support of the Treasury Committee for Studentships in Foreign Languages and Cultures, London (the 'Scarbrough' Committee). I am happy to acknowledge once again the Committee's generosity and tolerance. I have given elsewhere an account of the conditions I worked under and the methods of research I used while in Bunyoro (Beattie 1965). Like most of my generation of social anthropologists, I lived in, and as far as possible as a member of, the communities I studied: after the first six months or so I worked almost wholly through the Nyoro language, and I obtained information by observation, interviews (mostly informal and 'unstructured'), the collection of texts, and, in a few contexts, but only during the later stages of my field-work, the use of questionnaires.

Also during these later stages I engaged locally a few research assistants, though never more than two at a time, and without their help my findings would be even more exiguous than they are. Messrs. Perezi Mpuru and Lameki Kikubebe, both, alas, now dead, were young men of outstanding ability and with a genuine interest in their own culture. I owe much, also, to Messrs. Edward Byaruhanga, Michael Bahandagana, Yasoni Isoke, and H. K. Bakanoba.

I should also acknowledge the help of the then Mukama of Bunyoro, Sir Tito Winyi Gafabusa IV, C.B.E.; without his co-operation and his tolerance of an inquisitive stranger in his country, my work in Bunyoro would have been impossible. I received much willing assistance, too, from many of his senior officials, past and present, especially Messrs. John Nyakatura (the distinguished Nyoro author), Petero Rwakaikara, and Laurenti Muganwa. Many of the county, sub-county, and 'parish' chiefs took much time and trouble to answer my sometimes impertinent questions, and I received special help from Mr. Ernest Kwebiha, then sub-county chief of Mutuba IV, the area in southern Bunyoro where I began my field research.

I and my family also received much assistance and many
kindnesses from the officers of the Uganda Protectorate Administration of that time, and their wives, also from the representatives of the Church Missionary Society (now the Native Anglican
Church) at Bunyoro's capital, Hoima. I am also greatly indebted to the then director (Dr. Audrey Richards, C.B.E.) and
fellows of the East African Institute of Social Research at
Makerere University College, Kampala. Although for the
greater part of my time in Bunyoro I was not officially associated
with the Institute, they provided me generously with both
hospitality and intellectual stimulus. In more recent years
Sir Archibald Dunbar, M.A., then agricultural officer in Uganda
and the author of *A History of Bunyoro-Kitara*, has put me in his
debt by his kindness in providing me with information about
events in Bunyoro since Independence.

In Oxford my major obligation is to Professor E. E. Evans-
Pritchard, without whose early support and encouragement I
should not have become a social anthropologist, nor have had
the opportunity to go to Bunyoro. I am also indebted to Dr. John
Peristiany, Professor I. Schapera, F.B.A., Dr. H. Meinhard,
Dr. A. I. Richards, C.B.E., F.B.A., Dr. R. G. Lienhardt, and
Dr. R. Needham, all of whom have at various times read and
commented helpfully on earlier drafts of some parts of this book.
I am especially grateful to Dr. M. Southwold for his valuable
criticisms of a draft of Chapter 11. Belated though this book's
appearance is, it is unlikely that it would ever have been written
at all but for the continued generosity of the Center for Advanced Study in the Behavioral Sciences, Stanford, California,
where I not only held a fellowship during 1959–60, but was
granted a further term of hospitality in 1966–7.

All social anthropologists are indebted to their predecessors
in the field, where there have been any, and of the various works
relating to Bunyoro which were of particular use to me (all
of them are listed in the Bibliography) the missionary-anthropo-
logist John Roscoe's book *The Bakitara or Banyoro*, published in
1923, served as an indispensable base-line for my own researches.
Although it was based on only a brief visit to the country and
contains numerous errors there is much of interest and importance in it, and it is still an essential source for the student of
Bunyoro.

However, my greatest obligation is to the people of Bunyoro of all classes, whose patience, tolerance, good humour, and, often, friendship not only made my work possible, but also made my stay in their country one of the most pleasant periods of my life. In the hope that what I have written here and elsewhere may be of some interest to them and to their children after them, I dedicate this book gratefully to them.

Some of the material presented here has previously been published, mainly in article form. But all has been extensively revised and for the most part completely rewritten for the present work and I have incorporated a good deal of hitherto unpublished data. None the less I should like to thank the following for permission to use in revised form work originally published by them: Messrs. Holt, Rinehart, and Winston, New York (Beattie 1960a, chapters 1–4); Messrs. Faber and Faber, London, and the East African Institute of Social Research, Kampala (1960b); and the editors of the *Journal of African Administration*, now the *Journal of Local Government Overseas* (1954 a, b), of *Africa: Journal of the International African Institute* (1959), of *Civilisations* (1961a), and of the *Journal of African History* (1964a).

JOHN BEATTIE

Oxford

CONTENTS

LIST OF PLATES

The Frontispiece and Plates 2 and 3 are from photographs by the late Dr. A. T. Schofield, and were originally published in *The Uganda Journal*. I am grateful to Mrs. Zebiya Rigby, of Makerere University College, for obtaining prints of them for me from the Archives Division of the Makerere University College Library, and to the Library authorities for permitting me to use them. Plate 1 is from a photograph by Hunting Aerosurveys Ltd., and first appeared in Beattie 1960a. Plates 5 and 6 are from photographs by the Uganda Protectorate Department of Information.

LIST OF MAPS

Map 1 first appeared in Beattie 1960a. Map 3 is from J. H. Speke, *Journal of the Discovery of the Source of the Nile*, 1863. Map 4 is from *Uganda: Report of a Commission of Privy Counsellors on a Dispute between Buganda and Bunyoro* (the 'Molson Report'), Cmnd. 1717, HMSO, London, 1962, by kind permission of the Controller of H.M. Stationery Office.

LIST OF FIGURES

1

INTRODUCTION

ON 9 September 1862 the first Europeans to reach Bunyoro, Captains J. H. Speke and J. A. Grant, arrived at the court of the Nyoro king Kamurasi. A little over one hundred years later Uganda became a Republic, and on 8 September 1967 the Prime Minister, Mr. Obote, signed an Order abolishing the four Bantu kingdoms of Uganda, of which Bunyoro was one. By this act he brought to an end four interrelated African monarchies, whose dynastic histories stretch back for several centuries, and whose origins are lost in the mists of traditional history and legend.

So this book is in a sense a requiem. The state which it describes no longer exists, except in the measure in which it is 'incapsulated' in the new Uganda, through the ideas, values, and institutions of living Banyoro. What follows is a description of the political institutions of the kingdom of Bunyoro, or Bunyoro-Kitara, in western Uganda, as they were when I carried out research there in the early 1950s.[1] My work was a good deal less complete than I would like it to have been, and there are many gaps in my understanding of Nyoro society and culture. I have acknowledged these elsewhere, and given some

---

[1] The ancient name of the kingdom is said to have been Kitara (a word which also means 'sword'), hence Roscoe (1923) entitled his book about it *The Bakitara or Banyoro*. In some recent documents and publications (e.g. the *Bunyoro Agreement* of 1955) the kingdom is referred to as Bunyoro-Kitara. But in historical times the name Bunyoro has been the one commonly used, and I retain it here.

Bunyoro is the kingdom; *Banyoro* (or *Abanyoro*) (sing. *Munyoro* [or *Omunyoro*]) are the people; *Runyoro* (or *Orunyoro*) is the language; and *kinyoro* is the Nyoro way of doing things. In accordance with ordinary usage I retain all these prefixes (*ba, mu, ru*) except in the case of the last term, which is less often heard, where I simply use the stem *Nyoro* as the adjectival form of the name. With regard to the use of the initial vowel in all Nyoro verbs and substantives, it is extremely difficult to be consistent, as Banyoro themselves use it or omit it in accordance with rules which have still to be clearly formulated. In the interest of simplicity I have usually omitted it, writing *Munyoro*, not *Omunyoro*, *Runyoro* and not *Orunyoro*, and so on, retaining it only in those few words which would look (and sound) strange without it to a Munyoro.

reasons for them (Beattie 1965). But it seems worth while to put on permanent record what I did learn about the Nyoro kingdom. Every human society is unique, and although Bunyoro in the 1950s showed many resemblances to other kingdoms in Africa and elsewhere, it also differed from them significantly. Also, I believe that its polity was one of particular interest, though I may be prejudiced on this point.

Of course there have been vast changes in Bunyoro since I lived there fifteen years ago, as there have elsewhere in Uganda, and throughout Africa. In this book, though I say something of recent developments, I make no attempt at an analysis of the contemporary scene. But today is the child of yesterday, and I do not doubt that many of Bunyoro's traditional political values and usages still survive, and will continue to do so. Also, social anthropologists need feel no qualms when the work they have done turns out to be social history.

When I knew it, the kingdom of Bunyoro had been radically affected by more than half a century of close contact with the West, and many of its traditional institutions and values had become much modified. But it was still a viable social and cultural unit. As such, it was evidently as worthwhile a subject for systematic investigation as any organized human community anywhere. Moreover, as one, perhaps the oldest, of the several traditional Bantu states which for centuries have occupied the interlacustrine region of east central Africa, an account of its polity should have some comparative ethnographic value. The fact that even in the 1950s it was doubtful whether, and for how long, these ancient kingdoms could survive in anything like their forms at that time added a sharper edge to my interest in them.

There is a further consideration. The study of small-scale centralized polities like Bunyoro, which retained many pre-European features, may have some relevance to more broadly based comparative studies of political institutions. An interest which is more than merely local attaches to a first-hand understanding of the ways in which a preliterate people, lacking developed communications and an advanced technology, have dealt with the task of achieving and sustaining a political order. The problems of government in small-scale societies may be handled in many ways, but the possibilities are not unlimited.

So it is not surprising that the Nyoro state shows many analogies with the medieval states of Europe and elsewhere: I mention a few of these resemblances in this book. Analogies are dangerous if misused, but they are valuable if they suggest lines for further research. And it may reasonably be claimed that the findings of social anthropologists, who observe the institutions they study in action and at first hand, may have at least some relevance for historians of Europe as well as of Africa, who study, through documents, institutions in at least some respects comparable. So, at any rate, at least a few historians are beginning to think.

The very fact that Bunyoro was undergoing rapid social change during the time that I worked there gave an added interest to my research. No society is in a state of perfect equilibrium; conflict is always present, not merely between individuals, but also between institutions, and, in individual people, between the values associated with these institutions. These conflicts may vary in nature and in intensity, but where new institutions and values are incorporated into a traditional system with very different ones, often incompatible with the new, the strain is likely to be severe. In what follows I say a good deal about such conflicts, and about the kinds of solutions to them which Nyoro culture offered.

Nyoro society and culture form a unity, though one that is by no means wholly integrated or harmonious. Of course this does not mean that it can be studied as a 'whole', though like Banyoro we may sometimes so conceive it. For us, as for them, 'Bunyoro' is an extended complex of interconnected institutions, values, and beliefs, and obviously we cannot describe all of these at once. The problem is one of exposition rather than of analysis: as field-worker the anthropologist can and indeed must pursue his inquiries simultaneously on many fronts; as author he can only say one thing at a time. In this book, therefore, I describe some of Bunyoro's characteristically political institutions: I hope in two further volumes to deal more fully than is possible here with the relationships and values of the Nyoro local community, and with Nyoro ritual and symbolism.

Such a division of ethnographic labour is inevitably somewhat arbitrary. To begin with, political relationships and 'community' ones interpenetrate at all levels, and both are

associated, in certain contexts, with symbols and rites. No one of these three broad themes can be considered in total isolation from the other two. Also, in societies which lack the degree of functional specialization and official 'departmentalization' characteristic of modern, western-type bureaucracies, it is often impossible to distinguish institutions sharply from one another as specifically 'political', 'economic', 'ritual', and so on. The same institution, kingship, for example, or clanship, may at the same time be important politically, economically, ritually, and in many other ways.

So my division of topics is not based simply on a classification of institutions themselves (though such a division can be made in Bunyoro very much more readily than it can in many African societies); it is based also on a classification of *aspects* of institutions, which themselves are not exclusively one thing or the other. Thus I am not concerned only with such obviously political institutions as the kingship and the system of territorial chiefship; I take account, also, of 'economic' institutions such as the land tenure system, and 'judicial' ones like the system of native courts. For such institutions have, or may have, political importance.

For purposes of this study, I do not define the term 'political' too rigidly. Very broadly, I take it to refer to the maintenance of social order (in so far as social order *is* maintained) between the different categories and groups of persons in a community, and to the ordering of relationships between that community and other 'outside' ones. I also take it that such institutions may, although they need not, involve the idea of *authority*; some kinds of people may have a socially acknowledged right to make decisions and give orders in matters which have a bearing on social order or on inter-group relations. There were many such authorities in Bunyoro, and their various roles and significances will be discussed.

But this definition is still a little too wide. For almost all social institutions have *some* bearing on the maintenance of social order. This is because institutionalized behaviour itself implies sanctioned conformity to rules. Thus the institutionalized role of the father in maintaining domestic discipline, or a socially sanctioned system of marriage regulations, contributes to, among other things, the maintenance of an orderly system

of intra-community relationships. So here I follow Radcliffe-Brown in taking as a further criterion of what it is useful to regard as 'political', a reference, explicit or implicit, to territory.[1] I take authority to be 'political' only when its applicability depends upon, among other things, the occupation of a certain territory by the persons who acknowledge and are subject to it. This fits the Bunyoro kingdom well enough; the authority of the king and his chiefs, no less than that of the superimposed National Uganda Government, was over people who lived in politically demarcated and named areas. This is not the case with, for example, domestic authority; a man's acknowledgement of his father's authority over him depends not, or not primarily, on where he is, but on what he is, that is, a son.

Radcliffe-Brown follows Max Weber and others in including in his definition of 'political' the sanction of 'the organized exercise of coercive authority through the use, or the possibility of use, of physical force'. When we are dealing with the maintenance of territorial order by these means we are no doubt concerned with political authority, and in Bunyoro's centralized polity a wide range of persons exercised authority which was backed by the force of the Mukama's government and, ultimately, by the British Protectorate itself. But even in a kingdom like Bunyoro other factors besides the organized use or threat of force might help to sustain a political order, and in this book I do not restrict myself to an account of Bunyoro's formally appointed rulers, although I am centrally concerned with them.

Law, in the sense of 'social control through the systematic application of the force of politically organized society' (Pound, R., quoted by Radcliffe-Brown 1952, p. 212) may evidently also be regarded as an aspect of political authority, at least where such control is found. But it is generally more useful for social anthropologists to think in terms of social sanctions (of which 'law' is one kind) than simply in terms of law, since many societies lack law in Pound's sense. Bunyoro does, however, have law in this sense, and in this book I say something of the native

---

[1] For Radcliffe-Brown, political authority is concerned with 'the maintenance or establishment of social order, within a territorial framework, by the organized exercise of coercive authority through the use, or the possibility of use, of physical force' (Radcliffe-Brown 1940, p. xiv).

court system, and of the part it plays in maintaining social order. However, I do not here discuss informal methods of dispute settlement at 'village' level. It is more convenient (if perhaps not altogether consistent) to consider them in the context of 'community' rather than of 'state'. For Banyoro they belong unambiguously to the former, not to the latter.[1]

A division of Nyoro society and culture into distinct spheres of 'state' and 'community' is not entirely arbitrary. It reflects a distinction which was constantly and explicitly drawn by Banyoro themselves. A central task of the social anthropologist is to achieve as full an understanding as possible of the concepts and categories of the people he is studying, and then to translate this understanding into terms of his own culture. But what he says must still make sense in terms of the culture he is describing. Most of his readers want to learn about the people studied, not about the anthropologist's theories concerning them. No doubt the distinction between these two things is not always easily drawn, but it is valid and important. In what follows I present, as best I can, Banyoro's view of their own social and cultural institutions, rather than, or at least as well as, my own ideas about these institutions.

The notions of 'state' and 'community' are, then, as familiar to Banyoro as they are to Western sociologists.[2] Banyoro quite explicitly distinguished 'kingship' (*bukama*)[3] and 'government' (*bulemi*) on the one hand, from 'neighbourhood' (*butahi*), 'clanship' (*bunyaruganda*), and 'kinship' (*buzaranwa*) on the other. They thought of these two dimensions of social life as quite separate, indeed as standing in opposition to each other, for the claims they made often conflicted, and the differences between them were often referred to in everyday conversation. *Bukama* is the abstract form of the word *mukama*, which means the owner or master of anything and denotes, in particular, Bunyoro's hereditary king, who was traditionally thought of as the owner

[1] There is a brief discussion of them in Beattie 1957*b*.

[2] The state, as 'the body politic as organized for supreme civil rule and government' (*Shorter Oxford English Dictionary*) is often opposed to the community, as in Tönnies's celebrated distinction between *gemeinschaft* and *gesellschaft*. The notion of a community implies no such organization; we may speak of it 'wherever the members of any group, small or large, live together in such a way that they share, not [just] this or that particular interest, but the basic conditions of common life' (Maciver and Page, pp. 8–9).

[3] Or *obukama*. See p. 1, n. 1.

as well as the ruler of his country and of everything in it. *Bukama* refers specifically to the system of authority which was centred on the king, and the hierarchy of territorial chiefs who wielded authority in his name. Likewise, *bulemi* implies the notion of 'ruling' (*kulema*), but it also involves the idea of 'weight' (*bulemezi*), and so of something that is difficult, even oppressive. Banyoro think of political authority as something heavy and burdensome, superimposed on and external to the multifarious and mostly face-to-face relationships which subsist between neighbours and kin who live in the same community and share the same background, interests, and values. Ideally such 'community' relationships are close and friendly, and numerous proverbs and stories emphasize this. Occupants of the same settlement area (*kyaro*, literally 'a place where people stay') ordinarily possess a strong feeling of local unity, both in relation to other similar communities and, even more, as against the superimposed 'government'. I say little of such relationships in this book, though in Bunyoro the notions of state and community imply one another; I hope to give a fuller account of them in a second volume.

Associated with the pervasive distinction between 'government' (*bulemi*) and community is a strong emphasis throughout Nyoro culture on the ideas of superordination and subordination. Almost every social relationship has, or is believed to have, a hierarchical or 'unequal' aspect. This 'premise of inequality', to borrow Maquet's useful phrase (1961), is summed up by Banyoro in the popular saying 'people are equal in the grave' (*baingana biituro*)—and, it is implied, nowhere else. It is usually expressed in the language of 'ruling' (*kulema*), and ownership. Fathers are said to rule their children, husbands their wives, a woman's agnates her husband, a sister's son his mother's brother. A superior is addressed as *mukama wange* (my master), *waitu* ('sir': literally 'our'—'master' understood), *isebo* (their father), or just *tata* (father). An inferior may refer to himself as *mwiru wawe* (your slave or servant), or *mwana wawe* (your child), and is addressed as *mwana wange* (my child), or his personal or *mpako* name may be used.[1] These and similar terms

[1] One of the eleven or so *mpako* names, which are supposedly of Nilotic origin, is given to every Munyoro shortly after birth. Their use implies both a measure

are constantly used in ordinary conversation by Banyoro, even when there is no evident difference of rank between the speakers.

Of course I am not saying that all social relationships in Bunyoro were inegalitarian, though many were; nor am I saying that the Nyoro state was less egalitarian than most other African societies, though it may have been. What I am asserting is that social relationships in Bunyoro were, and probably still are, pervaded by the *idiom* of inequality, and that this has coloured Nyoro thinking, both about themselves and about other people. This way of thinking about social relationships is consistent with the emphasis in traditional Bunyoro on ascribed, as opposed to achieved, status: we shall see that this emphasis is justified by myth, and that it still affected political relationships in important ways up to the time when this study was made.

of intimacy and respect. For a discussion of their origin see Crazzolara 1950, pp. 97–100.

2

THE COUNTRY AND THE PEOPLE

THE Banyoro are a Bantu people; that is, they speak a Bantu language, Runyoro. This is one of the main languages of the interlacustrine region of east-central Africa,[1] and dialects of it are spoken by the neighbouring Batoro (essentially the same people as the Banyoro), the Banyankore of Ankole district, and, in Tanzania, by the Bahaya, the Bazinza, and the Bakerewe, all of whom live on or near the southern shores of Lake Victoria.

When I was there in the 1950s, the kingdom of Bunyoro was coterminous with the administrative district of the same name, one of the four districts (the others being Toro, Ankole, and Kigezi) of Uganda's Western Province. Since then the size and population of the district have been much increased by the return to the parent kingdom in 1964 of the 'Lost Counties' of Buyaga and Bugangaizi in Mubende district to the south: I discuss the 'Lost Counties' dispute with Buganda, and its belated 'solution', in Chapter 4. In 1953 Bunyoro's boundaries lay between 1° and 2° 30' north of the equator, and between 30° 30' and 32° 20' east of Greenwich. They enclosed a land area of 4,735 square miles, of which about 2,350 square miles were available for African occupation and use, the remainder being taken up by National Park and sleeping sickness reserves, and by uninhabited forest and swamp. The kingdom was bounded on the west by Lake Albert, beyond which lies the Congo; on the north and east by the Victoria Nile and the Acholi and Lango districts, and until 1964 its southern boundary was the Kafu–Nkusi river system, which separated Bunyoro from the neighbouring Buganda kingdom.

Most of the Bunyoro lies at an altitude of between 3,000 and 4,000 feet, and is fertile and well watered. But in the north the

---

[1] Cf. C. M. Doke: *Bantu Modern Grammatical, Phonetical and Lexicographical Studies since 1860*, London, 1945. According to Doke the other main Bantu languages of the interlacustrine area are Luganda, Kirundi, Konjo, and Gisu.

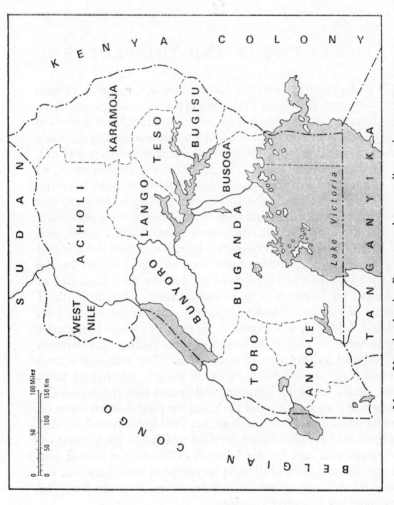

MAP 1. Uganda, showing Bunyoro and surrounding regions, 1955.

country falls to undulating savannah, rich in elephant and other game and mostly now included in the Murchison Falls National Park, and in the west it descends by a steep escarpment to the shore of Lake Albert, in the dry Western Rift Valley, about 1,000 feet below upland Bunyoro. Over most of the district rainfall averages over 45 inches a year, though it is a good deal less in the escarpment areas and in the Rift Valley, and in the northern savannah. Precipitation is fairly evenly distributed throughout the year; only January, February, and March are comparatively rainless months. There are two areas of rain forest in the district, Budongo and Bugoma, both of them easterly extensions of the great Congo rain forests to the west. But most of the country, where it is not cultivated or papyrus swamp, is covered by light deciduous forest and dense stands of elephant grass 6 or more feet tall. In inhabited areas much of the grass is burnt off every year at the end of the short dry season, opening up unexpected or forgotten vistas, but during the rest of the year visibility in most parts of the country is generally restricted to a few yards.

The characteristic topographical pattern in upland Bunyoro, though not in the low, flat areas near the lake shore or in the northern savannah, is one of clearly defined areas of more or less raised ground, separated from each other by swampy streams which often contain extensive stands of papyrus. These raised areas vary in extent from one to several square miles, and they are known in Runyoro and related languages as *migongo* (sing. *mugongo*), a word which primarily means 'back' or 'ridge'. The human settlement pattern is to a great extent determined by this topographical feature. Homesteads, normally one or two mud-and-wattle houses with a central courtyard of beaten earth, are scattered fairly evenly over these raised areas. Banyoro do not like to live cheek by jowl with one another, and except in one or two lakeside areas they do not live in compact villages. Each homestead is surrounded by its own gardens and plantain grove, and it is likely to be within shouting distance of one or more neighbours, though probably invisible to them during most of the year. *Migongo* are often coterminous with the settlement areas or *byaro* (sing. *kyaro*) which are the residential units of the Nyoro community, but larger *migongo* may contain two or even more such settlements. In any event, the swampy boundaries of the *migongo* mark them off, and the communities

that live on them, as separate units, and so give visible expression to each neighbourhood's strong sense of local identity. An idea of the pattern of residence can be gained from Plate 1.

To the eye, at least, Bunyoro is a well-favoured country. The undulating landscape and its scattered ranges of hills are green for the greater part of the year; most of the country is well wooded and there is plenty of shade; there are numerous swamps and streams, and in upland Bunyoro the fertile soil and ample rainfall combine to produce a luxuriant vegetation.

Banyoro sometimes say that in former times each *mugongo* was occupied by a separate 'clan'. Every Munyoro acquires in the paternal line membership of one of Bunyoro's 150 or more clans (*nganda*, sing. *ruganda*). Except for the royal Bito clan, of which more will be said later, clans are exogamous. Every clan is associated with one, sometimes two, animate or inanimate objects, called *miziro* (sing. *muziro*)—the word *kuzira* means to respect or avoid, and clan members must respect and avoid injuring the avoidance object of their clan. It is believed that if a Munyoro should eat or otherwise harm his *muziro*, he will become ill and may even die, though I was told that this would be unlikely to happen unless he did so on purpose.

Nowadays clan members are widely dispersed throughout Bunyoro and far beyond it, and it seems unlikely that clans as such were ever compact, territorially distinct units. It is, however, likely that *lineages* were (as indeed they still were in 1955 in one or two isolated lakeside villages). What is meant by the assertion that each *mugongo* was formerly the territory of a specific clan seems to be that in traditional times each such area was dominated (though not occupied exclusively) by a group of agnates. This nucleus of fellow-clansmen would give their clan name to the settlement area or *kyaro* which they occupied. A similar process can be seen in operation today, though rarely, as nowadays brothers are less likely than was formerly the case to continue to live together after they grow up. Certainly many *migongo* and divisions of *migongo* are named after one or other of Bunyoro's many clans, even though there may be few or even no members of the eponymous clan now living in the area so named.[1]

---

[1] When I lived in the village of Kihoko in southern Bunyoro in 1951–2, four brothers, members of the Bahenda clan, lived in neighbouring homesteads at one end of the settled area. Though they were by no means the first settlers there, by

PLATE 1

Comparatively densely settled area of Bugahya country, Bunyoro, a few miles south of Hoima. The headquarters of the sub-county chief Mutuba I are on the right of the main road in the upper part of the photograph.

Scale approximately 3 inches to one mile

Banyoro attribute the breakdown of the alleged traditional association between territory and clan to the disturbances caused by the wars with the British and the Baganda towards the end of the last century, and although, as I have said, it is unlikely that clans were ever completely localized, there is evidence that locally based patrilineages were a good deal more important in pre-European times than they are now.

In 1948 the total African population of Bunyoro was estimated at 108,380; in 1959 it had risen to 126,875.[1] This 17 per cent increase in population over a period of eleven years was one of the lowest in Uganda, far below the national average increase of 31 per cent. The Bunyoro figure also includes 20,000 or more immigrants, mainly Lugbara from the West Nile district and Alur from the Congo, but also some Baganda. Also included in the total are the 6,000 or so Jopalwoo or 'Bachopi' who live in northern Bunyoro but speak a Nilotic language and are close relatives of the neighbouring Acholi.

If we compare Bunyoro's population at mid century with Sir Harry Johnston's estimate of its population at the turn of the century, when he considered that it did not exceed 110,000 (1902, vol. ii, p. 591), it becomes quite plain that even allowing for a wide margin of inaccuracy Banyoro have increased very little, if at all, during the past half-century or so. Bunyoro's general annual fertility rate (144 per 1,000 women aged 16 to 45) is well below the average level for Uganda as a whole; only one district in Uganda has a lower one. Its annual infant mortality rate (180 deaths under one year per 1,000 births) is well above the national average of 160. In 1959 Bunyoro had a lower percentage of small children (under 6) than any of the other Western Province districts. Banyoro were well aware of their comparative infecundity, and as we shall see they had several explanations for it.

There were, however, a further 34,000 Banyoro in the 'Lost Counties', which were until 1964 parts of the Mubende district

---

the time that I came to Kihoko the *kyaro* where they lived had come to be known, half jokingly to begin with, as Kihenda. It is likely that even after the brothers die or disperse (in fact at least one has since died) the area will continue to be known as Kihenda, at any rate for a time. For a fuller account of the Nyoro clan system, see Beattie 1957a, pp. 319–25.

[1] These and the other demographic data given in this chapter are from the *Uganda Census 1959; African Population*, Uganda Protectorate, 1961.

of Buganda. Most of these lived in the Buyaga and Bugangaizi
(Bugangadzi in Luganda) counties, where they outnumbered the
Baganda by about seven to two. After a long campaign by the
Mukama of Bunyoro and his chiefs, these counties, originally
part of Bunyoro, were restored to the parent kingdom in 1964
(an account of these events is given in Chapter 4). Thus the
total population of the Bunyoro District is now something over
170,000. In 1959 there were altogether over 188,000 Banyoro in
Uganda, and they made up 2·9 per cent of the total African
population of the country. Among the thirty-one Uganda tribes
listed, the Banyoro ranked eleventh in order of population.

In 1959 the population density over the whole of Bunyoro
(excluding the Murchison Falls National Park) was 32·4 per
square mile, by far the lowest figure for the Western Province.
But in fact the population was mostly confined to relatively
closely settled areas, where the density was a good deal higher,
often up to and above 200 to the square mile.

Bunyoro is often said to have been traditionally a pastoral
country,[1] but for many years trypanosomiasis has been enzootic
in the district, and except in a very few localities cattle do not
thrive. When I was in Bunyoro there were a little over
6,000 head of cattle in the country, most of them in the fly-free
Bugungu area in the north-west, and in the neighbourhood of
Bunyoro's two towns, Hoima and Masindi, where periodic
prophylaxis was available. The ratio of cattle to humans over
the whole district was thus about one to eighteen, compared
with the average for the whole Protectorate of one to two. So
by no stretch of the imagination could Bunyoro in the 1950s be
described as a pastoral country. The alleged decline in cattle
population over the past century or so was said by Banyoro to
be due mainly to war, trypanosomiasis, and rinderpest. It
was also attributed by many to the deliberate intention of the

[1] See, for example, Roscoe 1923, p. 3, and other writers. But see also Samuel Baker
1874, p. 150: 'None of the general public [of Bunyoro] possess cattle', and (p. 212)
'In Unyoro, cattle are scarce, and they belong to the king'. It seems that except
perhaps in the extreme south of the country (which was the centre of the ancient
kingdom) a pastoral way of life has not been widely practised for many generations.
It may be noted also in this connection that the size of the great earthworks
associated with the Bacwezi suggests that they were intended to enclose cattle as
well as people. Some of them, including one in the Bugahya county of modern
Bunyoro, are today overgrown with substantial forest, infested with tsetse fly. But
when they were constructed the country must have been open grassland.

Protectorate Government. The Veterinary Department's attempts to control rinderpest in the 1930s by preventive inoculation were not very successful; the vaccine used seems to have been defective, and it is said that the treatment killed more cattle than the disease itself. But even though in the 1950s not one Munyoro in a hundred owned cattle (though the proportion who did was gradually increasing) and many had never tasted beef or milk, values associated with cattle still had an important place in Nyoro thought, and their language is rich in words and idioms associated with them. The loss of their presumed ancient herds was still deeply felt and mourned by almost all Banyoro, especially by older people, and not least by those whose forebears were unlikely ever to have owned any, at least for many generations back.

Apart from the few cattle-owners, and a still small (though growing) class of officials, professional people, and businessmen and traders, the typical Munyoro, in the 1970s as in the 1950s, is a small-scale agriculturalist, who cultivates an area of from 4 to 8 acres, and owns a few goats, some chickens, and perhaps one or two sheep. The main food crop is eleusine (finger millet), called *buro* in Runyoro. It is eaten daily, cooked as a stiff porridge, and is regarded as Bunyoro's staple and traditional food. Sweet potatoes, cassava, and various kinds of peas and beans are also much eaten. As was noted above, almost every homestead has its grove of plantain trees, but unlike the Baganda, Banyoro do not use these much for food, preferring to make them into plantain beer (*mwenge*), for which purpose they grow certain beer-making varieties. A good deal of *mwenge* is consumed, and it is an important source of protein. The Munyoro farmer grows cotton and sometimes tobacco as cash crops, the former especially in the drier escarpment areas, often a long way from his home. From the proceeds of these crops he may make a cash income of 200 shillings or so a year, sometimes considerably more. He is likely to have a few coffee trees by his house, but he uses the fruits of these mostly for drying and chewing, and for offering to guests on formal occasions. If he has a surplus he may do a small retail trade in them, but coffee has never been an important cash crop in Bunyoro, as it has in Buganda. The average agricultural holding, with provision for fallow land, has been estimated at about 15 acres.

In the 1950s there had not as yet been much attempt by private individuals to develop large units of land by modern agricultural methods, though a few wealthy and progressive farmers were developing substantial holdings with paid labour. Co-operative farming was being successfully introduced in some areas, and some of the wealthier growers' societies were beginning to have sufficient resources to purchase or hire lorries and tractors, as also, more recently, have some wealthy individuals. The co-operative movement in Bunyoro got off to a rather slow start, mainly because the mutual confidence required was not always forthcoming. Many Banyoro engage in petty trade, and a number nowadays have substantial businesses. But in the 1950s retail trade was mostly in the hands of the immigrant Indian community, which numbered about 800 in 1955. At that time, also, an important trade in dried fish was carried on by the inhabitants of the few lakeside villages. The local bus service between Hoima and Toro had been owned and operated by Banyoro for many years.

In 1953, adult male Banyoro paid flat-rate taxes amounting to about 26 shillings per annum, but a graduated tax was introduced in 1954, after which most Banyoro paid about 40 shillings in taxes a year.

Today most Banyoro live in rectangular two-, three-, or four-roomed houses of varying sizes and degrees of solidity. Most are still made of wattle and clay (sometimes just wattle and grass) and thatched with grass, but more and more brick houses are being built, and thatch is increasingly being replaced by corrugated iron. Iron roofing is preferred to grass not only because it is stronger and lasts longer but also because it is not inflammable: arson is common and much feared in Bunyoro, and it is widely believed that the house of a man who shows himself to be richer and more progressive than his neighbours is likely to be burned down. But although rectangular, iron-roofed houses are steadily increasing, the gleam of corrugated iron through the plantain groves is not yet so typical a feature of the rural landscape in Bunyoro as it is in Buganda. In the remoter areas, some people still live in the typical old-fashioned 'beehive' type of house (*kisu*), which can be built in a few hours.

In comparison with most other parts of East Africa, social services in Bunyoro in the 1950s were above the average. The

country is well provided with roads. Of the two main ones, the first runs from the port of Butiaba on Lake Albert in the west (the port has, however, been out of action for several years owing to an extraordinary rise in the level of the lake) through Masindi, one of Bunyoro's two towns, to Masindi Port on the Nile in the east, and the second runs from the Atura ferry, connecting Bunyoro with Acholi district and the north, through Masindi and Hoima to the southern boundary of Bunyoro, and thence to Toro district. There are also main highways direct to Kampala from both Hoima and Masindi, and a good new road from Masindi to the Murchison Falls and the National Park, as well as hundreds of miles of lesser but still motorable roads. Off these there is an intricate network of foot and cycle paths.

Education in Bunyoro was almost wholly in the hands of Bunyoro's two Christian missions, the Native Anglican Church (deriving from the Church Missionary Society) and the Roman Catholic White Fathers. The Christian two-thirds of the population of Bunyoro in 1959 was fairly evenly divided between these two denominations (35 per cent were Protestant, 29 per cent Roman Catholic); most of the remainder, apart from a tiny handful of Moslems (2 per cent), were 'pagans', mostly older people who had never thought it worth while to be baptized. As in other parts of Uganda, from the earliest days of the British presence the Protestants wielded an influence on the local rulers out of all proportion to their numbers; the Mukama of Bunyoro was a Protestant, and so were the great majority of his territorial chiefs.

During the colonial period, competition between the two missions led in some areas to the close juxtaposition of schools of the rival denominations, to the educational detriment of more neglected areas. Education had to be paid for; in the 1950s school fees started at about 6 shillings a year, and increased rapidly with the standard reached. Books and school clothes also had to be bought. Many Banyoro parents pleaded poverty as a reason for failing to educate their children beyond the first or second standard. Nevertheless literacy in Bunyoro was the highest in the Western Province: 45 per cent of males and 19 per cent of females over the age of 6 had received some schooling, a figure appreciably higher than the national average

for Uganda. In 1955 there were fifty-eight schools in the district of which four provided secondary education.

There are modern hospitals in Hoima and Masindi, and dispensaries at several points throughout the district. For several reasons, not all of these were as popular as they might have been, though they were becoming more so. Some people still distrusted European-sponsored medicine and medical techniques, also references were frequently made to the extortions of the subordinate medical staff. Banyoro are not, on the whole, particularly healthy. There is a good deal of venereal disease, and yaws and other infections are common. Hookworm and bilharzia are endemic. Few Banyoro can afford to eat meat otherwise than as an occasional treat, and fish are little eaten except by the fishing communities who live on the lake shore, and who are of conspicuously better physique than upland Banyoro. Chickens and eggs were formerly prohibited to women, but are now being increasingly eaten by both sexes. However, the diet of most Banyoro was, and probably still is, seriously deficient in protein, as it consisted almost entirely of starchy foods such as millet, cassava, and potatoes.

In the 1950s Bunyoro was, as it still is, almost wholly African. Non-native estates occupied only about 29 square miles, and all but one of them were owned by Indians. Most were strung along the Masindi–Butiaba road, on the edge of the Budongo forest, and were mainly devoted to coffee. Altogether there were about 140 Europeans in the district, most of them in the employment of the Uganda Railways and Harbours Administration, which handled traffic between Masindi and Butiaba and across Lake Albert. (This route, in the 1950s the main link between Uganda and the Congo, has since been suspended due to the rise in the level of the lake referred to above.) Apart from these, and the handful of European missionaries, most of the other Europeans in Bunyoro at that time were officials of the Protectorate Government. The central administration was represented in Bunyoro by a district commissioner stationed at Hoima, the capital, assisted by two or three assistant district commissioners, one or two at Hoima and one at Masindi. These officials, all of whom have, of course, been replaced by Africans since Independence, were assisted by substantial staffs of clerks, accountants, typists, interpreters, and messengers. There were

also a few departmental officers, each with his own subordinate staff, who were responsible for such matters as agriculture, veterinary affairs, game and fisheries, marketing, co-operative development, and police work.

During the colonial period, the Bunyoro Native Government, with the hereditary ruler of Bunyoro, the Mukama, at its head, operated under the general supervision and control of the British administration. The Mukama's capital was at Hoima, about a mile from the district commissioner's headquarters, but he also maintained a private palace at Masindi, and he has been living there since his office was abolished in 1967, and his palace at Hoima taken over by the government. Until Independence, he was assisted by a secretariat consisting of the Katikiro (the term is a Luganda one), who combined the functions of prime minister and chief secretary, the Muramuzi or chief justice (the verb *kuramura* means to adjudicate or settle a dispute), and the Muketo or treasurer. All of these officials were supported by staffs of assistants, clerks, and messengers. After Independence, the structure remained basically the same until the abolition of the kingdom, except that the Katikiro's post became primarily a political appointment, being held by a nominee of the ruling Uganda People's Congress: the administrative work connected with the post was taken over by a new office-holder, the permanent secretary to the Katikiro. In 1955 the Mukama was also advised by a council consisting of seventy-two members, mostly chiefs appointed *ex officio*, but containing also a number of elected members.

For political and administrative purposes the territory of Bunyoro was divided into four counties or *sazas*, each under the control of a *saza* chief. The *sazas* were divided into sub-counties or *gombololas*, of which in 1955 there were twenty-five, each under a sub-county (*gombolola*) chief. Their disposition and titles (see below) are shown on Map 2. *Gombololas* are further divided into *miruka* (sing. *muruka*), a term which is usually translated 'parishes', each with its own chief. In 1955 there were sixty-five *miruka* chiefs. *Miruka*, finally, were sub-divided into *matongole* (sing. *butongole*), under paid headmen called, nowadays, *batongole* or *bakungu*.[1] In English, these units are

---

[1] All of these terms (except *bakungu*) are Luganda ones, introduced when the local administration was reconstituted, on the Ganda pattern, at the beginning of

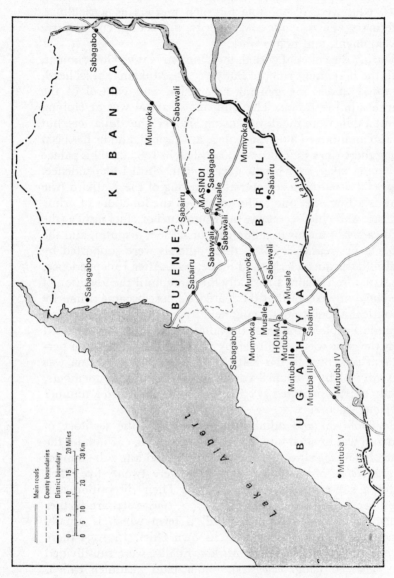

MAP 2. Bunyoro, showing counties and sub-county headquarters, 1955.

usually and conveniently called 'villages', and their chiefs referred to as 'village headmen'. There is no objection to this, provided that the term 'village' is understood to refer not to a compact cluster of dwellings, as it might in Europe, but rather to a fairly extensive area of dispersed settlement, such as is illustrated in Plate 1.

These *matongole* constituted the lowest order of units officially recognized for administrative purposes, and the *batongole* or *bakungu* were the lowest rank of salaried chiefs. But in fact *matongole* were yet further divided into settlements or *byaro*, which, as we noted above, are social rather than political units. In each *kyaro* a man, usually of some local eminence, acted as the chief's informal representative, and he derived some prestige and occasional perquisites from his position. These men received no official salaries, and were sometimes jokingly referred to (and referred to themselves) as *ndyamuki*, a term which is based on the interrogative form of the verb *kulya*, to eat, and which may be very roughly translated as 'what do I get out of it?'

Below *saza* level, the official chiefs, and by extension the territories they administered, were called by a series of six titles in order of rank, the series being repeated at each of the three levels of chiefship concerned. In descending order of priority, these titles were *Mumyoka*, *Sabairu*, *Sabagabo*, *Sabawali*, *Musale*, and *Mutuba*. Again, these are not traditional Nyoro titles, but were adapted from the Ganda system.[1] Bunyoro's four *saza* chiefs had special titles of their own. The functions and inter-actions of these various grades of political authorities are described in later chapters; here we need only note that in the early 1950s Bunyoro was still, at any rate formally, a centralized, hierarchically organized state, with the Mukama at the apex of the traditional pyramid of authority, and the 150 or so village headmen at its base. In traditional times the Mukama was

the century. In its Runyoro form *gombolola* is *ibohorra* (pl. *mabohorra*). I use the simplified Ganda spellings (strictly, in Luganda *saza* should be written *ssaza*, *gombo-lola ggombolola*, and *muruka muluka*) because they are often used by Banyoro, and are familiar in the literature.

[1] The Ganda titles mean respectively 'second in command', 'head of those who serve', 'head of the shield-bearers', 'head of the slaves', 'arrow', and 'barkcloth tree' (a species of fig) (Fallers 1964, p. 73). If there were more than six chiefs at any one level they were known as Mutuba I, Mutuba II, and so on. All these titles were replaced by a set of Runyoro ones in 1963 (personal communication from Sir A. Dunbar).

thought of as the ultimate ground and source of all political power in the kingdom; in this century most people knew that he was subject to the superior authority of the European Protectorate government. This had, of course, affected traditional attitudes towards the Mukama and his chiefs in many important respects.

From 1933 to 1955 (and so during the period of my field-work) relations between the Protectorate Government and the Bunyoro Native Government were based on the Bunyoro Agreement of 1933. This 'Agreement', which as Lord Hailey has remarked is properly to be regarded rather as a declaration of Protectorate Government policy than as a treaty between two freely contracting powers (Hailey 1950, p. 46), acknowledged the Mukama as 'the native ruler of Bunyoro-Kitara'. At the same time it prescribed that he should follow the Protectorate Government's advice, and that Bunyoro should be subject to the Protectorate's legislation. The right to appoint, promote, and dismiss all the higher grades of chiefs was vested in the Mukama personally, but his decisions were subject to the Governor's approval. He was to be assisted in his administration by councils of prescribed composition.

During my stay in Bunyoro, the 1933 Agreement was being increasingly criticized by the growing class of educated Banyoro, including some of the chiefs themselves, on the ground, in particular, that it excessively strengthened the Mukama's personal power in the appointment, promotion, and dismissal of chiefs. Partly as a result of these criticisms it was replaced in September 1955 by a new Agreement, in which the Mukama's powers were drastically curtailed, and he was effectively reduced to the status of a constitutional monarch. These Agreements and some of their implications are discussed in Chapter 7.

Little is known about the origins of the Banyoro people or their kingdom, and it is unlikely that we shall ever have a clear picture of its earliest times. Some further light is being thrown on these matters by current archaeological work in the region, though so far the importance of this is largely negative, showing that evidence for some formerly accepted theories is lacking. The usual view, which originated with the early European explorers in the 1860s, is that the Banyoro, like other peoples of the interlacustrine region, represent a mixture of at least two

different physical and cultural strains. Even this, however, is far from certain, and it has recently been argued that the distinctive physical types associated with the widespread distinction between pastoral Bahima (Bahuma in Bunyoro) and agricultural Bairu may well have emerged locally from a common stock through processes of social and natural selection (Posnansky, p. 6).

According to the commonly accepted view, the area was at one time occupied by a more or less negroid agricultural, or possibly hunting and gathering, people (on the whole less interest has attached to the question of where *they* might have come from). It is supposed that over several hundreds, perhaps thousands, of years successive waves of immigrants of different racial stock, probably from the north and possibly speaking Hamitic languages (of which in the interlacustrine area no trace whatever remains), intruded into the region, each wave producing cumulative modifications in both the physical type and the culture of the indigenous inhabitants. Such a version of Nyoro prehistory provides a ready and easily intelligible explanation (though not necessarily the correct one) both of the wide variety of somatic type and of the dual system of socio-political organization (which I have broadly labelled the opposition between community and state) which characterize the whole region today. It gains some support, also, from the traditional histories of the interlacustrine kingdoms, as we shall see in the next chapter. Even today, some Nyoro clans are distinguished as 'those that were found here' (*basangwa*) from those clans, or divisions of clans, which are said to have arrived later. It is supposed that some of these newcomers brought cattle with them; perhaps, at a very early stage, the lyre-horned 'Ankole' type still found in some parts of the interlacustrine area, though no longer in Bunyoro itself.

The structural duality which these hypotheses and myths imply, and which, whatever its origin, still characterizes the interlacustrine states, enables us to see Bunyoro as exhibiting, like its neighbours, a sometimes uneasy synthesis between the centralized rule traditionally associated with the newcomers, and an originally segmentary, lineage-based type of social organization, characteristic perhaps of the indigenous agriculturalists. The dualism is also expressed in the Bahima (or

Bahuma)–Bairu distinction, still recognized throughout much of the interlacustrine area. In many parts of the region, such as Ankole, Rwanda, and Burundi, the Bahima (called Batutsi in the last two countries), though always a small minority of the total population, assumed the role of overlords, dominating and exploiting the agricultural Bairu majority (called Bahutu in the southern kingdoms). In these countries the opposition between the state and the community and that between the pastoralists and the agriculturalists tended in some measure to coincide.

But the clear-cut distinction between pastoral rulers and agricultural peasants is not valid for Banyoro. In Bunyoro, Bahuma have always regarded themselves, and been regarded, as superior to Bairu, and this is still the case in so far as Bahuma can still be identified. But the distinction between Bahuma and Bairu has little of the importance that it possesses, for example, in Ankole. Although some Banyoro still proudly claim Huma descent, today practically everyone, whatever their pedigree, shares the same way of life and the same interests and values. Indeed, in Bunyoro in the 1950s the term Huma had in ordinary use come to have a primarily functional significance; it no longer referred to a particular high-status group. Any man who owned a herd of cattle was likely to become known as a Muhuma, whatever his ancestry, and anyway most Banyoro claim some Huma forebears. Also, to claim Huma status without owning any cattle would be for most people an empty boast, and few Banyoro today would bother to do so.

The distinction between Bahuma and Bairu probably had a good deal more force in Bunyoro when there were more cattle in the country, but it is now quite unimportant, and it is doubtful if it was ever so important as it has been in some of the other kingdoms. We shall see in Chapter 6 that in Bunyoro political authority seems always to have been associated with the grant by the ruler of rights over specific areas of land and the people on them, rather than with patron–client relationships based on cattle grants. And whatever importance the distinction between Bahuma and Bairu did possess in traditional times was no doubt effectively weakened by the destruction of Bunyoro's herds in the wars of the last century. Conscious though Banyoro are of status differences, the rigid, caste-like discriminations described for Ankole and traditional Rwanda are not found in

Bunyoro. Marriage between Bahuma and Bairu was not prohibited, and it has always been possible (though not necessarily
easy) for Banyoro of commoner origin to rise to high position in
the state. Many have done so in historical times.

The story of Nyoro origins is complicated by the appearance,
in Bunyoro's myth and tribal history, of two other elements.
First came the Bacwezi, a mysterious race of quasi-divine rulers,
who are said to have taken over the country from an earlier and
even more shadowy dynasty, called the Batembuzi. This event
is ascribed to the fourteenth or fifteenth century, an attribution
which has received some confirmation from recent archaeological research at Bigo, in Mubende district, a site traditionally
associated with the Bacwezi. Radiocarbon dating has provided
a date of around 1350–1500 for the occupation of the extensive
earthworks there (Posnansky, p. 5). The Bacwezi, who are
believed to have been light-complexioned and to have performed many wonderful feats (as well as constructing the
remarkable earthworks at Bigo and elsewhere) are said to have
ruled the country for a generation or two and then mysteriously
disappeared. Whether they were invaders from the north—from
Egypt, Meroe, or Ethiopia, or even, as has been suggested
(Nyakatura, p. 28) from Europe; whether they were merely a
militant offshoot of the already dominant Bahima; indeed
whether they really existed at all (though certainly *somebody* built
and inhabited the ancient earthworks in Mubende); these are still
matters for speculation, and are likely to remain so for some time.

However, there is very much less doubt about the arrival of
the next dynasty, the Babito, who were a Nilotic clan, or perhaps a group of clans, from north of the Nile. They took over
from the Bacwezi, peaceably according to tradition, and they
provided Bunyoro's royal line until the end of the kingdom in
1967. The Babito are relatives of the present-day Acholi and
Alur and, more distantly, of the Shilluk of the upper Nile. To
the Babito, as rulers, attaches much of the prestige and authority
associated in the more southerly kingdoms (which the Babito
did not reach) with the Bahima. But according to the Nyoro
historian, J. Nyakatura (p. 65), some traditionally minded
Banyoro still regard the Babito as *parvenus*, 'just Bairu!'

Bunyoro's traditional history is further discussed in the next
chapter. Here we need only note in passing that Roscoe, the

author of the first full-length study of the Banyoro, was mistaken
in asserting that the ruling class in Bunyoro were Bahuma, and
that the Bahuma were 'pastoral nomads' (1923, p. 6), thus
conveying the quite erroneous impression that Bunyoro is—or
was—ruled by a hereditary élite of cattle-herding chiefs. The
facts are that the king and the 'princes' were not Bahuma but
Babito (though it is said that they often married Bahuma); that
the chiefs held explicitly territorial authority and so cannot have
been nomadic; and that the Bahuma, though they claimed and
were accorded special prestige and could become chiefs, were
not, as Bahuma, rulers, but cattle-men, who typically attached
themselves to the great chiefs. Sir Samuel Baker, although he
could hardly be accused of sympathy with the Banyoro, understood the situation better, at least in this respect. He had written,
many years earlier:

> There is a curious custom throughout Unyoro; a peculiar caste
> are cattle-keepers. These people only attend to the herds and the
> profession is inherited from past generations. They are called
> *Bahooma*, and they are the direct descendants of the Gallas who
> originally conquered the country, and, like the reigning family, they
> are of an extremely light colour. If the herds are carried off in battle,
> the Bahooma, who never carry arms, accompany them to their new
> masters and continue their employment. Nothing but death will
> separate them from their cattle (1874, pp. 148–9).

In Bunyoro chiefship was traditionally not based on descent,
but on the Mukama's personal gift, and he could and did
confer political office on Huma and non-Huma alike. The role
of the Bahima in Ankole was, of course, very different; the
king of Ankole was a Muhima, and so provided a focus and symbol of Hima political ascendancy in that country: the king of
Bunyoro was not a Muhuma but a Mubito. In Bunyoro the
Bahuma, though they claimed and were accorded high status,
have always, as Bahuma, lacked major political importance.

Banyoro believe, and so far as the evidence goes they are
certainly correct, that in former times their kingdom was very
much larger than it was in its last years. Even as late as Speke's
visit in 1862 it was a great deal more extensive than neighbouring countries (see Map 3). But in historical times its territory
was much reduced by the incursions of their traditional enemies
the Baganda, latterly aided by the British, and there is reason

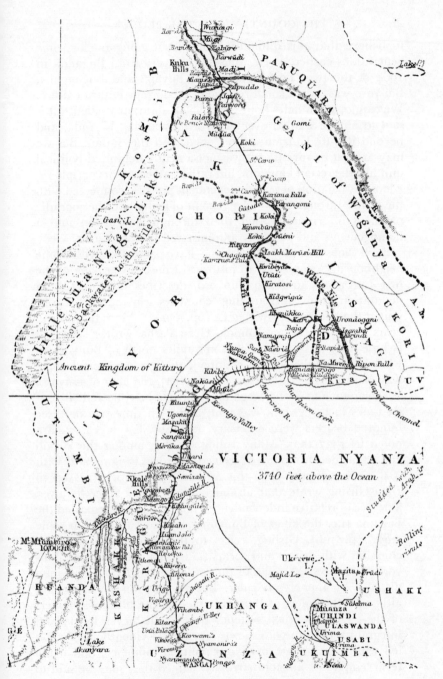

MAP 3. Bunyoro ('Unyoro') and surrounding regions (1862).
Scale approximately 66 miles to one inch.

to believe that this diminution had been going on for some generations earlier. Even after the recovery from Buganda in 1964 of the two 'Lost Counties' of Buyaga and Bugangaizi, Bunyoro was only a small residue of the former Kitara empire. We cannot say much about this ancient state; at its zenith it is said to have extended over most of present-day Uganda, and beyond it into Tanzania, the Congo, and the Sudan. But we may at least be sure that it was not a neatly delimited political unit like the recent kingdom, but rather, at least at its periphery, a loose association of semi-independent polities, connected with the centre through acknowledgement of fealty and the sporadic payment of tribute, rather than through integration into a homogeneous and centrally administered unitary state.

Such 'loose' political relations have subsisted with some neighbouring peoples up to historical times. Speke, one of the first Europeans to reach Bunyoro, describes how in 1862 a deputation from surrounding countries (including Acholi) visited the king's court with gifts (pp. 530–2). More than thirty years later the Italian Romolo Gessi Pasha wrote: 'Wadelai [whose area was on the Nile some miles north of Bunyoro in what is now Acholi-Madi country], though a powerful chief, was the vassal of Kaba Rega [Kabarega], the king of Unyoro. Wadelai gave to Kaba Rega all the ivory he collected; five or six times in the year it was sent, and each time two or three hundred bearers were necessary' (p. 106). Father Crazzolara noted in 1937 that 'Many ruling families among the Acooli and Aluur declare to have received the royal insignia and with it the royal dignity from this *Mukama*' (1937, p. 13). And in 1960 Girling wrote that although each Acholi ruler 'enjoyed a degree of relative independence', many of them 'regarded the Bakama [i.e. the kings of Bunyoro] as their suzerains in some sense' (p. 126). Girling, refers to the association of Acholi chiefship with drums and spears said to have come from Bunyoro, and gives examples of the settlement of Acholi accession disputes by the Nyoro ruler. But he goes on to stress that although 'the rulers of Bunyoro acted as the ultimate arbiters of the Acholi political system', the Acholi 'never formed an integral part of Bunyoro society' (p. 172). Evidently the Acholi fell within the sphere of Nyoro political influence, and if the term 'empire' is not too narrowly defined they may be said to

have formed a part of the Kitara empire. The position seems to have been similar with regard to the Alur chiefs of the areas near the north-western shore of Lake Albert, who recognized what Southall calls 'their ritual subordination' to Bunyoro, by going there 'for confirmation of their title after accession to kingship'. According to Southall, all Alur claimed 'that the Bunyoro kings were their kinsmen despite their different language and changed customs' (pp. 218–19). It is not, in all these cases, a question of simple inclusion or exclusion, but rather of the degree of suzerainty acknowledged. We are concerned with expanding and contracting spheres of political influence, not with sharply bounded, unitary states.

Although detailed information is lacking for other areas, it seems likely that similar relationships of political dependency without integration existed in other peripheral areas of ancient Kitara. In any event, inclusion in it was largely a matter of degree; and it need not be supposed that the links of dependence of the kind just described were necessarily very enduring. Revolts and declarations of independence were probably frequent in outlying areas, and it is likely that the borders of the empire were always shifting and fluid. They have indeed been so right up to historical times. The neighbouring kingdom of Toro achieved independence early in the nineteenth century (though it was later reconquered and finally regained its independence only through British intervention) when its Mubito ruler Kaboyo, a son of the Nyoro king, revolted from the parent kingdom. And during the latter part of the last century the northern part of Bunyoro, which was ruled by another Mubito chief, Ruyonga, was constantly, though unsuccessfully, in revolt against the Nyoro king Kamurasi and his successor Kabarega.

In the 1950s Banyoro were very conscious of their former greatness, and of the drastic decline in their fortunes in more recent times. Most of them considered the past far superior to the present, and all of the dozen or so Banyoro who wrote essays for me on 'the state of the country' (*burungi bw'ensi*), in response to an essay competition I organized in 1953, considered Bunyoro's present state an unhappy one; all extolled the past and denigrated at least some aspects of the present. Banyoro are a very historically minded people. Also, many traditional political values and attitudes survived into the greatly changed

socio-political world of the 1950s, and I think it is likely that they survive still. Thus any full understanding of modern Bunyoro requires some knowledge of its traditional political organization, and of its history since the first contact with the West over a century ago. In Chapter 4, I summarize this history, of which fuller though for the most part piecemeal accounts are available elsewhere.

It is no part of my purpose to describe Nyoro 'character' (even if it were possible to identify such a quality); as I have said elsewhere, as individuals Banyoro seemed to me to be much like the members of any peasant-based community anywhere. During my time with them I was impressed on many occasions by their good temper, courtesy, tolerance, and generosity. If, in addition, they showed some reserve and, in particular, a deep underlying fear and distrust of Europeans, this should not surprise anyone who is acquainted with the history of Nyoro–European relations. When I was in Bunyoro, it was widely believed among the less-educated majority that Europeans disliked Banyoro and were uncompromisingly opposed to their interests. We shall see that the historical record, and indeed some aspects of the contemporary situation in the 1950s, provided some ground for these opinions.

In any event, it is certain that ever since the very first contacts a century ago, Europeans have constantly passed judgement on the Nyoro character, and almost always their judgements (there are a very few exceptions) have been adverse to a remarkable degree. As these opinions quickly came to be incorporated in the official record, and undoubtedly influenced later British attitudes and policies towards the Banyoro, some account must be taken of them here. We shall see in Chapter 4 that it was Bunyoro's misfortune, due both to its geographical position and to historical accident, that ever since the first contacts in the 1860s relations with Europeans were almost uniformly hostile. For Baker, in particular, no strictures were too severe for the 'villainy' of the Nyoro king or for the 'treachery' of the people of 'this accursed country' (1874, pp. 316, 320). Most later assessments of Nyoro character owed more to his choleric opinions than to any first-hand knowledge of the people themselves.

A typical comment is that of a Victorian author, the Revd. J. G. Wood, who in 1868 described the Banyoro (whom he had

never seen) as 'forming a very unpleasant contrast to the people of Buganda, being dirty, mean-looking, and badly dressed'. He went on to describe their character as being 'quite on a par with their appearance, for they are a mean, selfish, grasping set of people, sadly lacking the savage virtue of hospitality, and always on the look-out for opportunities to procure by unfair means the property of others'. The reverend author airily sums up, from the depths of his Victorian armchair: 'they seem, indeed, to be about as unpleasant a nation as can well be imagined' (1868, p. 467). This kind of comment, evidently based on Baker's writings, set the tone for subsequent views about and attitudes towards the Banyoro, and indeed after such descriptions had gained currency, rehabilitation might well be difficult. Thus Mrs. A. B. Fisher, the author of one of the best early accounts of the Banyoro and by no means unsympathetic to them, wrote in 1911 that 'work is repugnant to the Banyoro, and nothing proves an irresistible attraction save indolence and ease' (p. 34). Numerous reports by Government officers refer to their 'apathy', their 'habits of intemperance' and addiction to drink, their 'naturally apathetic and individualistic outlook', and their 'evident sense of inferiority'. Their temperament was described by one official as 'not well fitted to overcome' the moral tribulations which (he acknowledged) they had suffered. Even in 1953 missionaries and European officers regarded the Banyoro as idle, unenterprising, and decadent, compared with other African peoples of Uganda. During my first few days in the country the head of the White Fathers' mission in Hoima told me categorically that there could be no future for Bunyoro; the people were diseased and apathetic, and the country was going from bad to worse. Some members of the Church Missionary Society held similar views. The district had for years been regarded by government officers as a dead end.

It is scarcely surprising that this almost unanimously derogatory opinion, combined with Banyoro's painful memories of their defeat by the Baganda and British, should have come to be reflected in some degree in their attitudes to themselves. In my first conversation with Bunyoro's Katikiro (prime minister) he explained to me at some length that Banyoro's spirit was broken. '*Roho imekufa*', he told me in Kiswahili, '(our) spirit is dead'. I was told in 1953 that most of the few Banyoro who

enlisted in the military forces during the Second World War described themselves as Baganda. Although traditionally their hated enemies, everyone knew that the Baganda were a clever, enterprising, and progressive people, admired and respected by Europeans. I mentioned earlier Banyoro's infecundity as compared with other Uganda tribes during the past sixty years or so; when I was in Bunyoro they were very conscious of this, and many of them believed that the Europeans were actively concerned to maintain this state of affairs, so that eventually the Banyoro people would die out, and the Europeans could take over their country for themselves. These factors, allied with a profound nostalgia for their country's glorious past, combined to create an impression of Nyoro lack of confidence, self-disparagement, and mistrust, which contrasted strongly with the confident and forward-looking demeanour of other East African peoples with whom I was acquainted at that time, not least the Baganda. This impression was largely dissipated as I got to know the Banyoro better, and in any case Nyoro fortunes had been steadily improving over recent decades. But I believe that it was valid, as far as it went.

3

MYTH AND TRADITIONAL HISTORY

BUNYORO's rich and complex mythology, and the legends about its early kings, gradually merge into traditional history, and so link up with historical times. This material is of interest on several grounds. Regarded simply as oral literature, Nyoro tales of the creation, of the origin of the kingship, and of the first Bakama, can be read and enjoyed for their own sake. Regarded as exemplifications of perhaps universal mythical themes, found in a variety of forms throughout a wide range of human cultures, they may contribute to the interpretative and comparative study of myth, an interest somewhat neglected by the functional anthropologists of the 1920s and 1930s, but which has now come into its own again. Regarded as an adjunct to history, if a people's tribal histories are supplemented by (or used to supplement) existing historical or archaeological information, and if they are carefully collated with the traditional histories of neighbouring and related peoples, they may add to our knowledge of past events, or at least suggest plausible hypotheses about them. This is so especially for the more recent period when traditional histories merge into the period of written records, which began with the coming of the Europeans.

Thus in Bunyoro there are circumstantial accounts of the reigns of the later kings of the Babito dynasty, some of which (for example Bikunya, K. W., Nyakatura) have been published in Runyoro by Nyoro authors during the past forty years or so. The defeats and victories described in these accounts are still discussed around Nyoro firesides, and the places where they occurred are pointed out: the capitals and tombs of former kings are well known to everyone. But naturally the further one goes back in time the less reliable these accounts become, and the more they reflect Nyoro beliefs about and attitudes towards themselves and their past, rather than historical 'fact'.

But, for most social anthropologists, the central interest of myth is still in its current, contextual significance. A people's myths and traditional histories are contemporary phenomena, and the beliefs and values which they express can usefully be related to other existing aspects of the culture. Almost always they express social values, judgements about what the people who have the myth think desirable and proper. In particular, they often confirm and validate an existing social or political order. In Maciver's words, 'at the core of every myth-structure lies the myth of authority' (1947, p. 39). Nyoro myth justifies Bunyoro's system of social and political stratification, and so provides a 'mythical charter', in Malinowski's phrase, for the inequalities the system implies, and for the Nyoro kingship on which it is centred. But we shall see that it has other kinds of significance as well.

Several authors have given accounts, varying in length and detail (and not always mutually consistent), of Nyoro myth and traditional history.[1] In what follows I present only a summary version based mainly on the writings of Fisher, who gives a translation of a very full (though unhappily expurgated) account written for her early in this century by the kings of Bunyoro and Toro; Bikunya, a former prime minister of Bunyoro, who follows Fisher fairly closely; K. W., who is the former Mukama; and Nyakatura, also a former minister in the Mukama's government. I make no attempt here to correlate these stories with the traditions of neighbouring countries, or to assess their usefulness as guides to 'real' history.[2] My interest is in what they mean for modern Banyoro in their contemporary social and political setting, and we shall see that in the 1950s they both glorified Bunyoro's past and explained some aspects of its present condition.

Nyoro myths of origin describe a first 'family', though little is said of a first wife or mother in these accounts. In Fisher's (and Bikunya's) version the head of this family is called Ruhanga, which is the word nowadays commonly used for 'God': in Runyoro the word *kuhanga* means 'to create'. For Nyakatura the

---

[1] For example Fisher, chaps. 6–12; Czekanowski, chap. 3; Gorju, chaps. 2–5; Roscoe 1923, chap. 14; Bikunya; K. W.; Nyakatura; and Dunbar, Part 1. The contributions of some of these authors are briefly but usefully assessed in Dunbar, pp. 6–8.

[2] A beginning has already been made at these tasks: see, for example, Oliver 1955 and Posnansky.

story begins with the arrival from elsewhere of the first inhabitants of Bunyoro, led by their king, Kintu. *Kintu* is the Runyoro for 'thing': the prefix *ki*- sometimes conveys the notion of great size, and the root *ntu*, 'being', is the same as that in *muntu* (pl. *bantu*), 'person' or 'man'. Nyakatura says that Kintu arrived with his wife Kati (the word simply means 'woman'), but this is all we are told about her.

Fisher and Bikunya describe in detail the creation of the world. Ruhanga, who was accompanied by his brother Nkya Mba and the latter's four sons (in Nyakatura's account there are only three sons), was the creator, who after a time abandoned the world he had made. Nkya was the Adam of the Nyoro story; the first man and the progenitor of the human race. Bikunya entertainingly describes Ruhanga's piecemeal creation of the world and of the essentials for human existence, as Nkya asked one by one for the means of livelihood. First sky and earth were one, and they had to be separated; then Ruhanga created the sun, night and the moon, a fowl (to announce the dawn), grass and trees (to build houses with and to carve utensils from), tools (knife, axe, and hammer), sheep and cattle, gourds, and fire to cook with. It is not unlikely that in telling this story Fisher's informants, the kings of Bunyoro and Toro, were influenced by the biblical account (both were converts of the Anglican Mission), but the order of priority, and the way in which the story is told, are certainly Nyoro rather than Hebraic. So the creation was completed, and everything essential for man's needs on earth was provided.

The eldest of Nkya's four sons was called Kantu, literally 'little thing' (in Runyoro the word *kantu* is used for the evil, anti-social element in human nature, as we might say 'something' got into a person). But the three younger sons were not distinguished by separate names, and their undifferentiatedness is indicated by all of them sharing the same name, Kana, which means 'little child'. So Nkya asked Ruhanga if he would give the three boys separate names: 'my children are too much for me', he said, 'because of their having only this one name Kana; when I call one Kana another Kana comes, and when I give them something they all fight over it' (Bikunya, p. 4).

Ruhanga agreed to do so, and the next day he subjected the three boys to two separate tests, to decide how they should be

named, and which of them was to be his heir. He called the boys
to him (he now lived in a different place from Nkya, the boys'
father) and he presented each of them with a wooden milk pot
(*kisahi*). He then sent them home, but on the way he placed six
things: an ox's head, a cowhide thong (for tying cattle with),
a bundle of cooked millet and sweet potatoes, a grass head-ring
(used for carrying loads on the head), an axe, and a knife. When
the boys came upon these things, the eldest immediately picked
up the basket of food and began to eat. His brothers told him
to leave off, saying 'you are eating other people's food; will they
not curse you?' So he stopped eating, but he put the bundle of
food on his head and took it with him, using the grass head-ring
for this purpose. He also took the axe and the knife. The
youngest brother took the ox's head, and the middle brother
took the leather thong, and he also carried his brothers' milk
pots as well as his own.

When they reached home they showed these things to their
father, who asked which of them had been eating the food. The
elder confessed that he had; the other two denied having done
so, adding, somewhat self-righteously, that they had told their
older brother not to.

That evening Ruhanga came to their house and subjected the
boys to a second test. After the cows had been milked he told the
three of them to sit on the ground with their legs stretched out
in front of them, and he filled each boy's milk pot with fresh
milk, and placing the pots on their laps, told them to hold them
safely in that position until morning. 'If I find that you have
drunk my milk, the same way as you ate my food, you'll see
(what will happen to you)', he said; 'I'll see you with it in the
morning' (Bikunya, p. 5). And he left them.

At about midnight, the youngest boy began to nod, and a little
of his milk was spilt. He awoke with a start, and begged his
brothers to give him some of theirs. They agreed, for they loved
him very much and anyway he had only spilt a very little, and
so his pot was full again. Just before dawn the eldest of the three
suddenly spilt all his milk. He asked his brothers to give him
some of theirs, but they refused, since his pot was quite empty
and it would need more than both of them could spare to fill it.

When Ruhanga came in the morning, he found the youngest
boy's pot full, the second boy's nearly full, and the eldest's quite

empty. He asked the second brother if he had drunk some of his, and he said that he had not, but had given some to his younger brother. So Ruhanga named the three boys. The eldest was always to be a servant to the other two, and so were his descendants after him. His lot was to be peasant cultivation, an occupation of low status, and so he was named Kairu, little *Mwiru*. Throughout the northern part of the interlacustrine area the term *mwiru* (pl. *bairu*) refers primarily to members of the agricultural peasant class, as distinct both from the rulers (*banyoro* or *balemi*), and from the cattle-keeping Bahuma. The term *mwiru* has other associated meanings too; often it can be roughly translated as 'servant'. Thus a dependant might say to his master '*ndi omwiru wawe*', 'I am your servant'. But always it implies the idea of social inferiority and subordination. The eldest son had showed himself fitted for no better fate, for he had chosen (and eaten) the millet and potatoes, the food of peasant cultivators, and he had taken up the load and the grass head-ring, thus accepting a role of subordination and servitude. Also, he had lost all of the milk entrusted to him, and so had shown himself unworthy to have anything to do with cattle.

The second boy and his descendants were to occupy the honourable status of cattle-keepers and herdsmen, so he was named Kahuma, little *Muhuma*. For he had chosen the leather thong for tethering cattle, and he had come home bearing his brothers' milk pots as well as his own. Also, he had spilt none of the milk entrusted to him, but had only given a little to his younger brother.

The third and youngest boy was to be his father's heir, and he and his line would always rule over his brothers and their descendants. For he had taken the ox's head, which was a sign that he would be at the head of all men. Even today, the person who is given the head of a slaughtered animal is specially honoured. At a feast the head is always given to the 'sister's son' (*mwihwa*) of the host; in many contexts a sister's son is said to 'rule' his mother's brother.[1] Also, only he had been able to show a full pot of milk in the morning, because of the service rendered

---

[1] The word *mwihwa* does not in fact mean 'sister's son'; it denotes the child of any woman of the speaker's lineage (of course including sisters' sons). See Beattie 1958*a*, pp. 17–22.

to him by his two older brothers. So Ruhanga named him Twari
(ruler), or Kakama (little *Mukama*), and he was to succeed his
father and become the ruler of the Kitara kingdom. Ruhanga
then told the two older boys that they should never leave their
younger brother Kakama, but that they and their descendants
should stay with him and serve him and his descendants for
ever. And he told Kakama always to rule sympathetically and
wisely.

The story relates that Kantu, Nkya's first son, disgruntled at
having been left out of this naming ceremony, accused Ruhanga
of discriminating against him. 'Because you didn't give me a
new name, I shall go and do wrong', he said. Then (in Bikunya's version) he went and found a piece of wood, took it to
Ruhanga, and asked him to make some holes in it. Ruhanga
agreed, and made thirty-two holes in it in four parallel rows of
eight. Kantu then picked up sixty-four small pebbles, and thus
was invented the game of *rusoro*, popular throughout Uganda,
and (under various names) throughout much of Africa.[1] Kantu
and Ruhanga began to play, but Kantu cheated, scooping up
all his uncle's pieces and placing them on his side of the board.
When Ruhanga remonstrated with him, he said that he was
doing wrong because he had been disinherited and discriminated against. Ruhanga later asked Kantu's mother why he
behaved so badly, and she replied that it was his fault for not
having created him well.

This made Ruhanga angry, and he ascended into the sky to
escape from the evil that had come into the world. At that time
the sky was joined to the earth by three columns, one of iron,
the other two of wood; of these one was a barkcloth tree
(*mutoma*), the other a Uganda coral tree (*muko*). After Ruhanga
had ascended, the iron pillar fell and was shattered, but the
barkcloth tree and the Uganda coral tree grew and flourished
and trees of these kinds can still be seen today. Small pieces of
the iron pillar are still found on the ground, and are sometimes
made into ornaments.

For Banyoro, this myth explains many things. It tells how the
world was made, how evil came into it, and (as so commonly in
myths of origin) how God, disgusted with the world he had

---

[1] For a recent account of its Uganda form see Nsimbe. *Rusoro* is called *omweso*
in Luganda.

created, withdrew from it and from any further close contact
with men. It also explains the origin of the popular game *rusoro*.
But, most important of all, it explains and justifies the 'premise
of inequality' (in Maquet's phrase) which characterized almost
all social relationships in Bunyoro, as it did in the other interlacustrine kingdoms. For it provides a 'mythical charter' for the
traditional stratification of Nyoro society into distinct social
categories, membership of which is, for the most part, acquired
by descent. The implication of the myth is that in the beginning
there were no such distinctions; the fact that the three boys had
no separate names or identities meant that all were equal. But
this led to confusion, and the solution was not only to distinguish
them by name, but more importantly still, to differentiate them
permanently in terms of both role and status. The same myth
is found among the formerly even more stratified Ankole and
Ruanda peoples to the south.

In recent years the distinction between Bahuma and Bairu
has decreased greatly in importance in most of the northern
interlacustrine area, and it is doubtful if it ever had the force in
Bunyoro that it had in the more southern kingdoms. Anyway,
it is said that in Bunyoro most of the Bahuma left the country
when the cattle died out. Also, the standing of the Bahuma
relative to the ruling Babito dynasty is by no means clear-cut.
Nevertheless, the distinctions of status which the myth justifies,
and the restriction, ideally at least, of high status to those
qualified by birth to occupy it, were important values in Nyoro
thought, and for the more traditionally minded, probably still
are. In the last resort, what the myth validates is not just
this or that particular kind of status difference, but rather the
'rightness' of all such distinctions based on birth. Although in
the myth the original discrimination was based on achievement,
what it validates is a system in which statuses are ascribed and
not achieved. So the subordination–superordination theme discussed in Chapter 2 is validated by a myth of the origin of
separate social classes. Inferiors may find subordination less
irksome, and superiors may exercise authority more confidently,
when both accept that the difference between them is something
determined by God, given for all time from the beginning of
things. A young and highly educated Munyoro, a member of
the Bito ruling class, assured me with conviction that it was

right that he and his agnatic kinsmen should hold and retain power, for had they not inherited the ability to govern from their ancestors?

The myth has a further meaning for Banyoro: it illustrates and validates the approved pattern of inheritance. In Bunyoro, status and property are inherited in the male line, and a man, or, if he is dead, senior members of his clan, usually close agnates, may nominate any son (or a brother, if there is no son) as his heir. But if a man has two or more sons, the eldest is rarely selected; in the case of the kingship he cannot be. The Mukama's eldest son is debarred from the succession, and traditionally assumes the office of Okwiri, or head of the Babito (his role is discussed in Chapter 5). Ideally, the youngest son should inherit, even though he is still a child: the older brother should occupy the role of sponsor and guardian until the heir is mature enough to take over his inheritance. This pattern of inheritance is still common. It may and often does lead to dispute, for when an heir grows up he may accuse his eldest brother of having 'eaten' his patrimony. But it serves also to ensure that occasions for the transfer of property and status (the second was especially important in Nyoro eyes) occur as infrequently as possible. Evidently a young boy may expect to live longer than his older brother, who in a polygynous family may be middle-aged. Regarded from this point of view, the myth may be seen as expressing and justifying the secondary, even subordinate, role often allocated to eldest sons. Nkya's oldest son Kantu was deprived of any inheritance and came to represent the force of evil in the world, and to Kairu, the eldest of the three unnamed brothers, Ruhanga gave the lowest status in the traditional Nyoro hierarchy. We shall see below that the same theme is expressed in the story of the coming of the Bito rulers.

The shadowy line of kings descended from Kakama is called the Batembuzi dynasty. The word appears to be associated with the verb *kutembura*, 'to build in a new place' (Davis, p. 169), and so it might reasonably be translated as 'the wanderers', those who continually build in new places. In fact until the second half of the last century Nyoro kings have moved to a new capital on accession, and often at frequent intervals during their reigns as well. Recent lists give the names of about eighteen of these early kings; their number has expanded considerably since the

first accounts were published about half a century ago.[1] Most of them are names only, but stories, some with contemporary morals, are told of the more famous of them.

Of these stories, one has particular relevance to Nyoro political and social values. It stresses the responsibility that goes with authority—a common theme in Nyoro thinking about politics—and it concerns the last (in Nyakatura's version the second from last) of the Batembuzi kings, Isaza, who succeeded his father Ngonzaki.[2] When Isaza first came to the throne he was young and irresponsible. He paid no respect to the old men whom his father had left to advise him, and he refused to consult them or to listen to their advice. Instead he drove them from the country, replacing them by gay young men: accordingly he was nicknamed Rugambanabato, which means in Runyoro 'he who talks with small children'.

He was a keen huntsman, and one day while he was hunting with his young friends they killed a zebra. Isaza was so delighted with the gaily striped hide that he insisted in being dressed in it at once. So a needle was found, and there and then the skin was sewn on to him with leather thongs. He was greatly pleased with his appearance and with the congratulations of his friends. They continued to hunt throughout the day, and gradually the hot sun dried the hide on Isaza's body, so that it shrank and began to squeeze him almost to the point of death. When he called on his young men for help they did not know what to do; they simply laughed at him and told him not to complain, saying, 'You're drying it up for your royal drum!' (Bikunya, p. 8).

Two of the old men whom his father had left behind to advise Isaza had not yet gone from the kingdom, and now Isaza sent a message to them, begging for help. First they refused, saying

[1] Thus in 1947 Nyakatura named eighteen Batembuzi successors to Kakama, in 1923 Roscoe listed eight, and Fisher, twelve years earlier, only four. For a useful comparative table see Dunbar, p. 15. The tendency of Nyoro royal genealogies to lengthen with successive publications may have indicated a desire to keep up with neighbouring kingdoms, but it also undoubtedly reflects increasing interest in and study of Nyoro myth and tradition.

[2] Ngonzaki was so named because he was said to have possessed enormous wealth, so that when a subject brought him a gift he would not bother to turn round to look at it, but would just say 'ngonzaki?' 'what should I want?' since his palace was already overflowing with goods. According to popular Nyoro etymology Isaza's name is commemorated in the term, in both Runyoro and Luganda, for a county (saza, pl. masaza), since he is said to have been the first to divide his kingdom into formal administrative divisions.

'What should we know about the matter? Let him consult his young men.' But at last one of them relented, and he told the young men to throw Isaza into a pond. They did so, and the moisture stretched and loosened the hide, so that it was possible to cut the thongs and release the king.

He was so grateful for the old man's practical advice that he called back all his father's old advisers, gave them a great feast, and reinstated them. At the same time he admonished his young companions, telling them that they should always respect their elders, and quoting the well-known proverb 'a household without a senior man in it cannot thrive' (*eka etali mukuru tetungwa*). From that time onward, the story goes, Isaza constantly consulted his old men and discussed things with them, and he ruled his kingdom wisely and well.

The story of Isaza and the zebra hide is popular, and it expresses values which are still important for Banyoro. First, it points the obvious moral that young people neglect at their peril the advice of their seniors, and that old men ripe in experience are generally wiser than ignorant youths. But it also stresses, what we have already noted in the first myth, that there is nothing inappropriate in young people possessing authority. There is no suggestion in the myth that Isaza should have been replaced by an older and more sensible ruler; only that he should be willing to take advice from his seniors. The wisdom of the old and the respect due to them are stressed, but their part is to advise, not to rule. The old should be spared the arduous responsibilities of making political decisions, but it is right that they should advise those who have those responsibilities.

Traditional Nyoro attitudes to kingship are consistent with these ideas. Thus, it was said that like 'divine kings' elsewhere, a king who grew too old to govern effectively was expected to kill himself by taking poison, or he might be put to death by his wives (Fisher, p. 124; Roscoe 1923, p. 121). It is also said that a king could formerly be required after he had reigned for nine years (nine is an auspicious number in many Nyoro contexts) to perform a special rite in the course of which he relinquished most of his powers, leaving the making of major political decisions to his chief ministers.[1]

---

[1] Fisher, p. 130; Bikunya, pp. 52–4. This institution is further discussed in Chapter 5.

I turn now to the series of myths which link the early Batem-buzi kings with their more famous successors the Bacwezi, and these with the even more celebrated Bito dynasty, whose reign ended with the last Mukama. These stories represent the Nyoro royal line as having continued in unbroken male succession from the creation of the world until the present day.[1] They thus merge with the traditional history of the Bito rulers, and so, chronologically regarded, link up with the 'real' history of Bunyoro which effectively begins with or shortly before the coming of the Europeans. The stories are rich in descriptive detail; here I give a somewhat contracted account.[2]

The story begins by telling how towards the end of his reign Isaza was approached by a messenger from the Underworld or the World of Ghosts, which was called Okuzimu (the ghost of a dead person is *muzimu*). The king of Okuzimu was Nyami-yonga—*muyonga* means a black smut. Nyamiyonga wished to enter into an alliance with the Nyoro king, and his messenger presented Isaza with a series of riddles from their master. These were too difficult for Isaza and his advisers, despite their age and wisdom, but they were solved by a little serving maid called Kazana (*kazana* means 'serving maid') who explained that Nyamiyonga wanted Isaza to enter into a blood pact (*mukago*) with him.[3] After the riddles had been answered, the messenger was asked what else he had brought, and he produced a small

---

[1] The view has recently been expressed that (as far as the Babito are concerned) the myth does not do this, but as this view is directly contradicted by the substantial volume of ethnographic evidence upon which it purports to be based, account need not be taken of it here. See Needham, pp. 438–42, and Beattie 1968, pp. 426–31.

[2] For more extended accounts see Fisher, chaps. 6–11; K. W. 1935, 1936, 1937a; also (in Runyoro) Bikunya and Nyakatura.

[3] Isaza was asked to identify the following: that which announces the dawn (*nterabuire*); the little door of poverty (*kaigi k'enaku*); the rope that binds water (*muguha oguboha amaizi*); that which makes Isaza turn (*kihindura Isaza*); that which does not finish the job (*ntamara mulimo*); and that which is not known (in the sense of 'unheard of') (*kitamanywa*). Kazana explained, with practical demonstration where appropriate, that the announcer of the dawn is a cock; the little doorway of poverty is the blood pact (*mukago*)—because if a man becomes poor he can rely on his blood partner for help; the rope that binds water is millet flour (which absorbs the water it is cooked in); that which makes Isaza turn is a cow which is brought into the courtyard and lows behind him; that which does not finish the work is a dog which is given a pipe to smoke; and that which is unknown is a baby which soils Isaza's mat, and wets him when he picks it up. See Bikunya, pp. 9–10; also Fisher, pp. 78–80. For a brief account of the blood pact in Bunyoro, see Beattie 1958b.

skin bag containing two segments of a coffee-bean, one with a little blood on it, a small knife, and a handful of a special grass called *jubwa*. Kazana explained that Isaza was to use these to make the blood pact with Nyamiyonga; he should swallow the blooded segment of coffee-bean, he should use the knife to make a small cut on his stomach, and after he had put a little of his blood on the other segment, he should return it to Nyamiyonga.

But Isaza's advisers said that it would be a dreadful thing for him to enter into a blood pact with a ghost, even with the king of ghosts; it would be much safer for someone else to do it on his behalf. So he called his chief minister Kwezi, who was not of the royal line, and giving him the knife and the two segments of coffee-bean, he told him to do what was required. Kwezi did so, and the bag and its contents were returned to Nyamiyonga.

Nyamiyonga was delighted that Isaza had become his blood partner, but he soon learned from one of his servants who had accompanied the messenger (and who had himself made a blood pact with one of Isaza's servants), how he had been cheated. He was very angry, not so much (the story goes) because he had been deceived as because he had been united in the blood pact with a commoner (*mwiru*). So he determined to get Isaza into his clutches.

He had a very beautiful daughter called Nyamata (*amata* is the Runyoro word for milk), and he sent her to Isaza's court with instructions to seduce him, but not to say who she was. When she was brought before Isaza he fell in love with her at once and married her. After a time she became pregnant, and she said that she wished to go home to her father Nyamiyonga's kingdom on a visit. She tried to persuade Isaza to accompany her, but he refused to be parted from his cattle. He loved Nyamata very much, he said, but he loved his big long-horned cows even more.

So Nyamata went home to the Underworld and told her father that she had failed to persuade Isaza to accompany her, because although he was not a bad man he was quite infatuated with his cattle. She did not return to Isaza, and some time afterwards she gave birth to a boy, who was named Isimbwa. Then Nyamiyonga thought of another plan to ensnare the Nyoro king. He chose two of his most beautiful cattle, a cow and a bull named Kahogo and Ruhogo (*ruhogo* means a reddish-brown

bull) which were larger and had wider horns than any of Isaza's herd, and he caused them to be found wandering near Isaza's capital. When they were taken to the king, he at once loved them more than any others of his herd, and swore that only death would separate him from them.

One day these two cattle were lost. Isaza was distracted, and he and his men searched everywhere for them. At last he caught a glimpse of their horns in a great hole in the ground, and after he had given directions that his palace doorkeeper, a commoner called Bukuku, should take care of his kingdom until he returned, he descended alone into the pit. At once he found himself in the Land of Ghosts, and after wandering for some time he reached Nyamiyonga's capital. Nyamiyonga received him hospitably and entertained him well, as a father-in-law should when his son-in-law visits him. He gave him a skin to sleep on, oxen to eat, cows to milk, and pots to cook with, but, the story relates, all of these were black, for black is the colour associated with ghosts and the Underworld. Soon Isaza was reunited with his wife and saw his young son for the first time, and his two cattle were restored to him, together with a large herd. But Nyamiyonga had not forgiven Isaza for having joined him with a *mwiru* in the blood pact, and he never allowed him to leave Okuzimu.

After all hope of Isaza's return was abandoned his deputy Bukuku took over the Kitara kingdom. But people did not like to be ruled by a *mwiru*, and for this reason many chiefs rebelled during his reign, and many people left the country. But Isaza had entrusted the kingdom to him, and anyway there was no one else of royal blood to rule.

Meantime Nyamata's son, Isimbwa, grew up at Nyami-yonga's capital, and his father Isaza married him to a girl called Nyabiryo, also a native of Okuzimu. They had a son, who was named Kyomya. Isimbwa was not confined to Nyamiyonga's kingdom as his father was, and he and his son Kyomya used to go on long hunting expeditions in the upper world of men. On one such trip he passed through Madi country (to the north of present-day Bunyoro) and leaving his son Kyomya there, he journeyed south and eventually reached Bukuku's capital.

Now Bukuku had a daughter named Nyinamwiru (a name which indicates her *mwiru* descent), and many years before,

when Nyinamwiru was a baby, the diviners had told Bukuku that he would have cause to fear any child that she might bear. They advised him to kill her, but he refused to do this, as she was his only child. Instead he confined her, attended only by her maid Mugizi, in a special enclosure to which the only entrance was through his own well-guarded palace. In one version of the story, when she grew up he put out one of her eyes and cut off one of her breasts, since she was a very beautiful girl and he wished to ensure that she would be unattractive to men (Nyakatura, p. 27).

When Isimbwa, the 'peripatetic voluptuary' as Oliver has aptly described him (1953, p. 136), reached Bukuku's palace, he was intrigued by this state of affairs, and wooed Nyinamwiru through her maid Mugizi, sending her with his compliments gifts of flowers and fruit.[1] At last, at Nyinamwiru's invitation and with the maid's connivance, he climbed into the enclosure by means of a ladder, accompanied, so the story goes, by his men and his dogs. He stayed there for three months, by the end of which time Nyinamwiru was pregnant. Then, after promising the infatuated girl that he would return two months later, he and his men departed, and he was not seen again for many years.

In due course, Nyinamwiru gave birth to a son, to Bukuku's consternation. He at once ordered that the child should be thrown in a river and left to drown. This was done, but by chance the baby's umbilical cord became entangled in an overhanging branch, and he was found there alive by a potter, Rubumbi (*mubumbi* means a potter), who was looking for clay. He brought the baby home, where it was cared for by his wife, who happened at that time to have a newborn infant of her own. Rubumbi knew that the child was Nyinamwiru's, and he let her know that it was safe. She was delighted, and contrived from time to time to give Rubumbi cattle so that the child would have plenty of milk to drink and would grow up strong and healthy. Bukuku had no idea that his grandchild was still alive.

---

[1] According to Bikunya (p. 16) the flowers were posies of a flowering grass with compact heads of white blossom, called *nseko y'ensi* (literally 'country laughter')—*kyllinga albiceps*; and the fruit was *kasekera*, a plant with edible purple berries (*lantana trifolia*); the name *kasekera* is probably also associated with the verb *kuseka*, 'to laugh'. I am indebted to Davis for these plant identifications.

So Isimbwa's son, Isaza's grandson, grew up as the potter Rubumbi's child. He grew into a very strong and spirited young man, and older people used to comment on his striking resemblance to their last king, Isaza. But he was constantly in trouble with Bukuku's herdsmen, for when they were watering the king's cattle he would drive them and their herds away, so that he could water Rubumbi's herd first. When the king's herdsmen protested he beat them, so that they were very much afraid of him, and at last they complained about his behaviour to their master. Bukuku was angry, and one day he went to the watering place himself with the intention of punishing the insolent youth. As usual, the boy drove the king's cattle aside. The king, who was sitting on his royal stool above the drinking place, ordered him to stop, and he called on his men to seize and beat him. But before they could do so, the young man ran around behind Bukuku and stabbed him in the back with his spear, so that he fell forward into the drinking trough and died. Then the youth sat down on the king's stool.

The royal herdsmen were astounded, and ran at once to Bukuku's daughter Nyinamwiru to tell her what had happened and to call on her to have her father's murderer killed. When Nyinamwiru heard the news she exclaimed 'my ears have heard both evil and good' ('amatu gampulire ebibi n'ebirungi'), for though her father had been slain, her son had inherited his grandfather's kingdom. Banyoro still use this saying when they hear news that is both good and bad. Nyinamwiru then gave orders that Ndahura, which is what the young man came to be called, should be installed on the throne of his grandfather Isaza, and everyone rejoiced that Kitara's royal line had been restored. Ndahura is known as the first king of the short-lived Cwezi dynasty, and he is said to have established his capital on Mubende Hill.

He soon recovered the areas which had seceded during Bukuku's reign, and he travelled widely over the whole of what is now Uganda and beyond, extending his empire wherever he went. But at last he too disappeared for a time: some say that he vanished into the Underworld like his grandfather Isaza. After an interregnum during which the empire was ruled by his half-brother Mulindwa ('the caretaker'), he was succeeded by his son Wamara, who was the last of the Bacwezi kings. As

we noted in Chapter 2, many stories are told of the marvellous wisdom and achievements of these rulers and their kinsmen, and many natural features such as volcanic crater lakes and strange rock formations, as well as the huge man-made earthworks at Bigo in Mubende district and elsewhere, are attributed to them.

But during Wamara's reign people started to rebel against the Bacwezi, for their rule was oppressive. Certainly, whoever constructed the great earthworks in Mubende and elsewhere, the task must have required a vast labour force. Also, dissension had arisen among the Bacwezi themselves. It is said that Nyangoma, a woman of the Basingo clan, and the mother (or mother's sister) of Mugenyi, Mulindwa's half-brother, attempted to murder Mulindwa. She was jealous of him because he and not her son Mugenyi had ruled the kingdom during Ndahura's absence, and she was afraid that he might succeed Wamara on the throne. To complicate matters further, Mulindwa was in love with Nyangoma. One day when he visited her he fell into a pit of boiling water which she had prepared for him in her house, but he was rescued from it, badly scalded, by Mugenyi, who appeared on the scene just in time. In Bikunya's account Mugenyi killed Nyangoma and many other members of his mother's clan in revenge, and ever since then members of the royal Bito clan have been forbidden to intermarry with the Basingo.[1]

Omens inauspicious for the Bacwezi began to appear: blood was found in the milk of Wamara's cows, and Mugenyi's favourite cow Bihogo, which he loved so much that he had sworn to kill himself if it died, had a fit and expired at a salt-lick. Mugenyi was only prevented from carrying out his threat by his brothers. Also, there were invasions from outside the kingdom and rebellions within it.

So Wamara summoned his diviners, and a small fattened bull calf (*enumi ente encwerano*) was slaughtered, after Wamara had rinsed his mouth with milk and the milk had been poured into the calf's mouth. When the diviners cut open the animal into order to examine its entrails, no trace of them could be found. The diviners were greatly astonished and did not know what to say.

---

[1] Bikunya, pp. 25–6. The rule has not been strictly observed in recent years: while I was in Bunyoro one of the Mukama's daughters was married to a Musingo *saza* chief.

Every time they attempted to divine in this manner the same thing happened. However, there happened to be present at that time a diviner called Nyakoka from Bukidi (the present-day Acholi and Madi districts north of the Nile), and he said that he would solve the mystery for them. But first he insisted, wisely as it turned out, on entering into the blood pact with one of the Bacwezi, in case they should wish to kill him if they were displeased with his interpretation. So he made the pact with Mulindwa. Then he took an axe, and cut open the legs and head of the animal, and at once the missing intestines fell out of these members. As they did so, a large black smut from the fire settled on them, and they were unable to remove it.

Nyakoka then said that the absence of the intestines from their proper place meant that the country would be left without rulers, for the reign of the Bacwezi in Kitara was ended. Their presence in the animal's legs and head meant that the Bacwezi would load up their belongings and would travel far away; according to Bikunya their presence in the head also meant that they would continue to rule over men through the spirit mediumship (*mbandwa*) cult, in which to this day the central figures are the Bacwezi hero-gods.[1] The black smut which could not be removed signified that the country would be taken over by dark-complexioned strangers from another country.

The Bacwezi were naturally displeased by Nyakoka's interpretation, and they would have killed him if he had not been warned of their intention by his blood-partner Mugenyi, and escaped. However, they gathered together their goods and their remaining cattle and left the country; some say that they disappeared into Lake Albert, others that they vanished from the earth altogether. They left their drums and spears and some other insignia in the care of certain peasant families near the lake, and they also left two old Bahuma women, said in some versions to have been wives of Wamara, who were familiar with palace procedure, at their royal capital in what is now Mubende.

Thus the Bacwezi vanished from Bunyoro. As we saw, little can be said about who they were or where they come from; indeed it has been questioned whether they really existed at

---

[1] Bikunya, p. 57. For a brief account of the Cwezi *mbandwa* cult see Beattie 1969.

all.[1] But rather more can be said about the distinct but connected meanings of the word 'Bacwezi' today. In its first meaning, the Bacwezi are the small group of rulers whom we have just been discussing, descended in the male line from the earlier rulers and, as we shall see, the progenitors of the later ones. Nine of them are specially well known, all sons or grandsons of Isimbwa, and there are sometimes said to have been nineteen of them altogether—as was noted earlier, nine is an auspicious number in many Nyoro contexts. Bikunya (p. 32), however, lists forty-seven of them, women as well as men, all descendants of the peripatetic and philoprogenitive Isimbwa. He also names at the same time twelve of the Bacwezi's most important herdsmen (bahuma), a clear indication that at least in the Nyoro view Bacwezi were not the same people as the Bahuma.

But in other contexts Banyoro think of the Bacwezi not just as a small group of rulers, links in the agnatic chain connecting the first to the third dynasty of Nyoro kings, but rather as a singular and distinct race, who came from somewhere else, probably from the north or the north-east, lived in Bunyoro for a while, and then disappeared. They are said to have been of very light complexion (early Europeans were sometimes taken to be the Bacwezi returning to their old kingdom), and (as we have seen) to have possessed marvellous skills and miraculous powers. The description of the Bacwezi given by Oberg in his account of the Ankole kingdom would also be accepted by Banyoro (pp. 122–5).

But for present-day Banyoro the term Bacwezi has yet another meaning. It denotes the spiritual powers which are the traditional objects of the Nyoro spirit mediumship cult. It is said that when the Bacwezi left the country they left behind them a cult of spirit mediumship of which they themselves were the objects. Through the cult Banyoro retain a permanent means of access to the magical wisdom and power of the Bacwezi, whose spirits can 'climb into the head' (kutemba ha mutwe) of their accredited mediums, and which are concerned, in particular, with Banyoro's well-being and fertility. But these spirits are not thought of as the ghosts of long-dead people; the word for ghost (muzimu)

---

[1] It has been suggested (Wrigley) that they are no more than personifications of certain elemental forces, like the earlier Greek gods. But *somebody* must have built the earth fortifications at Bigo and elsewhere!

is not applied to them. They are a class of spirits *sui generis*, each with its own individuality and special competence, and each identified with one of the Cwezi hero-gods. There are many other kinds of spirits besides the Bacwezi which can reveal themselves through mediums but the Cwezi spirits are the objects of the 'white' possession cult (*mbandwa ez'era*), which may be said to be Bunyoro's traditional religion. Thus regarded, they are contemporary spiritual powers, not merely long-dead heroes or even ghosts. The *mbandwa* cult is not an ancestor cult; Banyoro do not think of themselves as the 'children' of the Bacwezi, though they may speak of their ruling family as being so. The Bacwezi were rulers, not ancestors: the idiom of Bunyoro's traditional religion is political, rather than conceived in terms of kinship.

To add further to the confusion, one of Bunyoro's hundred and fifty or so clans is called the Bacwezi. But members of this clan are distinguished in no significant ways from members of other clans, and they claim no special connection with the mythical Bacwezi, though if pressed they will agree that there must have been some genealogical link. Banyoro are not conscious of any particular incompatibility between these various senses of the term. Bacwezi were a small group of rulers, they were a whole race of stranger peoples, they are, still, a powerful pantheon of individual spirits, and they are a Nyoro clan. Yet, in some sense all these are, at bottom, aspects of the same 'reality'; which aspect is referred to in any given case must be inferred from the context.

To return to our myth. After the diviner Nyakoka had escaped from the Bacwezi's vengeance, he set off for his own country of Bukidi, north of the Nile. When he reached its borders he met the four sons of the Mucwezi Kyomya, who were on a hunting expedition: Kyomya, Isimbwa's son by his first wife, had married a Mukidi woman, Nyatworo, of the Bakwongo clan, and his sons had grown up in that country with their mother. In the Nyoro story these four boys were called Babito, because when Nyakoka met them they were resting under a *bito* tree (in Nyakatura's version [p. 68] their mother's house was shaded by such a tree). This, however, is popular Nyoro etymology; nobody now knows what kind of tree a *bito* tree is. Very much more relevant is the fact that in Acholi the

term *bito* 'is used generally of the sons of an aristocratic lineage' (Girling, p. 154). From this and other evidence it is clear that whatever may be said of the earlier Batembuzi and Bacwezi dynasties, Crazzolara's claim that Bunyoro's Babito rulers are of Nilotic origin is certainly valid.[1]

According to the myth Nyakoka told the young men, Isimbwa's grandsons and the great-grandsons of the last Mutembuzi king Isaza, that they should go to the south and take over the abandoned kingdom of the Bacwezi. There were, in Nyakatura's version (p. 67), four brothers; Nyarwa, the eldest, the twin brothers Rukidi Mpuga Isingoma (*mpuga* is a cow with large white patches, and Rukidi is said to have been white on one side of his body and black on the other, a circumstance which for Banyoro symbolizes his mixed ancestry)[2] and Kato Kimera, and the youngest, Kiiza.

It is said that Rukidi and his brothers took the avoidance object or 'totem' (*muziro*) of their mother's clan, which was— and still is—the bush-buck (*ngabi*) because their father, the

---

[1] Crazzolara 1950, chap. 24. Further evidences for the Acholi (Nilotic) origins of the Babito are: (1) the *mpako* names, said to have been introduced by the Babito. There are about twelve of these, and every Munyoro is given one soon after birth. They are constantly used in everyday life, and imply both respect and friendly intimacy; they are only found in those areas where Babito are or have been. The same names are still found in Acholi, where they are called *pak*, meaning 'praise', and Crazzolara has argued convincingly that the Nyoro *mpako* are of Nilotic (Lwoo) origin. (2) Several of the names of the Bito kings of Bunyoro are Lwoo, like the name Bito itself; for example Winyi, Oyo, and Chwa. (3) The objects which make up the regalia of the Nyoro kings are distinguished as Cwezi and Bito in origin. For a list of the Bito ones see K. W. 1936, p. 77; some of them can, I understand, be identified with Nilotic artefacts. The Lwoo origin of the Babito is now generally accepted by historians; see, for example, Oliver 1963, p. 172, and Ogot, p. 46.

But Crazzolara's further claim (1950, chaps. 22, 23) that both Bahuma and Bacwezi were Nilotic too is not supported by the evidence. For (1) Interlacustrine Bantu tradition distinguishes Bacwezi from Bahima, and both from the Babito; (2) Bacwezi, unlike the Nilotes, are widely said to have been fair-complexioned; (3) Bunyoro's regalia are explicitly distinguished as Cwezi and Bito; and (4) no traditions link the famous earthworks in southern Bunyoro with the Babito. This last fact would be very surprising if they had had anything to do with them, for if such a claim had had any plausibility it would have been greatly enhancing to Bito pretensions.

[2] Needham (p. 445) considers this a 'rather superficial' explanation, and argues that Rukidi's dual colouring should be understood as an expression of 'the relation of complementary opposition'. It is, however, the Nyoro explanation. See, for example, Nyakatura, p. 67: 'Rukidi was so named because he had been born in Bukidi, and he was called Mpuga because one of his sides was very white like his Bacwezi father's, the other black like his Bakidi mother's' (my translation). For a fuller discussion of this issue see Beattie 1968, pp. 431–3.

Mucwezi Kyomya, had left them when they were infants. The kings of Buganda, who according to the Nyoro story were the descendants of the junior twin, Kato Kimera, respected their mothers' and not their fathers' 'totems', but in Bunyoro the bush-buck became the *muziro* of all of the Babito descendants of Rukidi Mpuga, who was the first Bito king.

The four brothers set out together for Kitara, guided by the diviner Nyakoka. In Fisher's version (pp. 113, 122) Rukidi and his younger brothers were afraid that their elder brother Nyarwa, who was much loved, might acquire the kingship. So after they had crossed the Nile into Bunyoro they tricked him into returning to Bukidi and went on without him. Nyarwa, disillusioned, climbed a mountain and ascended into the sky. According to Nyakatura (p. 67), Nyarwa accompanied his brother Rukidi to the Nyoro capital, where he was appointed *Okwiri*, head of the royal Babito clan, an office which continued to exist until the end of the kingdom and which was always held by an older brother of the Mukama. It is to be noted that it was not the eldest brother but the next after him who succeeded to their great-grandfather's kingdom.

When the Babito arrived at the former Cwezi capital they seemed strange and uncouth to the inhabitants. Having grown up as rough huntsmen, they were ignorant of courtly manners and of political diplomacy, and they had to be instructed in these matters by Nyakoka and by the two old women whom the Bacwezi had left behind. They knew nothing of cattle (with which their Bacwezi predecessors had been so obsessed): Rukidi was disgusted by the mire which the cattle made in his enclosure, and he only learned to drink milk after having been persuaded to take some unknowingly as a medicine. But gradually he assumed the values and manners appropriate to his new status.

Soon after he arrived, a messenger was sent to collect the regalia left behind by the Bacwezi. These included two drums, Nyalebe and Kajumba. The messenger was able to carry only one drum, Nyalebe, but when he reached the capital he was surprised to find that the other drum had followed him of its own accord, having rolled all the way by itself. This was regarded as a good omen for the new rulers. So was the fact that when Rukidi, at his formal accession, beat the great drum

Nyalebe it made a satisfactorily loud noise, and did not split or remain silent.[1]

Rukidi was the first of Bunyoro's Bito dynasty, of which Sir Tito Winyi Gafabusa, the last Mukama, claimed to be the twenty-sixth king. According to the Nyoro story, Rukidi divided the Kitara empire among his brothers and followers. In particular, he sent his twin brother Kato to govern the province of Muhwahwa, which later became Buganda (it was then very much smaller than it became afterwards), and his younger brother Kiiza to rule Busoga.

According to K. W., Rukidi and Kato lived in peace with one another; open conflict between Bunyoro and Buganda only began in the reign of the fourth Bito king of Bunyoro, Winyi I (1936, pp. 76–8). However, Fisher (pp. 122–3) and Nyakatura (pp. 86–7) say that Kato soon asserted his independence, assuming his second name, Kimera (from *kumera*, 'to grow or take root') as an indication that he intended to stay there permanently. It is said that Rukidi's advisers dissuaded him from taking up arms against Kato; it would be wrong for him to fight against his twin; also, if Rukidi was to have a kingdom then Kato should have one too, for there should be no discrimination between twins. So Kato Kimera became the first Kabaka, and Buganda was ruled by his patrilineal descendants until the deposition in 1966 of Kabaka Sir Edward Mutesa II, the thirty-fifth of his line. This, at least, is the Nyoro version of the founding of the rival kingdom, and its effect is to represent the Ganda state as junior and (originally) subordinate to Bunyoro. 'The Baganda are the children of the Banyoro' (*Abaganda abana ba Banyoro*), Banyoro say. Not surprisingly, most Baganda do not accept this account; they claim that their ruling line began many generations earlier with a first ruler, Kintu.[2]

Many stories are told of the Babito kings of Bunyoro, and these stories become more detailed and circumstantial as we approach historical times. Here I give only the briefest outline of the traditional history of the dynasty; first because, as a

---

[1] It was also convincing evidence of the legitimacy of Rukidi's claim (in the myth) to the Cwezi kingdom. According to Mrs. Fisher's text (p. 120), the satisfactory performance of the drum Nyalebe was proof that Mpuga was not an 'impostor', but was 'the true son of the Bacwezi', and so the proper heir to the kingdom.

[2] Roscoe 1911, p. 186. More is said of Ganda origins in Chapter 11.

detailed record of events and personalities it is perhaps rather less relevant to the understanding of contemporary Nyoro political ideas than the underlying body of myths which we have been discussing; and second, because detailed accounts of the early Bito kings are already available (K. W.'s is the fullest, but see also Dunbar, chap. 5).

Roughly, the era of Bito rule falls into two distinct periods. During the first of these, up to the time of the seventeenth Bito king, Duhaga I, the great empire said to have been inherited from the Bacwezi was maintained and even (it is claimed) extended. The fourth king, Winyi I, who evidently lacked the scruples of his grandfather Rukidi, fought against the Baganda (who had by now asserted their independence) and slew their Kabaka, though he permitted the defeated kingdom to retain its autonomy. The fifth and sixth Babito kings are said to have waged successful campaigns as far away as the borders of the Zande empire in the north-west, areas which are now in the Congo and the Sudan. The tenth king fought successfully against the Banyankole and the Banyaruanda in the south, though he did not succeed in holding either of these territories. However, a further war against Ankole took place during the reign of the sixteenth king, as a result of which, it is claimed, a large part of that country was incorporated in Bunyoro. During all of this period there were frequent campaigns against the small but increasingly aggressive Buganda kingdom, but the Banyoro almost always won.

The second period, from the reign of the seventeenth king up to the coming of the Europeans and the beginning of written history, is marked by a gradual decline in Nyoro power. This was brought about both by successful revolts in outlying parts of the empire, and by annexations by the expanding Ganda kingdom, which now began to acquire the political dominance which it retained until Independence. The process of Nyoro decline was not continuous; strong or popular Bakama sometimes temporarily reversed it. But on the whole more territory was lost than gained, and when the 'historical' period began just after the middle of the last century, Bunyoro was no longer comparable in size or importance with the great empire supposed to have been inherited from the Bacwezi. Dunbar (p. 37) points out that while only three of the first seventeen Bito

Bakama are said to have succeeded to the throne after a succession war, five out of the next six are said to have done so: this perhaps suggests greater instability during the later period. Also, during this time, the little dependency of Koki in the south-east revolted and was permanently lost to Bunyoro, and, more important, early in the nineteenth century Kaboyo, the son of Nyamutukura, the nineteenth Bito Mukama, revolted in the neighbouring and well-favoured Toro area. His independence was not seriously challenged until Kabarega's final effort to retrieve his ancient kingdom in the second half of the last century, an effort which was frustrated by the British and the Baganda, and Toro's existence as a separate kingdom dates from Kaboyo's defection.

So by the time of Mukama Kamurasi, who was on the throne when Speke and Grant reached Bunyoro in 1862, the great days of the Kitara empire were irrevocably over. Toro had asserted its autonomy, Ankole had long since been independent, neighbouring Buganda had grown into a strong and dangerous power and had already greatly extended its boundaries at Bunyoro's expense, and no more is heard of successful campaigns in Ruanda, the Congo, and the Sudan. But as the historical record of Kabarega's campaigns shows, Bunyoro in the second half of the last century was still very much a power to be reckoned with. We shall see in the next chapter that its final destruction and dismemberment were achieved not by the Baganda, or at least not by them alone, but by the British.

The series of myths which we have just discussed, merging into the traditional history of the last dynasty, do not give us very much information about the remote past to which they refer. But they tell us a good deal about Nyoro attitudes and values, and they have important social implications. We have noted that a main effect of the cycle of myths is to establish a genealogical connection, through the male line, between the ruling Bito dynasty and the dynasties which are supposed to have preceded it. These links are shown on Fig. 1. In Bunyoro, where hereditary status was of paramount importance, the acknowledgement of these putative links served significant social and political purposes. It evidently enhanced the prestige and authority of the Bito rulers, associated in other contexts with the naked and savage Bakidi (with whom the myth links

them by *maternal* descent), that they should be represented as directly descended from the mysterious and wonderful Bacwezi, a dynasty of hero-gods who are known and revered throughout the interlacustrine region. In fact, as we have seen, there is little doubt that the Babito were Nilotic immigrants from the north, and the Nyoro story stresses their ignorance and uncouthness

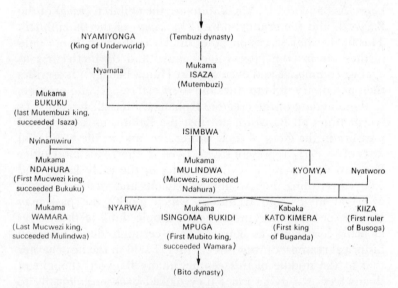

Fig. 1. Genealogical connection between Tembuzi, Cwezi, and Bito dynasties according to the Nyoro myth.

Note. It can be seen that Rukidi Mpuga, the first Bito king, is represented as being descended in a direct patriline from Isaza. A few early authorities (Fisher, Wilson, Bikunya) make Rukidi the son of Isimbwa by a Nilotic mother, omitting Kyomya from the genealogy.

when they first arrived from their uncivilized homeland. Even the superior Bahuma, who, according to Nyakatura, still look down on the Babito as *bairu*, do not in Bunyoro claim any genealogical connection with the Bacwezi. Like the Bahuma, the Bacwezi were cattle-lovers, and when they arrived in the country they found the Bahuma already there, and employed them to care for their herds. Bahuma have never been kings in Bunyoro, as the Bahima and Batutsi have in the other inter-lacustrine kingdoms to the south. Thus the Nyoro dynasty, and

by association with them the whole Nyoro people, were distinguished from the other rulers and kingdoms as being alone the direct descendants of the Bacwezi, and so the heirs of their great empire.

The genealogical connections specified by the myth not only link the Babito dynasty with the Bacwezi; they link both of them to the earlier and even more shadowy line of the Tembuzi kings. As Banyoro say, 'the Babito are the children (*bana*) of the Bacwezi, and the grandchildren (*baijukuru*) of the Batembuzi'. This further link serves purposes similar to the first. It not only further affirms the later rulers' unity and distinctiveness as against commoner and even against Huma lineages; it ascribes their hereditary right to rule, and to special respect and prestige, to the mandate of the creator, Ruhanga, himself. Up till very recent times all Banyoro, not just the Babito, took pride and pleasure in the glory of their ruling line, and in the wonderful feats of its early representatives. Even in the 1950s most older Banyoro were familiar with the tales of the early kings, and enjoyed recalling their wonderful exploits and victories.

Tribal myths and traditions which glorify the past may assume special importance when a people think of themselves as being in decline, as Banyoro have certainly done, for good historical reasons, during this century. I said in the last chapter that at the middle of this century many Banyoro thought of themselves as a dying race; they looked back nostalgically to their glorious (if mythical) past, rather than forward towards the future. In such circumstances, there is some consolation in the thought of past in default of present greatness. This preoccupation with the past and especially with the history of Bunyoro's royal line is also indicated by the fact that of the four books by Banyoro about their own country written within the past half-century, two recapitulate the history of the Bakama from the beginning, as their titles imply, one relates the history of one Mukama, and the other devotes several chapters to the history of the Nyoro kings.[1]

Like other royal genealogies, Bunyoro's has expanded rapidly in historical times. The list of pre-Cwezi kings grew from four or five in 1927 (Bikunya) to eighteen or more a decade or two later (K. W. 1935; Nyakatura). Even the Bito kings, of whom

---

[1] Bikunya, Nyakatura, Karubanga, Katyanku and Bulera.

Roscoe recorded only fifteen in 1923, total twenty-five in the later accounts. This tendency to expand is not surprising. A longer genealogy implies greater antiquity and so a claim to greater veneration; also, in the Bunyoro case, there was an element of competition with other kingdoms, especially with Buganda. It would not do for an ancient kingdom to have a shorter royal genealogy than a kingdom which it regards as its junior. We saw that the Baganda thought of their kingdom as being at least as ancient as Bunyoro. But, for Banyoro, Buganda was a mere offshoot of their kingdom, and their traditions put the upstart but (in recent years) more powerful, successful, and advanced kingdom in its proper, and subordinate, place. Banyoro believe that Buganda owed its separate existence to the forbearance of the parent kingdom. The Baganda are their 'children', and parents may claim some credit for their children's success.

But the main social importance of Bunyoro's cycle of myths was to establish and validate Bito rule. In doing this it resolved at the same time basic contradictions both in Nyoro ideas about their kingdom's past and in their evaluation of the kingship itself. On the one hand Banyoro believe that their country has been ruled by three separate and distinct dynasties, not just by one, and they think of these as having been quite different in kind. But on the other hand they claim that their Bito rulers were descended in an unbroken male line from the very first rulers, even from the Creator (or his 'brother') himself. If this were the whole story it might well be asked, as Crazzolara asks, 'How is it that the sons of the *Abatembuzi* came to be called *Abacwezi*, and again the sons of the *Abacwezi* came to be called *Ababito*?' (1937, p. 14). In other words, why are there said to have been three separate dynasties in Bunyoro, and not only one?

The question is a fair one, but it implies too literal and 'historical' an interpretation of the myths. It is now quite firmly established, thanks mainly to Father Crazzolara's own researches, that the Babito are of Nilotic origin. But there is no evidence at all that the Bacwezi were, and even less can be said of the origins or character of the remote Batembuzi. Whatever the 'real' connections, if there were any, between these dynasties, for Banyoro they were three dynasties, not one. So the effect

of mythically linking them in a single genealogy is not to reduce them to a single dynasty. As we have seen, its effect was rather to provide a genealogical charter for a contemporary political structure, a structure which was contemporaneous with the myths themselves.

Further, the myth resolves a fundamental contradiction in Nyoro values concerning their kingship and its history. The Bacwezi were civilized, fair-skinned, the owners of vast herds of cattle, and the rulers of a great empire. The Babito were identified through their founder Mukidi with the rough, black, and uncultured Bakidi, ignorant of kingship and cattle, and in other contexts looked down upon as untutored savages. Yet in the myth Rukidi was accepted, even welcomed, as Bunyoro's ruler; there is no suggestion that he achieved the kingship by conquest (as he may very well have done). And how could the proud and heredity-conscious Banyoro conceive themselves as submitting freely to so unacceptable an intruder and his fellow northerners? The detailed story of Rukidi's Cwezi origins, so central a theme in the myth, by showing that Rukidi was not *just* a Mukidi admirably resolves this basic contradiction.

It is worth noting again that the new blood, recognized in other contexts as having been brought in with the two dynastic changes I have described, is in both cases said in the myth to have been introduced through the maternal side. Thus the father of Isimbwa, the progenitor of the Bacwezi, was Isaza, the last of the Batembuzi kings; but his mother was Nyamata, the daughter of the mysterious and sinister king of the 'World of Ghosts' (it has been suggested that this may really have been an unnamed kingdom to the south). Likewise the first Mubito king was the son of the Mucwezi Kyomya, and the grandson of Isimbwa; it was from his mother Nyatworo, in whose country he grew up, that he is said in the myth to have derived his Nilotic blood. The ethnography of patrilineal societies provides many examples of the turning, by a sort of legal 'fiction', of matrilateral links into patrilateral ones in order to sustain the conceptual unity of groups of presumed agnates. In Bunyoro the change is made in the opposite direction, and what is recognized to be new blood, introduced by strangers from outside and associated with a different culture (and so likely to have been brought by men, not women), is represented as having been

injected into the royal line on the female side. In patrilineal Bunyoro, what it was sought to sustain was not (as for example among the Nuer) the corporate unity of existing agnatic groups: it was the continuity, in a political context, of a dynastic tradition. The conversion in the myth of what were presumably male newcomers into female ones provides an apt way of doing this. Thus the Babito are the sons of the Bacwezi, but they are the sister's sons (*baihwa*) of the Nilotic Bakidi, and so of their descendants the Acholi and the Alur, at least some of whom acknowledged, until recent times, the paramountcy of the Nyoro kings. And we noted that Banyoro held it appropriate for 'sisters' sons' to rule their 'mothers' brothers'.

4

RECENT HISTORY

HISTORY may be important in two ways for a social anthropologist studying a small-scale society. First, it may help him to understand how things came to be as they are: his central interest is in the present state of the society he is studying, but this can be better understood when something is known of the historical circumstances which led up to it. But, second, no less important for the social anthropologist is an investigation of the ideas a people has about its own past, and of the ways in which these ideas affect and are affected by other factors in the contemporary social and cultural situation. As sociologist rather than historian, he is centrally concerned with questions of this second kind; it is the fact that the beliefs that make up this 'incapsulated history' (in Collingwood's useful phrase) are often 'mythical', rather than being accurate representations of historical truth, that gives rise to what are for him the most interesting questions about them.

Often, when a preliterate culture is being studied, there is little or no evidence which could provide an answer to the question 'what actually happened?'—where this is so, there is evidently little point in asking it. But modern social anthropologists are increasingly studying literate, or largely literate, societies, in which there are extensive documentary sources. Where, as is very often the case, such material is relevant to their understanding of the institutions they are studying, they take, or should take, due account of it. Also, in the case of many preliterate or only recently literate communities, Western contact and the changes it has involved have provided documentary (though brief) histories—not always very happy ones—for societies which formerly had none. This has certainly happened in Bunyoro. When I was there beliefs about their country's recent past played a significant and constant part in Banyoro's thinking about themselves, their contacts with neighbouring

peoples, and their relations with the intrusive Europeans. So I could not have helped being interested in it.

In fact it is hardly possible in practice to keep separate the two kinds of historical interests which I have mentioned, though it is necessary to distinguish them analytically. For at every stage contemporary ideas about the past are influencing current, and subsequent, events; we shall see that recent Nyoro history provides many examples of this. So in this chapter I discuss both actual historical events (so far as the truth about these can be ascertained) and beliefs about these events, for both had combined to influence and define the social and cultural institutions which I sought to understand.

We generally assume that the truth about past events is at least in some degree ascertainable—it usually is a matter of degree—but we know, too, that history is influenced by those who write it as well as by those who make it. This is so especially when, as has often happened, the same people have done both, as they have in the case of many recently 'colonial' peoples in Africa and elsewhere. Inevitably, a central theme in Bunyoro's history from the first arrival of the Europeans to Uganda's independence a century later is Nyoro–European relations. During the first half-century of contact, these relations were for the most part far from cordial, and sometimes they were actively hostile. We shall not be surprised to find, therefore, that European and Nyoro ideas about them differ considerably. Since these differences are very relevant to the understanding of twentieth-century Bunyoro, I say something in what follows of the historical beliefs of both sides. In fact it would be possible to present the Nyoro and the European versions as two separate accounts, and it might be illuminating to attempt this. For from the time of the first contacts the same events were so differently regarded and recalled by those who took part in them that serious and growing misunderstanding developed, leading inevitably to sharper oppositions and, in the end, to physical conflict and the military subjugation of the Bunyoro kingdom. But such a dual presentation would be long and repetitious; and historically the story is one, not two. So here I attempt to combine some of the various evidences available, indicating as the story unfolds the more important points of misunderstanding between Banyoro and Europeans.

A full record of Nyoro history would require a book to itself.[1] The account given here is a summary one, noting only those events which are seen by both Banyoro and British as being the most important. This will provide the indispensable historical context for an understanding of Bunyoro's social and political institutions as they were in the 1950s. I use mainly secondary sources, but my understanding of Bunyoro's history owes much to long discussions with many senior Banyoro and, in a few contexts, to access to unpublished records.

The first Europeans to reach Bunyoro were Speke and Grant, who arrived from Buganda in 1862. At that time Mukama Kamurasi was exercising some sort of suzerainty over an area considerably larger than the present Bunyoro district (though a good deal smaller than the old 'Kitara' empire). It included much of present-day Buganda, as well as parts of the present Toro district and some of Ankole. As we noted in Chapter 2, Nyoro influence also extended some distance north and east of the Nile, and the Mukama's overlordship was acknowledged by at least some of the peoples to the west and north-west of Lake Albert. Speke's map (1863, see map 3 above) shows 'Unyoro' as occupying almost the whole of the area between Lakes Victoria and Albert ('Uganda' being restricted to a narrow coastal strip), and as extending south as far as the borders of Karagwe, now in Tanzania. Even Lugard (1893, vol. ii, map opposite p. 118), nearly thirty years later, put Bunyoro's south-eastern boundary many miles within what later became Buganda, and extended the country's southern limits (east of a Toro kingdom very much smaller than it is now) as far as the present-day Ankole boundary.

But it would be a mistake to suppose that all of this large area was subject to peaceful and uniform administration from Kamurasi's capital. Especially on the periphery, revolts, often led by 'princes' of the royal Bito line, were frequent. We have noted that Kaboyo, the son of a previous Mukama, had attempted with some success to establish a separate kingdom of Toro, and Ruyonga (Baker's Rionga), who was a constant thorn in the flesh of Kamurasi and his son and successor

---

[1] It has now acquired one in Dunbar (1965), which gives a very much fuller account than can be given here, especially of events during the present century up to 1962. It also has a useful bibliography.

Kabarega, was Kamurasi's father's brother's son's son. Supported by loyal chiefs, the Nyoro kings spent much time attempting, with varying success, to suppress such risings. At the close of the pre-European period, also, the neighbouring and hostile Buganda kingdom was, as we have noted, rapidly increasing in prestige and power, and there were frequent raids from across the border.

Speke and Grant came straight from the court of the Ganda king, Mutesa, and they stayed at Kamurasi's capital for two months, before moving on into what is now the Sudan. Both of these travellers recorded that Kamurasi was not given to daily executions and other atrocities, as Mutesa was, and they described him as 'not unkindly', and 'of a mild disposition compared with Mutesa' (Grant, p. 288; Speke, p. 525). But they were irritated by his constant suspicion of them, and irked by his repeated demands for gifts and for armed help against his cousin Ruyonga, who, as noted above, was in revolt in the north of the kingdom. However, they left Bunyoro safely, Grant at least confidently hoping (p. 289) that on account of the presents the king had received he would 'treat all future white men with due hospitality'.

Banyoro regarded this first encounter with Europeans with a good deal less complacency. Speke and Grant had come directly from the court of the hostile Ganda king, accompanied by an escort of Baganda, and as though this were not suspicious enough they had come separately and by different routes, just as though they had planned a two-pronged attack on the Nyoro capital. Further, the Baganda were anxious, then as later, to make as much trouble as possible between the Banyoro and the Europeans, both to discomfit their traditional enemies and also so that they could keep for themselves the new source of wealth represented by the white men. So they spread reports that the Europeans were cannibals, who required several men and women daily for their food, and also that they were in the habit of eating up mountains and drinking rivers dry. Absurd (or perhaps prophetic?) though these stories seem to us, it may be supposed that Kamurasi and his people, to whom Europeans were something entirely new, suspected that there might be something in them. Even in recent times some people in rural Bunyoro and elsewhere in Africa have believed that African

patients in government hospitals (or selected parts of such patients) are likely to be processed for use as food by Europeans. There is no tradition of cannibalism in Bunyoro, though witches (*basezi*) are said to be necrophagous, but far-away tribes are often reputed to be 'people-eaters' (*balyabantu*), and the trait was in former times readily imputed to foreigners. However, Kamurasi treated his white guests with fair hospitality and provided them with ample food and beer. If he was exigent in his demands for gifts and military help, this was natural enough when these alarming but apparently well-disposed strangers possessed what must have seemed an inexhaustible supply of firearms and other new and desirable things.

A little over a year later Samuel Baker and his indomitable wife reached Bunyoro. Unlike Speke and Grant they arrived from the north, not from the east, and in fact the four Europeans met at Gondokoro in the southern Sudan, Speke and Grant being then on their way home by way of Khartoum and Egypt. The Bakers spent an uncomfortable year in Bunyoro, in the course of which they discovered and named Lake Albert (it already had a Runyoro name, Mwitanzige, 'the locust-killer'), and sailed up its eastern coast. Baker (and his wife) possessed astonishing hardihood and remarkable physical courage, but he showed little tact or sympathy in his dealings with the Banyoro. Though his relations with Kamurasi did not involve open conflict, they were continuously strained. Baker must have known that Kamurasi had little ground for trusting him and his escort of northern Sudanese, but he made no allowance for this in his dealings with him. He wrote bitterly about the Nyoro king, accusing him of duplicity, cowardice, and greed (charges which he did not hesitate to make to his face), and describing his character as 'below that of the most petty chief that I have ever seen' (1867, p. 158). Baker's violent antipathy to the Nyoro ruler may perhaps be more understandable if it is remembered that until he reached Bunyoro his experience of African rulers had been confined to the comparatively minor headmen of the segmentary Nilotic societies to the north. The deviousness of an African court, and the evasive yet autocratic manner of the Mukama, the ruler of an area almost as large as England, were something new in his experience, and he may well have been disconcerted that Kamurasi did not conform to his idea of a

petty African chief. Had he come to Bunyoro by way of the very much more autocratic Ganda court, as Speke and Grant did, his reactions (and in consequence Bunyoro's future) might have been very different. The Bakers underwent much hardship and privation, but they left the country safely, which may be thought remarkable enough when the circumstances under which they arrived are considered.

These included the fact that shortly after the departure of Speke and Grant in the previous year a party of Sudanese had arrived from the north claiming to be these Europeans' 'greatest friends'. After they had on this account been hospitably received they suddenly, in collusion with Kamurasi's enemy Ruyonga, turned on their hosts and, according to Baker's own account, massacred about three hundred of them (1867, p. 34). Of course Speke and Grant were not personally responsible for this, though no doubt the raid was made possible by their information. But it is not surprising that thereafter Kamurasi and his people were somewhat suspicious of strangers, especially Europeans.

Nyoro reactions to the Bakers' visit were also determined by the fact that Baker was, from necessity rather than choice, closely associated with one of the several Sudanese gangs which were at this time raiding for slaves and ivory in what is now southern Sudan and northern Uganda. These large armed parties, whose guns gave them the advantage over any force of local tribesmen, operated with appalling savagery. They would ally themselves with one local ruler against another, taking as their reward for their armed assistance a handsome booty of slaves, ivory, and cattle from the defeated side. As likely as not they would then turn on their allies and after slaughtering as many of them as they could, they would then add their women and cattle to the spoil they had already gained. These raiders caused immense devastation, destruction, and misery through-out the area. Whole regions were depopulated, for many of those who were not killed or carried off perished from disease or famine, after their homes, crops, and cattle had been destroyed. Even though Baker tried to avoid participation in the raids and intrigues of his companions, Kamurasi was bound to regard him with deep suspicion.

Baker himself took little pains to counteract this inevitable impression. When Kamurasi displeased him, he did not hesitate

to threaten him with severe reprisals from these very raiders.
Baker himself reports that on one occasion the Mukama complained to him that one of the 'Turks' (that is, the Sudanese)
with whom Baker was associated had been insolent to him in
front of all his chiefs, and had even threatened to shoot him.
Kamurasi told Baker that he would have had this man and his
companions killed there and then, had he not been brought into
the country by him (Baker). Instead of apologizing for his
associate's offensive behaviour, or even undertaking to look into
the affair, Baker truculently 'advised Kamurasi not to talk too
big, as . . . he might imagine the results that would occur should
he even hint at hostility, as the large parties of Ibrahim and the
men of Mohamed Wat-el-Mek (two of Baker's Sudanese associates) would immediately unite and destroy both him and his
country'. Baker reports that 'the gallant Kamurasi turned
almost green at the bare suggestion of this possibility' (1867,
p. 194). This incident provides a good example of Baker's
manner of dealing with the Nyoro ruler, and further explains
the suspicion with which Kamurasi and his chiefs regarded him,
and by association all Europeans. One cannot help wondering
how this browbeating manner would have gone down at the
court of the pompous and autocratic Mutesa, who was very
much more respectfully treated by his European visitors.

Baker and his wife left the country in 1864. He returned eight
years later, this time not as a private explorer, but as Sir Samuel
Baker, the Governor-General of the Egyptian province of
Equatoria, at that time held to include Bunyoro. He found that
Kamurasi had died about six years after his first visit, and had
been succeeded by his son Kabarega, who had fought his way
to the throne after his father's death. Apparently unaware that
this was a traditional mode of establishing the royal succession,
Baker reviles Kabarega for his 'treachery' in securing his position by the assassination of a rival brother (1874, p. 179).

The visit lasted for only a few months, and during it there
was constant friction between Baker and Kabarega, culminating
in open conflict shortly after Baker, in the presence of Kabarega
and his chiefs, had formally proclaimed the annexation of the
whole of Bunyoro to Egypt. Baker claims that he had first
obtained Kabarega's agreement to the annexation, an assertion
(on the face of it improbable) which Banyoro deny. A few days

after this, according to Baker's version, the king sent poisoned beer to Baker and his men, many of whom became very ill and were only saved by the prompt administration of emetics. Baker and his party were then treacherously attacked, his account goes on, and after an affray in which Baker had to defend himself with a machine-gun, he and his men were compelled to beat a retreat northwards towards the Nile. Here Baker proclaimed the now ageing rebel Ruyonga (Kabarega's hereditary enemy), with whom he had entered into a blood pact, as the Egyptian Government's official representative in Bunyoro. Ruyonga was thus authorized to rule Bunyoro in place of Kabarega, who was regarded as having been deposed. No doubt this coup relieved Baker's feelings, but of course it had little or no effect on existing political relations within Bunyoro, though it did have important historical consequences.

It meant, most significantly, that Baker's successor Gordon entered into no direct relations with Bunyoro's real ruler, but dealt instead with Baker's puppet Ruyonga. Ten years later the missionary–explorer R. W. Felkin described Ruyonga as being 'very fond of the Egyptians, and . . . exceedingly proud of his flags with the crescent and stars'. Felkin goes on to say that Ruyonga had been 'an admirable ally to the Egyptians ever since he made blood brotherhood with Sir S. Baker' (Wilson and Felkin, p. 41). But of course he was in no way representative of the Banyoro people as a whole, and Kabarega's authority as the ruler of his kingdom was never significantly affected by his (Ruyonga's) recognition by the Egyptians.

The Nyoro version of these events differs very considerably from Baker's. I have referred to the ravages caused by the slave trade, and in the interval since Baker's first visit these had been carried into northern Bunyoro, especially the Bugungu area, Baker's 'Magungo'. These bands of slavers were known to have come from Khartoum, which for Banyoro was very much the same thing as Egypt. So when Baker returned in 1872 as an official representative of that country he could hardly have expected to be welcomed with open arms. Further, Banyoro writers claim (and these claims are amply corroborated by Baker himself and others), that Baker's Sudanese followers, who numbered several hundreds, inflicted revolting though usually unspecified cruelties and abuses on the people everywhere they

went (see, for example, Nyakatura, p. 151). Again, the manner of Baker's annexation of the country, just before he hurriedly fled from it, was hardly calculated to increase Nyoro confidence. The Nyoro version of this event is that Baker, without any consultation with the king or his chiefs, had the Nyoro flag lowered and raised the Egyptian one in its place, declaring Bunyoro to be henceforth a colony of Egypt. Surprised and indignant, Kabarega and his chiefs asked 'Are there then to be two kings in Bunyoro?'[1] According to the Nyoro story, Kabarega had been warned by an Arab friend of his father, named Ibrahim, that Baker had all along intended this unilateral annexation, and when Ibrahim's warning proved true there could be little ground for further trust in European good faith.

Banyoro deny Baker's allegation that Kabarega had sent him and his men poisoned beer; they say simply that the brew was particularly strong and that Baker's men drank too deeply of it. In the recriminations that followed, Banyoro assert, a messenger from Kabarega named Mboga was imprisoned and later 'executed' by Baker and his men.[2] In the hostilities which followed these events, it is said that Baker mowed down large numbers of Banyoro with a Maxim gun, and set fire to the king's enclosure and to neighbouring villages, before departing with his party for the north. He did not return to Bunyoro again.

Clearly we cannot now determine with any certainty the real course of events during those fateful days. But whatever really happened, it is plain that thereafter there existed two very different 'histories' of it, one accepted by Banyoro, the other incorporated in the 'official' European record. Certainly one or two later European writers have suggested that Baker's account might conceivably have told only one side of the story. Emin Pasha, writing five years after Baker's departure, said that he received in Bunyoro an account of Baker's visit 'curiously different from that given in Ismailia' (1888, p. 63), and the missionary–anthropologist Roscoe, who visited Bunyoro forty-five years later, also heard the story of the trouble between Baker and Kabarega 'from the Banyoro point of view. The

---

[1] This is the account given by the last Mukama in a memorandum entitled 'The Banyoro's Claim of their Lost Lands', which he addressed to the Secretary of State for the Colonies in 1948.

[2] See Nyakatura, pp. 151-2. Baker, however, simply asserts that the messenger 'disappeared' (1874, p. 320).

effect on Kabarega was serious', Roscoe wrote, 'and from that time he regarded all Europeans with deep suspicion' (1922, p. 138).

But by that time the damage had long since been done. Already in the 1870s two distinct and conflicting versions of Baker's encounter with Kabarega had 'incapsulated' themselves in the developing course of Nyoro–European relations. The ground had been laid for further misunderstanding and hostility, leading in the end to tragic consequences for Bunyoro and its king.

In 1874 Baker was succeeded as Governor of Equatoria by Colonel Gordon, and this famous soldier's attitude to the Banyoro and to their king Kabarega was largely determined by his predecessor's reports. As we saw, he made no attempt to come to terms with Kabarega but dealt instead with Ruyonga, who was not and (in terms of Nyoro ideas about succession) could not be the Mukama of Bunyoro, for he was only a grandson, not a son, of a king. Gordon's main and very laudable ambition was to stamp out the slave trade, and to this end he established forts in the more accessible parts of the country, mainly in northern Bunyoro, and staffed them with Sudanese and Egyptian soldiers. Kabarega and his chiefs were bound to consider the establishment of these armed posts in their country, without consultation, as provocative, especially as the soldiers who occupied them were if anything an even greater menace to the local population than the slavers themselves. Nevertheless, Banyoro say, Kabarega did not attack these forts, for he did not want to fight with the Europeans.

In 1878 Gordon was succeeded as Governor of Equatoria by the curious and complex German doctor known as Emin Pasha, who differed from his predecessors, and indeed from most of his successors, in being a trained scientist and scholar as well as an administrator. Alone among these early Europeans Emin got on well with Kabarega, and spoke highly of him. 'Kabarega is cheerful,' he wrote, 'laughs readily and much, talks a great deal, and does not appear to be bound by ceremony—the exact opposite to Mutesa, the conceited ruler of Uganda.' He describes him as 'a thoroughly hospitable and intelligent man' (1888, pp. 61–2). Emin's administration lasted for more than ten years, and seems to have been reasonably successful until

the repercussions of the Mahdi's revolt in the Sudan in 1884 led to his isolation and to the final breakdown of his authority. He carried on by himself for some years, out of touch with his head-quarters and gradually losing control of his province, until he reluctantly allowed himself to be rescued by H. M. Stanley in 1889.

Even though both Emin and, later, his assistant Casati—with whom, at least at the end, Kabarega's relationship was a good deal less happy (Casati, *passim*)—realized that Kabarega never completely trusted them or any other European, Emin's tact and good sense enabled relations to be maintained on a friendly enough basis throughout most of the period of his residence in the area. But with Emin's departure this relatively satisfactory state of affairs came to an end: Kabarega began a new series of raids into Buganda and, especially, into Toro (the province which had revolted three generations earlier) and from this time onward no further attempt was made by any European to enter into friendly relations with the Nyoro king.

The next phase in Nyoro–European relations opened in the following year (1890) with the arrival in Buganda of Captain F. D. Lugard, as the representative of the British East Africa Company, within whose sphere of influence Buganda and neighbouring areas now fell. Lugard approached Bunyoro from the south-east, by way of Buganda, and not from the north, as Baker, Gordon, and Emin had done. As we have noted, there was no love lost between Banyoro and Baganda, and naturally the Kabaka and his advisers did their best to prejudice Lugard against the western kingdom. It is clear from Lugard's own writings that he never even considered the possibility of nego-tiating with Kabarega; the Nyoro king was irrevocably cast as the villain of the piece. Lugard regarded him as having 'lost any claim to indulgence by his cruelties for years past', and sup-ported this judgement by reference to Baker's choleric account; it is, he writes, 'one which everyone who has any knowledge from Sir Samuel Baker's writings or elsewhere of that savage's character will be prepared for' (1892, p. 27). Lugard's judge-ment was further influenced by the fact that he had undertaken to install as king of Toro a young Mubito called Kasagama, a grandson of the prince, Kaboyo, who had earlier revolted against the parent kingdom of Bunyoro and asserted his inde-

pendence. When Lugard arrived in Buganda, Kabarega had recently been attempting, with some success, to reconquer Toro and reincorporate it in Bunyoro, and young Kasagama was a fugitive in Buganda.

Lugard combined this operation with an attempt to collect and re-enlist the Sudanese soldiers believed to have remained in the west of the country, near Lake Albert, after Emin's departure. His idea was to use them to help in maintaining order in Buganda, which was at that time in a very disturbed state. So he set out for Lake Albert, travelling by way of Toro, where *en passant* he installed Kasagama as king of that country. This undertaking inevitably involved some brushes with Kabarega's forces. Lugard in due course succeeded in collecting the six hundred or so Sudanese troops who in the year or so since Emin's departure had acquired large numbers of women, slaves, and hangers-on. On his way back to Buganda Lugard established a number of forts in Toro district, to protect the new king and his people from Kabarega's depredations, and he used some of his Sudanese soldiers to garrison these forts. These men, who since Emin's departure (and even before it) had become totally undisciplined, soon started to lay waste the country around the forts. This in turn inevitably led to further reprisals by parties of Kabarega's warriors from the north.

These events and circumstances combined to confirm Lugard's hostility to Bunyoro and to its ruler, Kabarega, and to intensify his existing conviction that there could be no possibility of an amicable settlement with him. Lugard acknowledges that envoys came from the Nyoro king to sue for peace but, he writes, '. . . I felt little inclination to come to terms; for years he [Kabarega] has exhibited a continued hostility to Europeans . . .'. The decision to conquer Bunyoro and drive out Kabarega by force of arms had been taken, and it was not to be influenced by any attempts at conciliation that the Nyoro ruler might now make. 'To conquer his country . . . and disarm his lawless bands' was now in Lugard's words, his 'pet scheme' (1893, p. 415).

The military invasion of Bunyoro was accordingly planned, to be undertaken with the help of the Baganda. In 1893 Colonel Colvile issued an ultimatum to Kabarega, telling him that 'unless in the meanwhile he had sent me guarantees for his good conduct in the future, and a substantial indemnity for damage

done in the past, I and my army would be across his frontier within 21 days of the date of writing' (Colvile, p. 70). It is plain enough that Lugard's enthusiasm for a campaign against Kabarega was fully shared by the young British officers who followed him. A fascinating glimpse of the sort of considerations which had to be taken into account in military policy in nineteenth-century colonial wars is afforded by an extract from a letter, written in September in the same year, by Captain Macdonald, then acting as British Commissioner in Uganda, to his subordinate Lieutenant Owen. 'I want peace for the next two months at least,' Macdonald wrote; 'I know you are most anxious that if there is a war against Kabarega it should be before your departure from Uganda. But you understand it is impossible that I should sacrifice the good of the country and plain duty to meet the private wishes of any member or members of the commission.'[1]

No reply seems to have been received to Colvile's ultimatum, and in December 1893 he entered Bunyoro with a force of nearly 15,000 men, of whom more than 14,000 were Baganda. The country was soon overrun, and Colvile quickly built a line of forts across Bunyoro (the present district headquarters at Hoima is on the site of one of them), thus effectively cutting the country in two. But the campaign thus begun dragged on for more than five years. Although constantly harried by the British and Baganda invaders, Kabarega carried on in retreat a protracted guerrilla warfare, sometimes north and sometimes south of the Nile.

Colvile withdrew from Bunyoro early in the new year (1894) and he decided that it would be expedient to hand over a large portion of southern Bunyoro to Baganda chiefs, to be ruled as part of Buganda. This area later became known as Bunyoro's 'Lost Counties', the most important of which were Buyaga, Bugangaizi, and Buwekula, south of the Kafu river (see Map 4). These counties had not in fact been overrun or 'conquered' by either the British or the Baganda. But Kabarega and his force were now effectively cut off from them, and the Baganda were not slow to take over the political control of this large area, which included the centre of the ancient Bunyoro kingdom. It appears that Colvile did not report this wholesale annexation

---

[1] Entebbe Secretariat: Macdonald to Owen, 29 September 1893.

to the British Government, though after it had received his report on the campaign, the Foreign Office instructed him that there was to be no further annexation of territory. By this time, however, the transfer was a *fait accompli*. The foundations had been laid for the 'Lost Counties' dispute, which embittered relations between Banyoro and Baganda for seventy years, and was only finally settled, after Independence, in 1964.

In 1894 Captain Thruston succeeded Colvile as commander of the invading forces, and he inflicted some major defeats on the elusive Nyoro king. Lugard wrote that he succeeded in capturing 'the throne and other insignia, which Unyoro superstition regarded as constituting the office of king, and the loss of which meant the fall of the dynasty' (1900, p. 146). In fact it meant neither this nor the end of the campaign. In the following year Major Cunningham led an even more enormous army against Kabarega, 'consisting of six companies of Sudanese, with two Hotchkiss and three Maxim guns, and twenty thousand Waganda' (Lugard 1900, p. 147). Quite apart from its military implications, the effects of this locust-like invasion on the already precarious resources of the country can readily be imagined.

In 1896 Cunningham reported that Kabarega had been driven out of the country, and many hundreds of cattle captured. But although the Nyoro state had been dismembered, its traditional organization had been reduced to chaos, and its long-suffering people were enduring great hardship, Kabarega still held out to the north of the Nile. He was at last captured in April 1899 in the south of Lango district, after a sharp engagement in which he received a severe bullet wound in the arm, which had later to be amputated. With him was Mwanga, the disreputable Kabaka of Buganda, who had fled from his country and joined his former enemy in common resistance to the British. Both kings were exiled to the Seychelles Islands, where Mwanga died a few years later. In 1923 Kabarega, then an old man, was given permission to return to Bunyoro, but he died *en route* at Jinja, a hundred miles from the Bunyoro border, without seeing his own country again. Many Banyoro believe that it was not intended that he should do so.[1]

---

[1] For a fuller account of the campaign against Bunyoro, and of Nyoro–Ganda–British relations during the last decade of the nineteenth century, see Dunbar, chap. 10. See also (for a Runyoro account) Katyanku and Bulera, chap. 4.

In 1900 Sir Harry Johnston concluded the famous Uganda Agreement, on behalf of Her Majesty's Government, with the three regents who were then administering the Buganda kingdom. This document laid down the principles which should govern political relations between the Protectorate Government and that kingdom. It also formally defined Buganda's boundaries, and within them it included the large and populous areas of Bunyoro, south and east of the Kafu river, which Colvile had alienated in 1893. Thus at a stroke Bunyoro was punished for its resistance and Buganda rewarded for its assistance to the British campaign, though this had not in fact been the primary reason for the annexation, which had been confirmed mainly for military reasons (Roberts, pp. 194–7). So from the turn of the century until 1964 about 40 per cent of the Banyoro people lived in Buganda territory and were subject to Baganda chiefs, a state of affairs which the Banyoro and their succeeding kings bitterly and increasingly resented.

At the end of the nineteenth century, then, Bunyoro's condition was desperate. Johnston refers to 'the appalling depopulation of the country consequent on civil wars and foreign invasions', and continues: 'as if the misdemeanours of their fellow negroes were not sufficient for their misery and destruction . . . Providence . . . visited this wretched country with appalling epidemics of disease'; he mentions in particular plague, dropsy, dysentery, smallpox, leprosy, and syphilis (Johnston, vol. ii, pp. 588–93). During and for several years after the war with Kabarega, there were periodic famines, during which, according to Mrs. Fisher (p. 50), 'girls and women were left (their husbands having been killed in the fighting) to roam about the country, selling their honour for a mere handful of grain'. The administration of the country, now regarded as conquered territory, was mainly entrusted to Baganda chiefs. With their king captured and exiled, their most important and favoured counties handed over to the Baganda, the remainder of their country devastated and depopulated, disease and famine rife, and their hereditary enemies lording it over them, the destruction of the ancient kingdom of Bunyoro-Kitara was almost complete.

Banyoro believe, as some Europeans have believed also, that the long-drawn-out military campaign against Kabarega was unjustified, and that their king was by no means as intractably

opposed to the spread of European influence as he has been generally represented as being. We have seen how radically the bad name given to him by Baker affected his subsequent relations with the British, and after the end of Emin's administration in the 1880s he was given little chance to rehabilitate himself. Banyoro say that Lugard, in particular, was deliberately misled by the Baganda, and they claim that there is evidence that Kabarega would have been glad to come to terms with the Europeans if he had been allowed to do so. As we have seen, the Baganda did profit handsomely from the downfall of their old enemy. The last Mukama has written: 'the Baganda for a long time had wished to conquer Bunyoro-Kitara but they had never been able to make any inroads into Bunyoro proper by themselves. Now with the assistance of the Protectorate Government they succeeded to gain what they had failed to achieve on their own.'[1] Banyoro point out that on several occasions Kabarega sent messengers to Lugard in Buganda, but always (as Lugard himself acknowledges) his overtures were repulsed, or else huge indemnities were demanded, as though Kabarega were doing wrong in occupying and defending his own country against foreign invasion. To quote again from the late Mukama, Tito Winyi: 'The Mukama Kabalega was not the aggressor. He fought only in defence of his territory. He was working under the natural instinct of self-preservation which motivates all nations and peoples. He would not have been held worthy of his position if he had not done so.'[2] Banyoro claim that throughout the campaign the king carefully avoided making any direct attack on the Europeans. Kabarega was not a fool; he realized that his only real hope was to come to terms with the British, and he tried to do so. But he failed, because his opponents had other plans, and in the end he was not brought down by the Baganda (or at least not by them alone), but by the protecting power.

A very few Europeans openly criticized the British action against Bunyoro during these years. In 1894 the Revd. R. P. Ashe, an Anglican missionary who knew the country well, wrote as follows about the Sudanese soldiers whom Lugard had posted

[1] In 'A Memorandum on the Parts of Bunyoro-Kitara which were taken by the Buganda Kingdom', addressed by the Mukama to H.E. the Governor of Uganda, 10 December 1945.
[2] Mukama to Secretary of State, 11 March 1948.

in forts in southern Bunyoro during the previous year: 'The frontier of Unyoro was laid waste by them, and it may be understood what just grounds Kabarega had for reprisals after these garrisons—left by the English—had been raiding, robbing, devastating, and doing in Unyoro such devilish deeds of hideous shame as one shrinks from writing down' (Ashe, p. 188). Later in his book (pp. 383–4) Ashe gives an account of Kabarega's attempts to come to terms with Lugard:

In the year 1891 Kabarega had sent to Mwanga, just before Lugard's expedition against the Muhammedans, to sue for peace. Captain Lugard, without giving the slightest proof, says that Kabarega's proposals were insincere, and that he was entirely opposed to Europeans. Some of the specimens of Europeans whom he had met with he had encountered under such circumstances of prejudice as hardly to give him the best opinion of them. . . .

He naturally dislikes militant Europeans who carry fire and slaughter into his country in the teeth of his earnest efforts at making peace . . .

On March 25th of the year 1892 Kabarega made another attempt to make peace, and sent a tusk of ivory to Lugard, and a bundle of salt to the Prime Minister of Buganda. Reverting to these overtures, Lugard again says he knew them to be insincere, but gives no word of proof of his statement . . .

A few years later (in 1896), William (later Sir William) Pulteney, then a junior political officer in the Mubende area, resigned when called upon to officiate in the transfer of the 'Lost Counties' to Buganda.[1] Another young administrative officer, Forster, also resigned for similar reasons. Lugard himself, after he left Uganda, seems to have recognized, somewhat grudgingly and belatedly perhaps, that Kabarega was not after all the unmitigated scoundrel whom Baker had depicted. In 1900 he wrote, comparing him with the former Ganda king, Mwanga: 'Kabarega seems to have had some good points, and Emin speaks highly of him, but Mwanga was in every way despicable and loose' (1900, p. 165). And two years later Sir Harry Johnston, the author of the 1900 Uganda Agreement, said, with notable understatement: 'When the British Protectorate was declared over Uganda [in 1894], it is to be feared that the Baganda chiefs, greedy for territory and spoil, rather threw

[1] Sir John Gray, letter in *The Times*, 27 July 1962.

difficulties in the way of Kabarega coming to terms with the British authorities' (vol. ii, p. 235). In 1947 a former Provincial Commissioner wrote in his autobiography: 'I like the Banyoro, and I do feel that their action in opposing foreign control hardly merited the consequences which have followed it.' And earlier in the same book: 'The inclusion of this [the Mubende] area in the Buganda kingdom is considered by many to have been one of the greatest blunders we committed in the past' (Postlethwaite, pp. 116, 90–1).

Famine continued to afflict the district periodically during the first decade or so of this century, and caused many deaths, but this period saw the beginnings of a settled and peaceful civil administration in Bunyoro, and the years since then showed slow but steady political and economic advance. Already in 1898 the British had appointed a young son of Kabarega, Kitahimbwa, as Mukama of Bunyoro, but apparently this youth failed to show promise as a potential ruler, and in 1902 he was replaced by another of Kabarega's sons, Andereya Duhaga. A Nyoro view is that Kitahimbwa was dismissed because he showed hostility both towards the Baganda chiefs who had been imported into his country, and towards the British, who had hunted and exiled his father (Bikunya, p. 78). Duhaga, who was a strong adherent of the Anglican Church Missionary Society and much influenced by it, reigned until his death in 1924, when he was succeeded by the last Mukama, Sir Tito Winyi IV, another of Kabarega's sons—Kabarega is reported to have begotten seventy-eight sons (and sixty-two daughters) in all (Bikunya, pp. 75–6). Sir Tito reigned until the abolition of his kingdom in 1967. Now an old man of over 80 years of age, he is at the time of writing living in retirement near Masindi.

In the early days of the British administration Bunyoro was composed of eight counties or *masaza*, but these were later reduced to six, and then to the four which made up the kingdom in its last years. To begin with Bunyoro was regarded as conquered territory, and the Administration had little concern to use or develop its indigenous political institutions, as they had done in Buganda. In any case little of them had survived the Kabarega wars. The Administration's aim, according to a contemporary government directive, was to be limited to 'efficient administrative control by the district officer'. It was thought

that this could be best achieved with the aid of the Baganda, and as we noted above Baganda were appointed to most of the major chiefships. The resentment which this caused led, in 1907, to a demonstration of protest led by most of the Nyoro chiefs in office, with popular support. The demonstrators refused to accept the authority of the Ganda 'foreigners' any longer, and demanded their dismissal and return to Buganda. This bloodless revolt, called *Nyangire* ('I refuse'), was firmly suppressed by the government, and several of the dissident Nyoro chiefs were deposed and exiled.[1] Banyoro say that the Baganda chiefs attempted to persuade the government that the revolt was far more serious and widespread than it really was, and also that the Mukama was implicated in it, in the hope that the Protectorate administration would decide to deprive Bunyoro of its separate existence and incorporate it in Buganda (Katyanku and Bulera, chap. vii). This was not done, but the Baganda chiefs remained, and a number of them continued to hold office in Bunyoro for many years, the last retiring in the 1920s. But no more Baganda were appointed to chiefships in Bunyoro, and by the end of the First World War the Native Government was almost wholly in Nyoro hands.

In 1933 the Bunyoro Agreement provided the kingdom with a political status comparable with (though less favourable than) those conferred on Buganda, Toro, and Ankole more than a quarter of a century earlier. In 1955 this was replaced by a new Agreement introducing a more democratic constitution more in keeping with current ideas about local government. The circumstances in which these Agreements were introduced and some of their implications are discussed in later chapters.

Banyoro believed that even during the half-century that followed the establishment of a settled administration in their country they suffered from disabilities and injustices not experienced by the neighbouring kingdoms, at least to anything like the same extent. I referred in Chapter 2 to the widely held belief that the loss of Bunyoro's (presumed) former herds was due not only to trypanosomiasis and rinderpest, and to the devastation of the wars with Kabarega, but also to the direct intention of the Protectorate Government, which, it was thought, wished to keep the Banyoro poor and submissive. Even the

[1] Dunbar (pp. 110–11) gives a fuller account of this affair.

activities of European missionaries were regarded by some pagan Banyoro as being directed to the same end. Despite half a century of missionary work and a considerable amount of nominal Christianity, the old religious cults still survived strongly when I was in Bunyoro, and I should be very surprised if they do not still do so. But their practitioners, when detected, were severely penalized by both missions and, through the native courts, by the Protectorate Government. Indigenous Nyoro religion centres on the *mbandwa* spirit mediumship cult, a main purpose of which is to ensure fertility. Many other rituals are directed to the same end, and to the health and prosperity of individuals and of groups of kin. Banyoro have often pointed out to me that there could be only one real reason for so ruthlessly suppressing these beliefs and practices: the Europeans did not wish Banyoro to increase in numbers, health, or prosperity. We noted in Chapter 2 that Bunyoro's population appeared to have remained stationary or even to have declined in European times, and it was natural that Banyoro's low birth rate, combined with a high rate of infant mortality (factors of which they themselves were well aware) should have been seen by many as due to the baneful influence of the Europeans.

Certainly the rigour with which Nyoro 'superstition' had been repressed, and continued to be repressed during the 1950s, was exceptional. All indigenous ritual practices were classed as 'witchcraft', and even to be found in possession of any of the paraphernalia of the mediumship cult, which in its traditional form involved neither sorcery nor witchcraft, was a criminal offence entailing on conviction a term of imprisonment. In the early 1920s the missionary–ethnographer Roscoe, writing about another type of ritual, said: 'rainmakers are forced to carry on their office in secret, for the government is determined to put an end to their practices, and is attempting to do so by vigorous methods of repression. This policy is to be regretted' (1922, p.154). This observation is particularly significant coming from an observer who was himself a Christian missionary. Roscoe would perhaps have been surprised to know that the cults which were so rigorously repressed are still widely practised; some of them indeed have proliferated widely in recent years (Beattie 1961*b*).

As well as perpetuating the 'Lost Counties' dispute (to which I return below), the 1900 Uganda Agreement gave rise to

Nyoro resentment on another ground. Among other things the Agreement, as is well known, provided that members of the Buganda royal family, as well as many chiefs and other important people, should receive what amounted to freehold rights over a large part of the country's populated areas. Afterwards it was recognized that this allocation was based on a misconception of the real situation, for most of the lands so allocated had not been the private and personal estates of the new beneficiaries, but had been held by them only *ex officio* and, often, temporarily. But by the time that this was understood it was too late to change things; the idea of private property in land had been irrevocably introduced, and naturally the *mailo* system (as it came to be called, from the English 'mile') had been welcomed by the members of the wealthy and ruling classes who had mostly benefited from it. In the other two kingdoms, Toro and Ankole, which had been granted Agreement status in 1900 and 1901 respectively, some similar freehold grants were made, though on a very much smaller scale than in Buganda. But after this the government was determined not to repeat elsewhere what it believed to have been an error, and despite frequent claims in later years by the Mukama and his chiefs, no similar grants of land were made in Bunyoro, which in any case did not achieve Agreement status until 1933. Not surprisingly the Nyoro rulers regarded this as a further act of discrimination.

But for all Banyoro the major ground of political dissatisfaction during the first sixty years of this century was the loss of their southern counties to Buganda. Their unremitting concern with this issue runs right through modern Nyoro history, and I conclude this chapter with a very brief account of the course of this dispute and its solution. This will illustrate an important dimension of Bunyoro's relationship with the British and Protectorate Governments during the colonial period; it will also exemplify the way in which, in the context of modern Africa, two neighbouring and in some respects similar peoples may think about themselves and about each other.

It will be remembered that the problem of the 'Lost Counties' originated in Colvile's unauthorized promise to the Baganda in 1894 that all of Bunyoro south of the Kafu river would be incorporated in Buganda, an undertaking which was ratified in

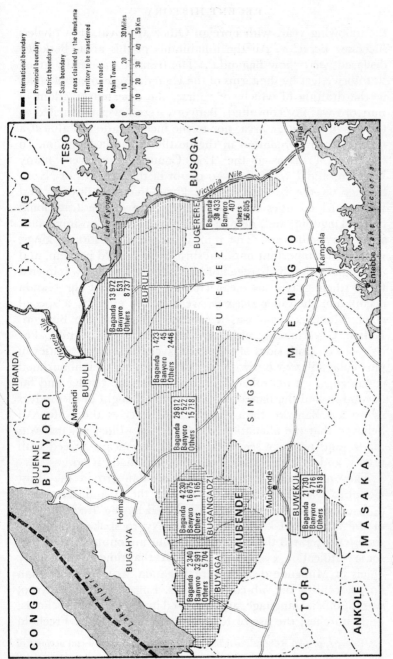

MAP 4. Bunyoro's 'Lost Counties'. (Note: 'Bugangadzi' is the Luganda spelling of 'Bugangaizi'.)

the following year, with Foreign Office approval, by Colvile's
successor Berkeley. All the inhabitants of this area, Berkeley
declared, were 'now Baganda'.[1] The transfer was finally given
statutory effect by the terms of the Uganda Agreement of 1900,
in the drafting of which, of course, the defeated kingdom of
Bunyoro was not consulted. Banyoro were never reconciled to
the loss of this large area, nor to the incorporation of almost a
third of their population in the hostile Buganda kingdom. In
the 1950s I discussed the 'Lost Counties' with very many
Banyoro, and I was left in no doubt of the strength of Nyoro
feelings on the issue. Everyone knew that the Buyaga and
Bugangaizi counties had been the centre of the traditional
Nyoro kingdom, and, despite their alienation, in an important
sense they still were. The tombs (*magasani*) of former kings,
which were important national shrines, were sited in them, and
although neither Kabarega nor his successor Duhaga was buried
there (their graves are near Hoima), throughout the Ganda
occupation the older *magasani* were looked after by a special
chief, Mugema, who was a salaried official of the Bunyoro
Native Government, although he lived in Mubende. For
Banyoro on both sides of the Kafu river, these two counties in
particular still *were* Bunyoro; ties of kinship and neighbourhood
extended in an unbroken continuum over the border and far
beyond it, and the Banyoro in Mubende thought of themselves
as no less Banyoro than their relatives across the Kafu. All
believed that the alienation was quite unjustified when it was
made (and we have seen that several Europeans agreed with
them), and that the passage of years had made it no less so.

They also claimed that the 50,000 Banyoro in the 'Lost
Counties' were discriminated against by their Ganda overlords,
and suffered from disabilities not shared by the 'free' Banyoro
of the attenuated kingdom. Official Nyoro spokesmen sometimes exaggerated these complaints, but undoubtedly they had
some justification, even in the 1950s. At that time all the county
chiefs in Mubende district were Baganda, as were more than
80 per cent of the sub-county chiefs. Luganda, not Runyoro,
was the official language, and was used in offices, courts, schools,
and churches; the use of Runyoro was discouraged. Freehold

---

[1] Roberts, p. 197. Roberts's article gives a concise and most useful account of
the circumstances of the annexation. See also Dunbar, pp. 86–7.

mailo estates were created in Mubende, as elsewhere in Buganda,
as a result of the 1900 Agreement, and almost all of these were
held by the Baganda minority, most Banyoro occupying the
status of *bakopi*, peasant tenants on Ganda-held estates, a state
of affairs which they naturally resented in what they regarded
as their own country. Banyoro I spoke to believed that their
fellow-countrymen in Mubende were constantly oppressed and
discriminated against by the Ganda chiefs, and it is likely that
they sometimes were, although there is no evidence that such
oppression was ever the deliberate policy of the Kabaka's
government (Molson Report, chap. 5).

Europeans generally failed to realize that Banyoro and
Baganda, as well as being traditional enemies and rivals,
differed culturally and socially in many important respects
(these differences are discussed in some detail in Chapter 11).
Thus the policy of assimilation which the British and Baganda
pursued in the 'Lost Counties' had little hope of success; certainly it had made negligible headway in more than half a
century. Throughout this period there had been sporadic unrest
in the area, especially in the counties of Buyaga and Bugangaizi,
where Banyoro outnumbered Baganda by about eight to one.
Such unrest was usually attributed by the local administration
to 'subversive propaganda' (for example by the Mugema, the
Nyoro chief in charge of the royal tombs). After a disturbance
in the 1930s a district commissioner in Mubende recommended
the removal of the Mugema and another dissident 'as they
represent the opinion of a very small fraction of the Banyoro
community in Buyaga, the vast majority of whom are living in
peace and contentment under the just and able rule of the
Baganda chiefs.' This rosy view was not, however, shared by the
Mukama and chiefs of Bunyoro, who saw their fellow tribesmen
across the border as 'serfs', 'enslaved' by their Baganda masters.
The Mukama made frequent formal requests for the return of the
'Lost Counties', addressing memoranda to the Uganda Government, to the Secretary of State for the Colonies in London,
and finally (in 1958) to the Queen. Many of these memoranda
were lengthy and well-prepared documents, containing references to most of the points noted above. The Mukama was
especially concerned to show that Mukama Kabarega had been
very much less intransigent than he had been represented as

being, so that the severe punishment meted out to Bunyoro, and
sustained after more than a quarter of a century's good behaviour by the inhabitants of that country, was unjust.

Representations at the very highest levels began in 1931,
when the Mubito Kosiya Labwoni (a son of the Ruyonga with
whom Baker had entered into a blood pact in 1872) made a
personal appeal to the Secretary of State in London, where,
with other Ugandans, he was giving evidence before a Parliamentary Commission on closer union in East Africa. The
character of the interview set the tone for later official reactions,
and what purports to be a partial record of it may be of interest:

Labwoni: My Lord, in Bunyoro Kingdom we have grievances that
is: most of our land was taken by the Baganda, which is the most
burning question. We pray and we want these grievances to be
righted by the returning of our land. In Bunyoro we do not enjoy
full liberty under the British flag because of this grievance, even
outside we appear to be enjoying liberty but it is not so in our minds.
But as I am now before the Crown and you have kindly arranged
this meeting, I presume that everything is all right and so I am free
to mention our grievances before you which we have in Bunyoro
Kingdom.

Secretary of State: Yes—but do you mean to say that the King will
simply order that your land may be returned?

Labwoni: Yes, my Lord, if possible.

Secretary of State: Do you know when this matter was done?

Labwoni: If I am right some time in 1907.

Secretary of State: Yes, about 25 years ago. It is a long time and this
matter was settled during the time of fighting, so we cannot now do
anything further in the matter.

Labwoni: My Lord, even if this matter happened a long time ago
it does not mean that we have no right now to claim our land.

Secretary of State: Yes, you can do whatever you like. If you like you
can put it before the Parliamentary Select Committee for Closer
Union—but I do not think they will do anything for you.

Labwoni: My Lord, I am only here before the Crown just asking for
justice.

Secretary of State: We will enquire to your Governor.[1]

At the ceremonial signing of both the 1933 and the 1955
Bunyoro Agreements the Mukama made formal public speeches

[1] Quoted in the Mukama's Memorandum to the Secretary of State dated
8 March 1948.

reasserting Bunyoro's claim to the 'Lost Counties'. On the latter occasion, which I attended, the Mukama spoke of 'the urgent necessity of resuming the question of the five and a half counties which were ceded by the pioneer Protectorate Government officials to Buganda for reasons unknown to the present generation and further generations to come, thus enslaving the people in those counties'. He went on to say, 'These counties were the core and substance of the Kingdom of Bunyoro-Kitara. Our kings were crowned there and the royal tombs of several kings are still in existence there. We all understand that slavery was extirpated and consequently now my people and myself petition Queen Elizabeth and her Government that these people in the said counties should be repatriated to their motherland, Bunyoro-Kitara.' (The Mukama meant, of course, that the counties themselves should be restored to Bunyoro.) The Governor, Sir Andrew Cohen, replied in the usual terms: 'On this I say what I and my predecessors have said before. I appreciate your feelings, but the decision of Her Majesty's Government has been made known to you many times.' He went on to say that he did not believe that the desire of the Rukurato (Bunyoro's central council) to send a deputation to London 'would bring any useful results for your people', but he undertook himself to receive Banyoro representatives and to explain to them why he thought this (*Uganda Argus*, 5 September 1955).

After this, there were no major developments for a few years, although pressures for the re-opening of the 'Lost Counties' question continued to increase in Bunyoro and Mubende, and there were numerous meetings and demonstrations. In 1958, after taking legal advice, the Mukama submitted a formal petition to the Queen asking that Bunyoro should be allowed to state her claims before the Judicial Committee of the Privy Council. This request was refused.

But in 1959 the door to negotiations at long last began to open. Late in that year the Governor, Sir Frederick Crawford, agreed to receive a delegation from Bunyoro to discuss their claim, at least in so far as it related to the Mubende counties. So on the very eve of Independence the government decided that Bunyoro's case, which it had refused to consider for more than half a century, might after all be worth examining. Events now began to move quickly. In 1961 the Banyoro were given

the opportunity of putting their case to Lord Munster's Relationship Commission, which was at that time touring Uganda with the object of reviewing constitutional arrangements prior to Independence. Now the tide had turned with a vengeance. In its report the Commission recommended that a referendum should be held in the Buyaga and Bugangaizi counties and in one other county of Banyoro's choice, and that any areas which opted for reunion with Bunyoro should be handed over at the time of Independence. This recommendation, which not surprisingly was wholly unacceptable to Buganda, was rejected by the government, but at a Uganda Constitutional Conference held in London later that year it was agreed that a Commission of Privy Councillors should be appointed to investigate the dispute, and a Commission, headed by Lord Molson, was appointed. Naturally all these developments caused mounting excitement in the disputed areas themselves, and from 1960 onwards there were numerous and increasingly serious incidents in the 'Lost Counties'.

The Molson Commission began its inquiries in Uganda at the beginning of 1962. Its report was completed early in March, but despite protest from Bunyoro its publication was delayed on the Commissioners' advice until after the election of Uganda's new government, on the ground that the Commission's recommendations might lead to a hardening of attitudes by the political parties, which might prejudice future negotiations. On 3 May 1962, by which time a national Uganda Government, headed by Mr. Obote, had been elected, the Commission's report was laid before the British Parliament.

It recommended the transfer to Bunyoro, before Independence (due on 9 October), of the Buyaga and Bugangaizi counties, where Banyoro constituted the large majority of the inhabitants. The other areas claimed, in which Banyoro were a small minority, should remain in Buganda, but the township of Mubende (within whose boundaries was included a sacred tree locally known as the Witch Tree, which was of ritual importance to neighbouring kingdoms as well as to Bunyoro) should be administered neither by Buganda nor Bunyoro, but directly by the Central Government. The Commission did not endorse the Munster Commission's recommendation that a referendum should be held in the Mubende district, on the

ground that in conditions as they then existed an attempt to do so could only lead to intimidation and probably violence. In any case the result, at least so far as Buyaga and Bugangaizi were concerned, would be a foregone conclusion. The Commissioners knew well that it was extremely unlikely that the Baganda would agree to the cession of any territory whatsoever (Ganda spokesmen had made this emphatically plain), but they none the less hoped for 'a generous act of statesmanship on the part of Buganda'. 'We can conceive of no other single act' [than the handing over of these two counties], they wrote, 'which would add more to the stature of Buganda within Uganda, or would contribute more to the stability of the Protectorate on the eve of independence.' If, however, the Baganda refused, the Commission urged that the main political parties in Uganda should attempt to persuade them to agree, and in any case the government should ensure that the problem was settled, in accordance with the Commission's recommendations, before Independence (Molson Report, chap. 8).

As anticipated, far from responding with the 'generous act of statesmanship' called for by the Molson Commission, the Baganda reacted to its recommendations with angry indignation. At a session of the Lukiiko (the Buganda Parliament) the day after the publication of the report members spoke heatedly of 'preparing for war' and 'fighting to the last drop of our blood' to retain the disputed areas. Telegrams were sent to the Secretary of State by the Kabaka and the Lukiiko rejecting the report and stressing that in no circumstances would Buganda ever agree to any transfer of territory to Bunyoro. A spokesman of the Ganda nationalist party, Kabaka Yekka ('the Kabaka alone') 'which was at that time in uneasy coalition with Mr. Obote's party, the Uganda People's Congress,[1] said that they would never agree to an inch of Buganda's territory being given away. In July the acting premier of Buganda said that the Kabaka's people had been prepared to invade Bunyoro if Britain had ordered any of the 'Lost Counties' to be transferred (*The Times*, 19 July 1962).

[1] As an American political scientist has emphasized in a perceptive (if not always strictly accurate) discussion of Nyoro local government, it is 'important to recall that Obote's U.P.C. was able to form a government only through coalition with the Kabaka Yekka—the Buganda party' (Burke, p. 83). But with defections from the opposition Democratic Party, Obote's party gained a slim majority, and its unlikely dependence on Kabaka Yekka soon came to an end.

Initial reactions by the Banyoro to the Commission's recommendations were unenthusiastic, for they had hoped to be awarded all three Mubende counties. But the Mukama early expressed himself willing to accept the compromise proposed by the Commission.

Faced by Buganda's intransigence and refusal to compromise, the British Government was left with a difficult choice. It could either call Buganda's bluff and impose the Molson recommendations before Independence, a course which would certainly have involved grave risk of serious disturbance, or it could leave the problem for final settlement, at some time in the future, in an independent Uganda. On the grounds that the atmosphere was quite unsuitable for holding a referendum in the short period available, and that to have forced the issue might have led to a breakdown in the arrangements for Independence, the second course was adopted. The Uganda Independence Order in Council, 1962, provided that a referendum should be held in the Buyaga and Bugangaizi counties, as the Munster Commission had recommended, but not until at least two years had elapsed, that is, not before 9 October 1964. In the referendum, persons on the electoral roll in each of these counties should be asked to vote for one of three alternatives. The first was that the county concerned should continue to be part of Buganda, the second was that it should return to Bunyoro, and the third was that it should become part of a new and separate district of Uganda. Until the referendum could be held, the two counties were to be administered not, as hitherto, by Buganda, but by the Central Government. It was thought that after at least two years of Central Government administration the peaceful holding of a referendum would be a very much more practicable proposition than it could be in the disturbed conditions of the eve of Independence.

This imposed 'solution' was quite unacceptable to the Baganda, who were determined never to cede any land to Bunyoro at any time. It was even less acceptable to the Banyoro, who believed (as did many observers sympathetic to Bunyoro, including the present writer) that if the referendum proposed by the Molson Commission did not take place before British protection was withdrawn from Uganda, it would never, in a Buganda-dominated Uganda, take place at all. As the Molson

Report put it: 'If a Prime Minister of an independent Uganda were dependent on the Baganda block for staying in office [as was in fact the case in 1962] he would find it difficult to support any concession to the Banyoro.' The British Government had been ultimately responsible for the problem in the first place. It had then, for more than half a century, refused even to examine it. Now, at the very last moment before Independence, having permitted it to be reopened and decided by an impartial tribunal in Bunyoro's favour, it was, it seemed, abandoning its manifest responsibilities in the matter, and leaving the new nation to hold this very prickly baby. To Banyoro, and to others, the government's decision looked like abject surrender to the more powerful and influential Buganda kingdom. The present writer, in a letter to *The Times* (7 July 1962), charged the government, perhaps a little intemperately, with 'pusillanimous surrender, on grounds of political expediency, to Buganda intransigence and refusal to compromise'. A *Manchester Guardian* leader spoke for many observers when, after pointing out that Bunyoro's claims had only lately been taken seriously, and had been found largely justified, it went on to say that it would be 'an act of cowardice to leave the people of Uganda to fight it out among themselves after Britain has left' (16 July 1962). Although Banyoro's determination to recover the Buyaga and Bugangaizi counties never wavered, at that time they saw little early prospect of this happening. The only hope, and that a very forlorn one, seemed to be that change of heart by the Baganda looked for, though not very hopefully, by the Molson Commission.

No such change of heart took place, yet in the end the British Government's policy paid off. On 4 November 1964 a referendum was held in the Buyaga and Bugangaizi counties, an overwhelming majority of the population voted for reunion with Bunyoro, and on 1 January 1965, more than seventy years after Colvile's unauthorized annexation, these two counties were formally restored to the Bunyoro kingdom. How did this come about?

The story can be quickly told. The new Prime Minister of Uganda, Mr. Obote, a Lango by birth and so with no 'tribal' attachment to either kingdom, had never made any secret of his intention to have the referendum carried out, in accordance

with Uganda's new constitution, as soon as the prescribed two-year period had elapsed. But the Baganda were determined to prevent this. Their Lukiiko continued its uncompromising stand, declaring that Buganda would never give up territory which they claimed (quite mistakenly, as we have seen) to have 'conquered'. Meantime, unrest continued in the disputed counties, especially in Buyaga, where early in 1963 the Kabaka of Buganda spent some time, with 300 attendants and bodyguards, on what was said to be a 'hunting trip'. Not surprisingly this gave rise to friction with the local Banyoro, and at the end of March Buyaga county was declared a 'disturbed area'. Through this and the following year the Kabaka spent a good deal of time at his 'hunting lodge' at Ndaiga in that county, where he launched an ambitious scheme for the resettlement in the area of some thousands of Baganda ex-servicemen. This injection of Baganda would, the Baganda hoped, go some way towards reinforcing their claims to the area. In April 1963 the Mukama of Bunyoro protested publicly against what he called this 'show of strength' by the Kabaka, and the presence of a Baganda force of about 2,000 armed ex-servicemen who were alleged to be in the disputed area at that time. However, the Mukama also called for restraint by Banyoro in the 'Lost Counties', and although there were some serious incidents during this period, in which a number of people were killed, the Central Government presence prevented any full-scale confrontation.

By mid 1964 Obote's ruling Uganda People's Congress, strengthened by numerous defections from the now declining Democratic Party, had been able to dissolve its improbable alliance with the Ganda nationalist Kabaka Yekka party, and relations between Buganda and the Central Government, never very cordial, began to deteriorate rapidly. In that year the Kabaka Yekka members of the Central Uganda Parliament did their best to obstruct the passage of the bill providing for the holding of the referendum, but one by one representatives of the other parts of the county, both Bantu and non-Bantu, came out in favour of it, and it was passed on 31 August 1964, after all of the Kabaka Yekka members had walked out of the assembly in protest.

In an independent Uganda, the Baganda were no longer in a position to enforce their will; without British support they

could not hope to retain the dominance which they had held
for so long. The writing was on the wall, but they refused to
read it. Their only hope of preserving an independent existence
in the new state was to accept the reality that the Central
Government was there to govern all Uganda, and to co-operate
with Parliament. But this they showed no inclination to do.
When the bill was passed, the Kabaka, as President of Uganda
(which high office he had held since Independence), refused to
sign it. His government, still unable to comprehend that they
no longer occupied the position of strength which they had held
for more than half a century, continued to insist that 'no one
in Buganda agreed or will ever agree to anything concerning
changes to Buganda counties' (*Uganda Argus*, 15 September
1964). The Lukiiko contested in the courts the legality of the
proposed referendum, claiming that all Buyaga and Bugangaizi
residents of more than six months' standing should be allowed
to vote, and not, as the government had ruled, only those whose
names appeared in the 1962 electoral register: had this been
accepted, the substantial number of new Ganda immigrants
into the Ndaiga area would have been able to vote on Buganda's
side. The Lukiiko also argued that without the agreement of the
Kabaka's government the referendum was *ultra vires*. These
claims were dismissed by the Uganda High Court and, later,
by the Privy Council, to which the Lukiiko appealed.

The referendum took place, without serious disturbance, on
4 November 1964. The results were announced the following
day. In Buyaga, 8,327 had voted for reintegration with Bunyoro
and 1,289 for retention by Buganda; in Bugangaizi the figures
were 5,275 for Bunyoro and 2,253 for Buganda. Only 112 people
voted for a separate district. This news was received with little
disturbance in the areas themselves, 'no incidents [being]
reported from the Lost Counties either during or after the
referendum' (*Uganda Argus*, 9 November). It was received with
satisfaction in Bunyoro, whose prime minister appealed for
calm, and issued a warning that there should be no reprisals.
But in the Kabaka's capital at Mengo in Kampala it was a
different story. Local Baganda, who had all along been misled
by their Lukiiko into believing that the referendum would never
take place, rioted, and a number of them were killed and
wounded by police fire. The Katikiro, Michael Kintu, had to

be rescued from an angry mob by the police, and his government, which was accused of 'deception, inefficiency, and betrayal', and of having 'sold' Buganda, resigned. In a public statement, Premier Obote issued a strong warning to the Baganda, reminding them that their Kabaka, as President, was sworn to respect the Constitution, including its provision for the Mubende referendum. He also declared that the government would be 'firm with lawless elements within the nation' (*Uganda News Review*, 16 November 1964).

On 1 January 1965, the Counties of Buyaga and Bugangaizi were formally transferred to the Bunyoro kingdom, and the 'Lost Counties' dispute was ended. Later developments in Buganda, the Kabaka's dismissal as President, the kingdom's abortive declaration of independence, and the tragic events of April 1966, when with much loss of life, the Kabaka's palace was stormed by the police, and he and his family driven into exile, do not concern us in a study of Bunyoro. The long story of Buganda dominance had had a bitter ending. No doubt in an independent Uganda its powers were bound sooner or later to diminish. But it may be argued that had the Baganda been willing to make the gesture asked for by the Molson Commission (which might well have had the effect of welding the four associated kingdoms into a powerful bloc in Uganda politics) and, more generally, had they been able to bring themselves to accept the hard fact that the Central Uganda Government was ineluctably there to govern all Uganda, the story might well have been different. But such speculations are beyond the scope of the present study.

The intractability of the 'Lost Counties' dispute showed clearly that even in the 1960s local patriotisms were a powerful and dangerous force for disruption in the new Uganda, as they have been in other African countries. The first loyalties of most Banyoro, equally with the Baganda, were to their own kingdom rather than to the Uganda State, which viewed historically was but a recent creation of the Europeans. In the next two chapters we examine in more detail some aspects of the traditional Nyoro kingdom, to which, as the 'Lost Counties' campaign so vividly demonstrated, Banyoro still attached such high and enduring value.

5

RITUALS OF KINGSHIP

LIKE other social institutions, the kingship of the Banyoro can be regarded both as expressing and sustaining a system of beliefs and values, and as the centre of a system of action, of institutionalized interpersonal relationships having causal implications for other coexisting social institutions. In reality, of course, these two aspects of the kingship were inextricably intertwined; for the ways in which people thought about the kingship, the Obukama, had important implications for their behaviour, and the social relationships centring on it could only be adequately understood when account was taken of how the parties to these relationships thought about them and about themselves. But the distinction is important analytically, for the two aspects imply different kinds of questions. In considering how the kingship was thought about, we are concerned primarily with meanings and symbols, and so, especially, with royal ritual: in thinking about the king as agent, we are concerned with consequences, with how the political system worked. In this chapter I am mostly concerned with the ways in which Banyoro thought about their kingship, and with some of the ceremonial and ritual usages through which these ideas were expressed. In Chapter 6 I discuss the king as agent, the nature and implications of his traditional relationships with his chiefs and people, and, no less important, with the British administration to which he and his kingdom were subject until 1962.

The Mukama's right to rule was grounded in his descent in the ruling line of the Babito clan; we saw in Chapter 3 how Bito pre-eminence was validated by myth and traditional history. Thus before discussing the rituals which are associated with the kingship, something more must be said about how the Babito as a group were regarded, and how they regarded themselves.

In Runyoro the term 'Bito' is an ambiguous one, for it applies both to the ruling dynasty and to the patrilineal clan (*ruganda*),

or perhaps congeries of clans, to which that dynasty belonged but which was not coextensive with it. Like other clans, Babito have a special avoidance object (*muziro*). For them, as for the aristocratic lineages of the Acholi to the north, this is the bushbuck, *ngabi* (Girling, p. 159). As a clan, they are not numerically stronger than a number of other clans, indeed in most country districts they are very poorly represented. But the Bito clan differs from all the other clans found in Bunyoro in two important ways. First, it might fairly be described as a group of associated clans (or perhaps sub-clans) rather than as a single unit. Thus Bikunya distinguishes no less than 156 Bito sub-clans (*bitabu*), though he insists that all are members of a single clan (pp. 59–61). No other Nyoro clan claims more than three or four such named divisions, and many have none. Secondly, unlike all other Nyoro clans, the Babito are not exogamous: it is said that Babito may 'marry their sisters', and (in the classificatory sense of the term 'sister') many do. But except for the Mukama's relationship with his 'official sister', discussed later in this chapter, such unions were not ordinarily between close agnates, and in any case no Mubito would marry a woman related to him through his mother: Babito 'avoid their mother's child' (*nibazira owa nyina*), Banyoro say.

Only those Babito who could establish a genuine agnatic relationship with the Mukama, usually by descent from a king who lived not more than three or four generations back, were accorded special prestige, and the closer the link, the higher the prestige claimed and acknowledged. Since recent Bakama have been notably philoprogenitive, there was in the 1950s a considerable number of such persons, and when the term Bito is used to distinguish members of the ruling clan from ordinary people it is this aristocratic class that is usually referred to. But there are many Babito who belong to one of the numerous divisions of their clan, and who have the bushbuck as their avoidance object, but who do not claim explicit genealogical connection with the ruling line, although all of them assert that they are descendants of its founder, the semi-mythical Rukidi Mpuga, or one of his brothers. These Babito are hardly, if at all, distinguished socially from members of commoner clans, unless perhaps by the slight *cachet* which attaches to the name Mubito. As members of their village communities, such 'non-royal'

PLATE 2

Mukama wearing crown: *c.* 1936

Babito are treated no differently from anybody else. Their social standing depends, like other people's, on their conformity to community standards and values, not on their agnatic descent. A Mubito neighbour of mine in Kasingo, a poor and ineffectual man with neither family nor property, was regarded by his fellow villagers with amused contempt. When it is wished to distinguish such 'ordinary' Babito from those superior ones who claim explicit genealogical connection with the royal line, they are referred to as 'just Babito' (*Babito kwonka*).

The category of Babito who claimed aristocratic status, and who (if it was wished to distinguish them from *Babito kwonka*) might be referred to as 'those Babito who are well known and respected', and 'those Babito who are near to the drum' (*ngoma*, standing here as in other contexts for the kingship), itself contained a smaller and even more exclusive group, the 'Babito of the drum' (*Babito b'engoma*). These were the actual sons of a Mukama, and only a *Mubito w'engoma* should succeed to the kingship. In the 1950s there were still many such princes of the drum, for a substantial number of Kabarega's hundred or more children still survived, and many were persons of importance. In what follows I adopt common Nyoro usage in referring only to members of these last two categories when I speak of Babito; I do not include those who are 'just Babito', and who make no claim to special distinction.

So defined, then, in the 1950s Babito still possessed and jealously sought to maintain considerable, though declining, prestige. They thought of themselves as a distinctive hereditary aristocracy, and in the past many of the more important of them had been granted large 'estates' in land by the Mukama. Since the grant of such estates traditionally implied also the grant of extensive political rights over their peasant occupants, this meant that many Babito were made into territorial chiefs. As we shall see in Chapter 8, the introduction during this century of salaried, 'civil-service' type chiefs had largely, though by no means completely, broken down the traditional identification of political authority with the possession of proprietary rights over land. Also, since the Bunyoro Agreement of 1933, the acquisition of rights of the latter kind has been less profitable, though hardly less easy, than it had formerly been. So although in the 1950s there were still many eminent Babito, as a class

they lacked much of the authority and wealth which they had formerly possessed. But they still claimed special privileges and prestige, and under the nominal headship of the *Okwiri*, the king's 'official brother', they still preserved the right to act, or at least to express themselves, as a group.

The Okwiri (or Mugamba, the title was a rotating one) to whom Roscoe oddly refers as Kasunsu Nkwanza and Mugurusi,[1] was traditionally the first son of the former king, and so the reigning Mukama's eldest brother. He was formally appointed after the king's accession, and his position as a salaried palace official was formally acknowledged in both of the Bunyoro Agreements. The Okwiri was said to 'rule' the Babito, just as the Mukama ruled the country as a whole. His office may thus be seen as a means of, so to speak, overtly 'detaching' the king from the exclusive Bito group of which he is the pre-eminent member, so facilitating his identification with the interests of all the people of his kingdom, not just with the Bito minority. This is a gap which has to be bridged whenever a ruling clan or other minority group acquires political dominance over a majority of supposedly different stock, and Bunyoro's traditional office of Okwiri provides one means of rendering the kingship acceptable to the mass of the governed.[2] So the king had no direct concern with the affairs of his Babito kinsmen, whose interests often conflicted with those of the people as a whole, as they still did in the 1950s: Bito affairs were the Okwiri's business.

As the Babito's mouthpiece and the protector of their interests, the Okwiri sat on the Rukurato or Central Council of the Bunyoro Kingdom Government at its biennial meetings, and resolutions relating to Bito interests, usually claims for special rights and privileges, were tabled by him. In recent years most of these resolutions had a quality of nostalgic

[1] Roscoe 1923, p. 272. *Kasunsunkwanzi* ('beaded cock's comb') is one of the king's crowns (*makondo*); *mugurusi* means any old man, and might well be used in casual conversation to refer to the Okwiri in his role as senior of the *Babito b'engoma*. Roscoe gives a reasonably full description of the kingship and of the ceremonial surrounding it (chaps. 5 and 6), though there are a few errors in his account.

[2] In the nearby interlacustrine Bantu kingdom of Ankole the same end was achieved by means of a very different institution. There the cult of the drum *Bagyendanwa*, which was said to be 'above' the king and to be accessible to Bahima and Bairu alike, provided a focus for national unity transcending the wide gap between the ruling pastoral Hima minority and the peasant Bairu (Oberg, p. 55).

unreality, being aimed at improving the economic position and enhancing the prestige of the 'princes', for whom there was little place in the increasingly bureaucratized political system of the 1950s. Thus in the half-dozen or so years before 1951 formal resolutions were tabled requesting special grants towards the school fees of Babito children, recommending that court cases against 'princes and princesses' should not be heard in the ordinary courts without having been first considered by their fellow Babito (on the ground that 'special consideration should be had for their rank'), and suggesting that special laws should be passed for the 'safeguarding' of princes and princesses 'in order not to be trespassed upon' (e.g. by lawsuits or prosecutions by commoners). It was also officially proposed that special allowances should be paid by the Kingdom Government to those Babito who were short of money.

In 1954 a county chief was taken to court, at the insistence of 'the Okwiri and all the Babito', for having spoken rudely to a Mubitokati, a daughter of the late Mukama Kabarega, after a cocktail party at the palace. He was alleged to have said 'go and call your father Kabarega from Mparo (his burial place) and let him come and distribute beer here for us at the palace' (*genda oyete so Kabarega Mparo aije agabe amarwa omu kikali*). His defence was that he was only joking, but the joke, if joke it was, was perhaps in rather poor taste. Anyway, he was fined 100 shillings.

None of these recommendations was accepted by the Rukurato, but the fact that they were made shows that Babito still regarded themselves as an aristocratic élite, claiming high ascribed status in the hierarchy of prestige. To them, and to many other traditionally minded Banyoro, there seemed nothing inappropriate in the notion that as a hereditary aristocracy they should enjoy privileges and rights not available to ordinary people.

Bito prestige was also marked in other ways. Babito who could establish a clear genealogical connection with the royal line had a right to claim from the Mukama a special brass ankle-ring (*kikomo*). They expected to receive deference and respect from commoners, and they generally did. Babito's right to exercise authority was not questioned, even though *qua* Babito, they no longer held political power. However, many

Babito still held large private estates (*bibanja*), and in the 1950s
the attitude of these Babito proprietors to the peasants settled
on their estates was often said to be particularly autocratic, as
compared with that of non-Babito landowners. Babito were
often said to be arrogant, demanding, and indifferent to the
rights of others. In fact many were not so, but in the 1950s some
undoubtedly were. In the largest of the village surveys which
I carried out in Bunyoro, the only household out of over a
hundred which actively resented my inquiries and completely
refused to co-operate was a Bito one. Sometimes Bito arrogance
was resented, but more often it was not. 'The Babito were
chosen long ago to rule us,' an old peasant informant told me,
'if it were not for them there would be no royal line to govern,
and to be governed by Bairu would be intolerable.' Thus the
mythical charter for Bito pre-eminence was still valid in the
1950s, and I should not be surprised if, for some, it still is. So,
like aristocracies elsewhere which have survived the social conditions in which they played an effective political role, the
Babito clung to the outward signs of their lost authority, and
lorded it over a peasant population which still showed few signs
of resentment. It might have been supposed that Babito, anxious
for the reality of power, would have sought positions in the
modern hierarchy of official chiefs. In fact, relatively few had
done so; Babito were hardly better represented in proportion
to their numbers than were several other clans.[1] This is quite
consistent with traditional Bito values. An elderly Mubito well
expressed their attitude: 'we are Babito; how could we allow
ourselves to be employed as subordinates to senior chiefs who
would probably be Bairu?' Like most traditional Nyoro values,
ideas about the Babito, and Babito's ideas about themselves,
were changing rapidly. But in the 1950s many still clung to the
older standards.

Corresponding to the Okwiri's position as head of the Babito
'princes' was that of the Kalyota or Batebe, a patrilateral half-
sister of the Mukama, whom he appointed, after his accession,
as the head of the Babitokati ('princesses'). There was a considerable number of these women, the most important (as with

---

[1] In 1955 one out of the four county chiefs was a Mubito (like the reigning king
he was a son of the former Mukama Kabarega); four out of twenty-five sub-county
chiefs, and two out of sixty-five 'parish' chiefs (*miruka*) were Babito.

their male clansmen) being those who were actual daughters of a king (*Babitokati b'engoma*), and they too were accorded high prestige. Many of them formerly ruled over areas allotted to them by the king, and so were themselves a kind of chief. In fact it was said that Babito princesses are 'like men'; traditionally they were forbidden to marry. In Bunyoro wives are expected to show great deference and submissiveness to their husbands, and it would have been unthinkable in traditional times for a king's daughter to assume so subordinate a role. Likewise, princesses were not allowed to bear children; the reason that Banyoro give for this is that it would be unlucky for a king to see his sisters' children. This is consistent with Nyoro ideas about the relationship between men and the children of their female agnates (characteristically between 'mothers' brothers' and their 'sisters' sons'). In Bunyoro sisters' sons are said to 'rule' their mothers' brothers, and even to be a source of ritual danger to them (Beattie 1958a, pp. 17–22): evidently it would be inappropriate for anyone to occupy such a status in relation to the Mukama. It will be remembered, also, that in the Nyoro myth, king Bukuku was killed by his daughter's son, who then replaced him on the throne. In Bunyoro, as in Buganda where a similar rule applied, these prohibitions prevented the development of potentially embarrassing lines of sisters' sons to the king, which might serve as focuses of disaffection: in this way they tended to preserve the exclusiveness and unity of the royal house.

In recent years the *Babitokati b'engoma*, like other Babito women, have been permitted to marry and have children, and such unions might have political significance. In 1953 one of the Mukama's daughters was married to a county chief who had recently been appointed Katikiro (prime minister) in the Bunyoro Native Government; another was married to the head clerk in the Native Government's central office. These influential officials were thus bound to the Mukama as sons-in-law (*bako*), and Nyoro culture is very explicit as to the obligations of respect and support owed by men to their wives' fathers (Beattie 1958a, pp. 13–14). But nobody who was not a chief nor otherwise important and wealthy would think of marrying a Mubitokati, for, an informant told me, 'they will not dig, or carry water, as ordinary women do, and they despise their husbands and call them "servants" (*bairu*)'. Also, bridewealth

is not paid in such marriages, for that would imply that Babito
and *bairu* could meet on equal terms: 'a Mubito's word should
be an order; how could a *mwiru* argue with a Mubito about
bridewealth?'

The Kalyota or Batebe (the title, like that of the Okwiri, is
a rotating one), who is the head of the Babitokati, is mistakenly
referred to by Roscoe as the 'queen'. In *The Bakitara* he
describes what he calls a ceremony of marriage between this
princess and the Mukama, and he writes of their relation with
each other as being that of husband and wife (1923, p. 136).
But it is plain from his own account that what he describes as
a marriage ceremony is really a rite of a very different kind, and
that the Mukama's relationship with the Batebe (who was
anyway, like the other princesses, forbidden to have children)
was in no sense a conjugal one.

The ceremony which Roscoe describes consisted in the formal
presentation to the chosen half-sister of certain insignia, including spears, knives, and other objects symbolizing political
authority. It is said also to have involved the ceremonial drinking of milk from the cows of the Mukama's special herd
(*nkorogi*), a rite also said to have been performed when major
chiefs were appointed, and which implied (as Roscoe rightly
says) 'a special dedication of the person to the service of the
king'.[1] Finally, the Kalyota is said to have kissed the Mukama's
hand, just as all other chiefs do on appointment to high political
authority (Roscoe 1923, p. 138). So what Roscoe is describing
was not any kind of marriage; the ceremony which the king's
half-sister underwent was rather a rite of accession to high
authority, and to the enhanced ritual status which in Bunyoro
this implied. The Kalyota, like the Okwiri, was a kind of chief;
she was appointed head of the women of the royal clan, just as
the king's eldest brother was appointed head of the princes. It
was traditionally her responsibility to settle questions of inheritance and precedence and other disputes between the princesses,
and she formerly held substantial estates in virtue of her office,
the peasant occupants of which she ruled just as other chiefs did,
and she derived services and tribute from them. In recent years
she has held little authority, but her status as official head of the

---

[1] 1923, p. 138. But there is some question as to whether milk was actually drunk
on such occasions. See below, p. 119.

women of the royal clan was acknowledged in both of the
Bunyoro Agreements (1933 and 1955), in which she is correctly
referred to as the king's 'official sister' (not as the 'queen').
Until the kingdom was dissolved in 1967 she received a small
salary, under the terms of the Agreement.

The Kalyota, then, was never the queen, in the sense of being
the king's consort. In European times she was socially overshadowed by the Mukama's true consort, the Omugo. She was
not a Mubitokati; the last Mukama married his Omugo in
Christian marriage, and she bore him several children, including his heir elect. It was the Omugo, not the Kalyota, who
accompanied the Mukama to Europe for Queen Elizabeth's
coronation in 1953, and she sat at his side at ceremonies and
other entertainments attended by Europeans. The Kalyota's
office was very different. One of her titles was *Omugole w'
omuchwa*, that is, bride or mistress of the house in the royal
enclosure which Roscoe refers to as her reception room (1923,
p. 141). She was 'married' to her office, symbolized by the
palace building *muchwa*, not to the king. If she ever did have
sexual relations with him, as Roscoe states, they were not part
of any kind of marriage. The union, if union there was, is best
regarded as symbolic, expressive of Kalyota's role as the female
expression or counterpart of the kingship. Sex may itself be a
symbol, as well as what is symbolized. It is said that traditionally
the Mukama could have sexual relations with any of his half-
sisters if he wanted to, though they were not allowed to bear
children. The Kalyota, then, was a political authority, not the
king's wife (the king's wives are discussed in the next chapter),
and though she owed her high status in part to her Bito descent,
her office, like that of other senior officials, was ceremonially
conferred on her by the Mukama.

So much, then, for the 'royal' clan, the Babito, for the ways
in which they were regarded and regarded themselves, and for
the manner of their representation at the king's court. I now
discuss some of the rites and ceremonies associated with the
kingship, and their significance.[1]

---

[1] I should say here that the information upon which the following discussion
is based derives rather from the scattered accounts and references in the ethnographic literature than from my own field investigations, which in this context were
a good deal less complete than I would have liked. For some reasons for this see
Beattie 1965, p. 47.

For my present purpose, I take the term 'ritual' to refer to formal and socially recognized procedures which are meaningful symbolically, rather than in terms of practical utility. Of course I recognize that many, perhaps most, procedures have both aspects, but here I am chiefly concerned with the former. What is symbolized I take to be some abstract quality or value, and I assume that there exists, or may exist, some kind of intelligible correspondence between this and the symbolic procedure in question. This is so even though the nature of the correspondence may be unknown to all, even perhaps to any, of the people who perform the ritual; it may even be no longer discoverable. Also, as Victor Turner and others have recently stressed, the same rite may have different symbolic significances at different levels, and may mean different things to different people. In the present context, I am interested in the nature of the correspondence between symbol and thing symbolized (where it can be ascertained), in the form which the ritual takes, and in its social significances. In the case of traditional royal ritual in Bunyoro, the matter is fairly straightforward. The king was thought of as the centre and source of all political power, as superior to and different from all other persons, and as ruler or master, not as 'father' of his people. So, basically, what Nyoro royal ritual is chiefly about is the notion of imposed but accepted authority, of legitimized social power, though it certainly has other significances too. It seems probable that in traditional Bunyoro the constant expression and reaffirmation in ritual of the hierarchical values implicit in Nyoro political relations contributed significantly to their preservation. Even in the rapidly changing Bunyoro of the 1950s, these values were still ubiquitous and pervasive.

So regarded, the ritual associated with the Nyoro kingship may be said to fall into three broad categories. First, there are those rituals which express the ways in which the kingship, as the traditional centre and focus of political authority, was conceived. Second, there are those formal procedures which relate to the acquisition, retention, and (at death) relinquishing of the kingship, the royal *rites de passage*. And third, there are those rituals which are concerned with the actual *use* of the Mukama's authority; the conditions under which he may exercise it, and the manner in which he may delegate it. These distinctions are

not absolute, and the categories based on them are not mutually exclusive. They none the less express the three main themes in Nyoro ritualization of authority, and in what follows I consider Nyoro royal ritual under these three heads.

In terms of the first of them, the central themes here are the king's identification with the country as a whole, and, consequently, his difference from and superiority to all other persons. In a sense indeed this latter theme is implicit in all the royal ritual, since it is the king's ritual and not anybody else's. But some rites and ceremonial usages do point directly to his uniqueness and superiority. Thus his symbolic identification with the country as a whole requires that he should maintain a state both of physical well-being and of ritual purity. The requirement that he should maintain himself in perfect physical condition meant that nobody who was ill could remain in the royal enclosure, lest the king's health, and so the country's well-being, should be affected. This prohibition applied even to the king's herds, and if one of the royal cattle became sick it was either sent away to be treated or it was killed, for it could not be allowed to die a natural death in the royal enclosure. All contact with death had to be avoided; the Mukama's absence from his mother's funeral in 1953, which I attended, was explained to me as being due to this prohibition. If the king himself became ill, this was kept a closely guarded secret and, according to tradition, if his illness seemed likely to be fatal he would be expected to hasten his end by drinking poison. It was believed that a king who suffered any physical injury involving mutilation or incapacity, such as a wound in battle, could not continue to reign; if the injury were not quickly fatal he would be given poison. When he grew old and feeble and was unable to carry out his duties properly he should either take poison or he would be killed by one or more of his wives.[1] It is impossible to be certain whether any kings actually killed themselves, or were killed, in such ways as these, though I think that it is not unlikely that they were. But whether they were or not, it is of interest that the kingship was thought about in this way. Like

[1] Roscoe 1923, p. 121. See also Emin Pasha 1888, p. 89: it was 'customary for the king, as soon as he falls seriously ill or begins to break up from old age, to be killed by his own wives, for according to an old prophecy, the throne will pass away from the dynasty of the Wawitu [Babito] in the event of the king dying a natural death.' See also Bikunya, p. 54.

the Mugabe of Ankole, the Mukama was not supposed to turn over while in bed, lest some disaster befall the country.

As well as keeping in good physical condition, the Mukama had to maintain a state of ritual purity, and for the same reason. This involved for him (and for others) some specific ritual acts and avoidances. He was required to observe certain food restrictions; he was supposed to eat no meat except beef, and certain low-status vegetable foods (sweet potatoes, cassava, and some kinds of peas and beans) were forbidden to him. The large number of servants and retainers who surrounded him (more is said about them below) also had to keep themselves ritually pure. Thus, for example, his female dairy attendants had to be virgins, and on ceremonial occasions they would smear themselves with white clay (kaolin), white here signifying goodness and purity, as it does in other Nyoro cultural contexts.[1] It is said that in former times a young woman—a virgin, who could not serve while menstruating—slept at the foot of the Mukama's bed to 'protect' him (Roscoe 1923, p. 92). He had a number of cooks who worked in turns, and they and his other personal attendants had to abstain from sexual intercourse during and for two days prior to their periods of service, which were for only two days at a time. The Mukama ate his meals alone; even the servants who gave him food and drink were not supposed to look at him while they served him. It would seem, however, that his cook must have been partially exempted from this rule, for he was supposed to place pieces of meat, impaled on a fork, in the king's mouth without, on pain of death, touching the royal teeth (Roscoe 1923, p. 103). The king's special herd of cows (nkorogi) had to be attended by a boy below the age of puberty who, despite his youth, had to avoid any contact with women while he was on duty. This boy had to be careful not to scratch or cut himself, for any injury to him would also adversely affect the king.

The Mukama's cattle ritual chiefly involved the parading of certain special beasts before him, his daily presence at the milking of some of the nine cows particularly dedicated to his use,[2]

[1] Roscoe 1923, p. 98. The Nyoro verb -eza means both to whiten and to make pure, and the association between whiteness and purity is explicit in many Nyoro cultural contexts. For a reference to some of these see Beattie 1968, p. 418.

[2] The association of the auspicious number nine with the king and the kingship is comprehensively testified to in the literature. Thus, to quote a few examples,

and his ceremonial drinking of the new milk. In addition, Roscoe describes a daily ceremony in which the Mukama places his head against the head of one of the two young bulls ceremonially presented to him each morning, saying 'may all evil be taken away from me' (1923, p. 93). These cattle rituals had to be performed daily 'for the good of the country', and in the 1950s the Mukama was meticulous in carrying out at least a part of the prescribed ceremonial every morning.

These and other rituals centred on the Mukama as head of the state and the source of all political power, and they stressed his symbolic identity with the country as a whole, and the consequent need for his physical and ritual well-being to be maintained. But they do not at all suggest that he was thought of as an intermediary, through whom his people might communicate with a spiritual power over and above the kingship. The Mukama was not 'the great high priest of the nation', as Roscoe asserts (1923, p. 90). He did not intercede with spiritual powers, of which there are many in the Nyoro pantheon, on his people's behalf, nor were communications from the spirit world mediated through him. These functions were performed by the *mbandwa* spirit mediums, members of the highly institutionalized spirit mediumship cult, which was Bunyoro's traditional religion.[1] Though the Mukama had his priest mediums, he was not a priest, nor (unlike the chiefs of the neighbouring Alur and other Nilotic peoples) was he a rainmaker, though he had his rainmakers, magical experts who were subject to his and his chiefs' discipline and control.[2] As I have stressed, the Mukama was first and foremost a ruler, and was so thought of. It appears likely that ritual and ceremonial clustered about the Nyoro kingship because it was the centre of secular power, rather than

there were nine royal drums (of which the ninth was 'especially his'), there were nine white cowskins on the royal stool in the palace dairy, and a royal drum was beaten for nine days after the king's coronation (Roscoe 1923, pp. 77–8, 98, 133); during the king's accession ceremonies he knocks on an axe nine times, and on a metal drum nine times, 'while the people rejoice', he also beats 'in nine different rolls' on his principal drum, Mpango, takes nine sips of milk, and cuts himself nine pieces of meat to eat (K. W. 1937*b*, pp. 290, 294, 295, 298); a king should reign, or at least exercise full powers of government, for nine years (Bikunya, pp. 52–4, see also pp. 113–14 below). It has been argued that the propitiousness of the number nine for Banyoro is 'dubitable' (Needham, p. 436), but this opinion is not consistent with the ethnographic evidence.

[1] For a general account of this see Beattie 1969.
[2] For an account of them see Beattie 1964*b*.

the other way about. In this respect, Bunyoro and similar states differed fundamentally from such classic 'divine kingships' as are represented by that of the Shilluk of the Upper Nile, in which some temporal authority seemed to have attached itself to an institution whose primary significance was religious and symbolic. Other ceremonial usages expressed the Mukama's separateness from and superiority to ordinary people. He was not greeted or addressed as they were. He was properly addressed in the third person singular, not the second, and he replied in the same person. Of the twelve *mpako* or praise-names, one of which is given to every Munyoro soon after birth, one, *Okali*, was reserved exclusively for the king.[1] He also had a number of special names and honorific titles. His official title, *Rukirabasaija Agutamba*, means 'he who exceeds all men, and who relieves distress'. This style of address was officially adopted as a slightly inferior substitute for the prefix 'Your Highness', granted only to the Kabaka of Buganda among the interlacustrine rulers, and its use 'on official occasions' was authorized by both Bunyoro Agreements. Other traditional titles, often used, and applied to no one else, were *Mwebingwa* ('he to whom people run for help and protection'), *Nyakanungi* ('good ruler'), *Mwegombwa* ('he who is loved and longed for'), *Kasorobahiga* ('the animal they hunt'—i.e. other rulers, who are jealous of his power and preeminence), and *Emanzi ya Karuzika* ('the hero of the palace'). Before midday, the Mukama might be greeted *Ngundu zona Okali*, 'you are the chief bull in the whole herd, *Okali*'.[2] He could be greeted at any time with the words '*Kaboneka Agutamba*' (or *Mwebingwa*, etc.), meaning '*Agutamba* (or *Mwebingwa*, etc.) has appeared'. After sitting down he might be further greeted '*Kahangirize Agutamba*' (or *Mwebingwa*, etc.), which means 'may *Agutamba* (or *Mwebingwa*, etc.) live long'.[3] The Mukama made no reply to any of these greetings, which were never used among ordinary people. Even in the 1950s the most senior officers of the Bunyoro Kingdom Government were expected to kneel down before the king if they wished to hand him anything or make any request of him in his palace.

[1] See p. 52, n. 1 above. There is a discussion of these names in Crazzolara 1950, chap. 22.
[2] Roscoe mistranslates this phrase as 'the whole world is yours' (1923, p. 95).
[3] Misspelt by Roscoe as *Kahangiriza agutema*, and mistranslated by him as 'sit down in health' (1923, p. 95).

The king's distinctiveness was also stressed by the use of a special vocabulary to refer to his person and activities. Thus his eating, sleeping, bathing, laughing, being ill, dying, and being buried were referred to by words different from the ordinary ones, as were his corpse, his grave, and the milking of his special cows. His cooks, his bed, his drums, his spears, and other persons and objects associated with him also had their special names. The list that follows is taken from Karubanga (p. 43). Where the special 'royal' word has a meaning in everyday Runyoro I have so indicated. Initial vowels and (in the case of verbs) infinitive prefixes have been omitted.

Verbs	Special term	Ordinary Runyoro	Everyday meaning of special term
bathe	-ambuka	-oga	cross a swamp or river
bury	-tabaza	-zika	make to go to war
die	-tuza	-fa	
eat, or drink milk	-boneka	-lya	become visible, appear
greet	-ramya	-ramukya	worship
be ill	-sasa	-rwara	be in pain
laugh	-era	-seka	be white. As already noted, whiteness is associated with goodness and auspiciousness.
milk royal cows	-koroga	-kama	possibly connected with koroga, to mix or stir.
sit down	-singa	-ikarra	overcome
sleep	-raihya	-byama	raise, elevate

Substantives			
royal barkcloths	ngaju	mbugo	a large cow with long horns
bed or chair	kihango	kitabu or kitebe	possibly associated with the verb hanga, to create
cook	mwokya	mucumbi	one who roasts or burns something
corpse	muguta	mutumbi	
royal drums	mpango	ngoma	possibly also connected with verb hanga
graves	magasani	bituuro	
spears	mahango	macumu	possibly also associated with verb hanga
large jar for beer	buliza	mbindo	

There were, also, extensive regalia associated with the kingship;[1] these included various drums, crowns, spears, shields, and other objects, many of them with their special custodians (of

[1] I use the past tense, though at the time of writing these regalia are being preserved at the district headquarters at Hoima. It is much to be hoped that it will be possible soon for a detailed study of these artefacts and their histories (a study which was not feasible during the latter years of the kingdom) to be made.

whom more is said below). Some of these artefacts were said to have been handed down from the Bacwezi, others to have been brought by the Nilotic Babito when they first arrived from the north to take over the kingdom. They included various drums, beaded and bearded crowns, trumpets, spears, shields, a bow and arrows with quiver, decorated staffs, and other artefacts.[1] The royal enclosure (*kikali*) was very much larger than any other in the country, and it was laid out on a distinctive and unique plan, centring on the main assembly hall or courthouse (*karuzika*), which contained also the king's sleeping place and the royal dairy. It also enclosed a large number of other buildings and residences, all with their special names and associations. As a fairly full account of these is given by Roscoe, I do not describe them in detail here (1923, chap. 5). I am not in any case in a position to add much to his description. The layout illustrated in his book was still quite closely conformed to in 1955, and many of the houses were still similarly named, but there were fewer of them. Many, including the *karuzika*, were comparatively large modern buildings, and the *kikali* was no longer surrounded by the houses of the great chiefs, as it had been in traditional times. Nevertheless, many present and past senior chiefs still had 'town houses' in or near the capital.

In the 1950s the Mukama's pre-eminence was also expressed in a more modern idiom. His photograph, together with Queen Elizabeth's, hung in every courthouse in the kingdom. His car, at that time a venerable Humber, was exempt from road tax; his emblem, a representation of two crossed spears and a drum, took the place of a registration number plate. And his chauffeur was provided with a special uniform.

I turn now to consider the second broad category of royal ritual distinguished above, that relating to the acquisition, retention, and relinquishing of the kingship. I give only a summary account, as detailed descriptions are available in the literature (Roscoe 1923, pp. 127–35; K. W. 1937*b*). First, accession ritual marked strongly and dramatically the new ruler's change of status. Traditionally, in Bunyoro it was not known which of the princes would succeed to the throne until some time after the old king's death. We noted that any son of the late king except

---

[1] A short list of the Cwezi articles is to be found in K. W. 1935, p. 160, and of the Bito ones in K. W. 1936, p. 77.

the eldest might succeed; which one did so would generally depend on the amount of support he commanded. It is said that often, in former times, two eligible princes, sometimes more, have competed for the succession after their father's death. Each would count on the support of his maternal kinsmen, and probably on that of the chief and people of the area in which he had been brought up—as in other similar kingdoms princes were not supposed to be reared in the palace (Roscoe 1923, p. 137). He would rely, also, on such popular support as he could muster. The last Mukama's father, Kabarega, succeeded after he had killed his brother. This mode of succession meant that in Bunyoro, as in some other kingdoms, the death of a king was followed by a period of lawlessness and confusion, an interregnum during which warring factions made life for ordinary people uncertain and dangerous. It may be supposed that this very fact brought home to everyone the kingship's importance as the indispensable conditions of security and national well-being. The fact that in principle any son (but one) of the late king might succeed meant that for the successful prince a major change of status was involved; previously he had been one of what was often a considerable number of equally eligible princes (since kings had many wives); now he had become king, the first person in the land. It is not surprising that this dramatic change in status was strongly ritualized.

Nyoro accession ritual stressed, in particular, two themes: the assumption by the new king of a special ritual status, and his accession to paramount political authority. Both of these themes are explicit. Rites expressing the first theme include ceremonial washing, haircutting, and nail-paring, anointment with what the late Mukama described as 'consecrating oil', asperging, daubing with white clay, the placing of the beaded royal crowns on the king's head (nine times in the case of the most important crown), the sacrifice of a white bull and a white cock, the beating of the royal drums by the king (nine times in the case of the most important one), the ceremonial drinking of milk from the royal cows, and the announcement of the accession to the people.[1] Also involved was the choosing of a younger brother of the new Mukama as a 'mock king' who took the real

[1] K. W. 1937b, pp. 289–95. The sacrifice referred to here is the only one I know of which is said to be made to the high god, Ruhanga.

Mukama's place for eight days, and was then strangled and buried in the king's throne-room, 'in order', according to Roscoe, 'that death might be deceived and the real king protected from evil' (1923, p. 130). It was also, it seems, thought necessary to shed human blood from time to time in order to strengthen the kingship, and Roscoe states that this was done secretly in the course of the ceremonies held monthly at the time of the new moon, the blood of the victims being smeared on certain of the regalia (1923, p. 108). At the annual *Mpango* ceremony (latterly held only once every two years) animal sacrifices were also made, likewise a white cow and a white fowl, and others of the accession ceremonies were repeated.

Equally conspicuous in the accession ceremonies were rites expressing the Mukama's accession to specifically political authority. He was handed various objects symbolizing the coercive aspect of kingship; these included a spear, a bow and quiver, a dagger, and a stick. At the same time he was appropriately admonished, and told to kill those who offended him, to exercise his power wisely, and to protect his people. At one point in the ceremonies an official raised the alarm and shouted: 'You enemies, you witches, you barbarians, why do you disobey this brave Mukama?' (K. W. 1937*b*, p. 292.) The former range of his political authority was expressed by the formal presentation to him by a man 'representing foreigners' (that is, people from Acholi and Lango districts, north and east of the Nile) of a tribute of an elephant tusk and two copper bracelets (K. W. 1937*b*, p. 293). In the course of the accession proceedings the Mukama acted out ceremonially the judicial settlement of a case in which a man sued another for debt (K. W. 1937*b*, p. 294). He also shot arrows in four directions with the bow he had been given, naming the countries which lay in these directions as he did so, and exclaiming 'thus I shoot the countries to overcome them'.[1] This rite was also performed at the two-yearly *Mpango* refresher ceremonies. In a further rite a hammer and a stone anvil were brought, and the new Mukama struck some iron on the anvil four times. According to the last Mukama, this signified that the king was at the head of all the ironsmiths, as well as implying that he was like a hammer himself. It is evident

---

[1] K. W. 1937*b*, p. 295. See also Roscoe 1923, p. 134. Seligman was struck by the similarity of this rite to one described for ancient Egypt (Seligman, p. 15).

from these and other rites that the Mukama's succession was not only, or even primarily, to ritual status: it was also, explicitly, accession to supreme political authority.

These two associated aspects of the ritual were also manifested in a traditional rite called *Njeru*, or *Kusimba Njeru* (Nyakatura, p. 265; the word *njeru* means a white ox or sheep, and *kusimba* means 'to pledge'). This rite, aptly called by Fisher 'a covenant of peace' entered into by the king with his people (p. 131), is said formerly to have been performed after a king had reigned for the ritually auspicious period of nine years. In Bikunya's account, the king and his entourage first visited a hill called Epyemi, in what is now the Mubende district, where a special royal herd of cattle was kept.[1] Two of these cattle were slaughtered, and skinned in such a way that the hides were gown-shaped and could be worn. These were treated until they were very soft, and then the king and a chosen sister of about his age were dressed in them. The Mukama was then required to swear that from that day forward he would not wage war, kill or beat people, decide cases, or be angry, envious, or quarrelsome (Bikunya, p. 53; Nyakatura, p. 266).

In Fisher's account this ceremony was associated with sacrifice, both animal and human, on an enormous scale, involving 'thirty thousand cattle, tons of beads, and 200 princes', the latter being killed by being cast into a big furnace. It also involved the killing of a chosen royal servant, called Nyamajuga in her account, by the king, who 'offered him up for sacrifice in his own stead' (Fisher, pp. 130–1).

According to Bikunya, the sacrifice, on an equally huge scale, took place at a second stage in the proceedings. After he had entered into the 'covenant of peace' on the hill Epyemi, the Mukama and the chosen sister were taken to Chope, at the other end of the kingdom, where at a place called Podya there was said to be a pit called Nyamutaijura—the word means 'that which cannot be filled up'. Wearing their special hides, the king and his sister, together with the chief minister, Bamuroga, entered the pit, whereupon a large number of people captured for the purpose were slaughtered, and their blood allowed to flow into the pit until it rose up to the necks of the royal pair

[1] Bikunya, p. 52. According to Nyakatura the rites of *epyemi* and *njeru* were different, the former being concerned only with accession ritual (pp. 264–5).

and their companion. When they emerged from the pit the Mukama was required to climb up to the top of the heap of corpses beside the pit and to swear the same oath again. After that he sacrificed a white bull (*enimi enjeru*), and handed over the effective government of his country to a council composed of his chief minister, Mugema (the chief in charge of the royal tombs), and two or three other senior chiefs (Bikunya, pp. 53–4).

There is, of course, no evidence that such a rite was ever performed (Fisher refers to it specifically only in her account of the fourth Bito king, Oyo Nyimba, though according to K. W. four kings underwent the ceremony,[1] still less that, if it was performed, it involved the holocaust Fisher and Bikunya describe. But it is of interest to us on two grounds. First, there is the suggestion, found only in Fisher's account, of a substitute killing of the king in the context of the *njeru* ritual. Comparable customs are of course found in other parts of the world, though not, so far as I know, in the interlacustrine area of Africa.[2] Second, and of particular importance in the present context, is the way in which these ideas reflect the complexity, even the ambiguity, of traditional Nyoro ideas about political authority. Even though the Mukama was seen as the supreme power in the land and the source of all political authority, his authority was not, and was not conceived as, absolute. Even he, the paramount ruler, held it conditionally and at the will of his people, and the fact that, in theory at least, he could in due time be called upon to relinquish it was expressed in the *njeru* rite. Bikunya, for example (p. 52), writes of kings being 'permitted' (*baikirizib-waga*) to rule for nine years, and then being 'compelled' (*bamuhambirizaga*) to perform the required ritual.

The kingship's dual aspect, at the same time both secular and ritual, was also expressed in the royal mortuary ceremonies. Like comparable rites elsewhere, these emphasized both the continuity of the kingship, and the breach of that continuity.

[1] These were the fifth, sixth, and eighth of the dynasty; Winyi I, Olimi I, and Winyi II, and the eighteenth, Duhaga I. The last, however, who took the oath 'on the advice of his people', later broke it, with fatal results for himself. See K. W. 1936, pp. 68–9, 71 (78–80); 1937a, pp. 74–5 (58). (The page references in parentheses are to the English translations of K. W.'s articles, published with the Nyoro version.)

[2] Frazer, for example, in his discussion of ancient kingships, refers to some hints in Scandinavian traditions that 'of old the Swedish kings reigned only for periods of nine years, after which they were put to death or had to find a substitute to die in their stead' (1911, p. 57).

In traditional times, the king's death was concealed from the public for a considerable period, sometimes for months (Bikunya, p. 55). Persons unconnected with the palace were simply told that the Mukama was unwell. The dead king's body was laid out by special officials, and his nails and hair were cut by a woman of the Bakwonga clan. Then a young cow from the king's herd, which had only calved once, was brought. A selected son of the king, perhaps the chosen heir if the dead king had made his preference known, reversed the barkcloth he was wearing so that it was fastened on his left shoulder instead of his right, and milked the cow into a new wooden milk pot (*kisahi*). He then poured some of the milk into the dead king's mouth.[1] According to Bikunya, if the son held between his fingers leaves of plants called *mubuza* and *mwetango* (the latter of which at least has a white blossom), this was an indication that he was the selected heir.

After a few days the king's corpse was opened, and the intestines and other organs removed: these were wrapped up in a barkcloth and buried separately, near water. His lower jawbone was also detached, and this was carefully preserved, according to Bikunya at the home of a Mubito princess in Chope, in the north of the kingdom. The body was then placed on a wooden framework and dried over a slow fire for four months. Bikunya says that a large pot was placed beneath the framework, into which dripped liquids from the corpse. This pot was then carefully preserved by the chief minister (Bamuroga), and after the new king had been enthroned, the liquid was mixed with the meat with which the new king feasted his chiefs and people. In this way, Bikunya states (p. 55), they can be said to have 'eaten their king' (*balire omukama wabu*).

When the time came publicly to announce the king's death—at the appearance of the fourth moon after he had died, in Bikunya's version—a man said to be a (classificatory) 'sister's son' of the Babito,[2] was told to climb to the top of the palace (*karuzika*) roof, carrying with him a milk pot full of milk. When

---

[1] Bikunya, p. 54. A comparable rite is carried out when any household head (*nyineka*) dies (Beattie 1961c, p. 171).

[2] '*Omwihwa w'Ababito.*' As princesses were not allowed to marry or have children this man could not have been a sister's son to the Mukama himself. The sister's son, as both outsider and near kinsman, also plays a destructive and 'inauspicious' role in the mortuary ceremonies of ordinary householders (Beattie 1961c, p. 172).

he reached the summit, he called out the alarm (a high-pitched ululation), and hurled the milk pot to the ground, together with the spear which always stood erect on the apex of the conical thatched roof of the palace. At the same time he cried: 'The place has lost its masters; the milk is spilt; darkness has come again; evil has befallen; the king is dead.'[1] As he descended he was speared to death, for a man who had made so terrible an announcement could not be allowed to live.

After this, one of the late Mukama's younger sons was installed as a 'mock king' (*muragwangoma*, 'he who will say goodbye to the kingship'). He was treated as a real king for some days and was then killed, either by the genuine heir or on his orders (Bikunya, p. 56). According to Roscoe, this was supposed to deceive death and to deflect any ritual danger from the real successor during the accession ceremonies (1923, p. 130). It may also be seen as stressing the continuity of the kingship, for once the death was announced the country could no longer remain without at least a nominal head.

When the heir had secured his succession, traditionally by defeating his rival brother or brothers, he had to come to claim the dead king's jawbone, which had been carefully guarded in its hiding place, which was known only to the Bamuroga and a few other senior palace officials. He then had to bury it at a chosen site near the traditional centre of the Bunyoro kingdom in Mubende, the area which later came to be known as the 'Lost Counties'. Here a large circular building was erected over the tomb, and some of the late king's regalia were kept there, in the care of a chosen member of the Babito clan. The rest of the corpse was buried separately, and with it, Banyoro writers say, were interred some of the dead king's favourite wives; also, according to some accounts, a number of retainers.[2] After some time this grave was forgotten; the tombs (*magasani*) which are remembered today and which are still national shrines of great importance, are those where the royal jawbones were buried.

The third broad category of Nyoro royal ritual includes those rites which express the conditions under which the Mukama may exercise political power, and the manner in which he may

---

[1] In Bikunya's version (p. 56), '*Ekyaro kyaburwa abakama, amata gatikire, obuire bwaira kabiri, ekibi kiguire, omukama atulize*'.
[2] Roscoe 1923, pp. 125–6. See also Fisher, p. 26; her account is the most lurid.

delegate it. For his power was not absolute, as Roscoe asserted; like other African rulers he could only retain it by giving some of it away. Some writers have considered kingdoms like Bunyoro and Buganda to be 'African despotisms',[1] but even though some African rulers have at times acted despotically, with widely dispersed populations, poor communications, and a simple technology (especially in regard to weapons) it is difficult or impossible to maintain, at any rate more than briefly, a very high concentration of political power. Always there are constraints and limitations on its exercise, and often these are ceremonially expressed.

Thus at his accession the Mukama of Bunyoro, like other African kings, was subjected to various admonitions by his senior administrative and ritual officials, who called on him to rule wisely and justly, not to abuse his position, and so on. According to Nyakatura, he was made to grasp a handful of grass (*kikarabo*), and to swear 'not to frighten his nation, to rule his people well, to welcome strangers who wish to settle in his country, to help all his people without distinction between poor and rich, to care for orphans left by his people, and to "cut cases" justly'.[2]

But perhaps of greater interest is the ritual associated with the delegation of royal authority. We have noted that political power, certainly in the context of tribal African kingdoms, is always limited by the fact that it must be distributed; the ruler has to confer some (often a considerable) degree of independent authority on his subordinates. Hence the loose nature of political bonds in many such 'pedestrian' African states as traditional Bunyoro; hence, also, the very real danger of rebellion (discussed above, p. 29). So delegation is inevitable, and it is especially evident in the Nyoro case that what was thought to be delegated was not only political power, but also what, following Radcliffe-Brown, we may call ritual status. The latter notion, denoted by the Runyoro word *mahano* (the plural form of *ihano*, which means anything especially strange or marvellous),

---

[1] Thus G. P. Murdock thinks that 'African despotism', of which the Uganda kingdoms are examples, is a kind of counterpart to oriental despotism, even though it is not 'hydraulically' based. See Murdock 1959, chap. 6.

[2] Nyakatura, p. 249. In Runyoro, '*obutatinirra ihanga lye, n'okulemaga kurungi abantu be, n'okwikirizaga abanyamahanga, n'okukonyeraga abantu be bona obutasororaga omunaku n'omuguda, n'okukuzaga enfuzi z'abantu be, n'okucwaga emisango y'amananu.*'

implies both a particular kind of power, and a special condition of ritual danger. This can as a rule only be relieved
by the performance of appropriate ritual. *Mahano* is associated
with many other conditions and objects besides the political
authority centred in the kingship, but common to all of them
is a quality of dangerous potency. What is *mahano* is to be feared
and respected, whether the power it implies is associated with
political authority, with spiritual forces, or just with what is
strange and out of the ordinary, and so in some measure
alarming.[1]

It is readily understandable why the Nyoro kingship, like
other kingships, should have been thought of as involving this
ritual and symbolic potency. We noted in Chapter 1 that
Banyoro are very conscious of the notions of power (*busobozi*)
and government (*bulemi* or *bukama*; the latter term may also be
translated as 'mastership' or 'proprietorship'). They think of
these forces, 'good' and indispensable though they may be,
as having a fearful and oppressive aspect. Rulers, from the
Mukama down to the household head (*nyineka*), are said to be
'feared' (*kutinwa*) as well as honoured and obeyed. Indeed the
word which denotes the honour and respect in which a ruler
or other important person is held (*kitinisa*) derives from the
same verb, -*tina*, and might equally well be translated 'fearful-
ness'.

In the political context, then, *mahano* is an aspect or expression
of political power, and this is especially clear in the ritual acts
which are associated with the delegation of royal authority.
Traditionally all positions of authority in the Nyoro state were
thought of as being, at least ideally, validated by the Mukama.
Thus not only did he formally delegate authority to the territorial chiefs when he appointed them, but the successors to
minor chiefships, and even to the headships of the small agnatic
descent groups (*nganda*, in one of the meanings of that term)[2]
which are said formerly to have constituted influential local
units, had also to be formally approved and confirmed by him

---

[1] It is associated, for example, with such ritually dangerous acts and situations
as incest, the birth of twins, death, and initiation into the spirit mediumship cult.
It is important to note that what is ritually dangerous is not necessarily 'bad' or
inauspicious. For some discussion of the concept see Beattie 1960c, also 1968,
pp. 438–9.

[2] For a discussion of Nyoro 'clans' (*nganda*, sing. *ruganda*) see Beattie 1957a.

or by his chosen representative. This confirmation consisted essentially in the performance of a ceremony called 'drinking milk' (*kunywa amata*) with the Mukama. It is said that in recent generations milk has not in fact been used although it was formerly; in later times the person who was being confirmed in authority received some dried coffee-beans from the Mukama's hands. Handing coffee-beans to guests to chew is an essential part of polite, formal social intercourse in Bunyoro, and to receive them, or anything else, from the king's hands was to be very highly honoured. The person upon whom authority had been thus bestowed should then kiss the king's hand, so expressing his attachment and loyalty.[1] All territorial authority in Bunyoro was traditionally held in this manner from the Mukama and by his grace, and its grant always implied also a major increment in the recipient's ritual status or *mahano*. In this context the latter was an expression of the former, so the two were inseparable.

The understanding of this makes clear the Mukama's relationship to a special category of chiefs known as the 'crown-wearers' (*bajwara kondo*).[2] Roscoe refers to them, not altogether appropriately, as the 'Sacred Guild', and describes them as 'a small body of special councillors', who were the king's 'special advisers and protectors' (1923, pp. 8, 51). He appears to have thought that they were distinguished from all other kinds of chiefs by the fact that they had to bind themselves to the Mukama by 'a special and very stringent oath which was taken by drinking some milk from cows which were sacred to the king himself' (p. 8). But, as we have noted, this ceremony was not restricted to the crown-wearers; it was carried out by all who succeeded to positions of political authority in the state. In fact the crown-wearers were chiefs, though specially honoured ones. Essential to their appointment, as to the appointment of all chiefs, was the bestowal on them both of political authority over specified territories and their inhabitants, and of

[1] Roscoe 1923, p. 303; also K. W. 1937*b*, p. 294. The kiss as part of the formal act of vassalage in medieval Europe had a similar significance (Ganshof 1952, p. 70).

[2] The crowns were elaborate beaded head-dresses, usually fringed with black and white colobus monkey skins, as 'beards'. Some of them are illustrated in Plate 3, and more are shown in Roscoe 1923, plate xiv (facing p. 112), and in K. W. 1937*b*.

enhanced ritual status. There is no evidence that they ever formed any kind of separate corporation or 'guild', or even that they were more influential as advisers than some other categories of chiefs and palace officials. The award of a crown implied the grant of high dignity and prestige, a kind of ennoblement, rather than appointment to a formal guild or council. Bikunya refers to the *kondo* as an extraordinarily high honour (*ekitinisa kya mahano*), conferring a special blessing, and the king's highest regard, on the recipient (p. 51). Both Bunyoro Agreements correctly define the *kondo* as 'an old established order or distinction', and it used to be awarded to persons, usually chiefs and often members of the Babito clan, who had performed some considerable service for the Mukama and the kingdom, such as winning a major military victory. A crown was also traditionally awarded by a new Mukama to his 'mother's brother' (*nyinarumi*), that is, to the head of his mother's agnatic lineage.

But Roscoe's use of the term 'sacred' to describe the *bajwara kondo* is rather more appropriate, for it points to the fact that, as we have just noted, the grant of a crown involved an enormous enhancement of ritual status. Banyoro express this by saying that crown-wearers, like the king himself, possessed an exceptional degree of *mahano*. Because of this they were subject to ritual food avoidances similar to those observed by the Mukama himself. They were not permitted to eat what are known as 'black' vegetable foodstuffs (*emikubi erukwiragura*), such as sweet potatoes, cassava, and certain kinds of peas and beans. Chickens and eggs were also forbidden to them.

Possession of a *kondo* was hereditary in the male line, and most of the few remaining *bajwara kondo* in the 1950s (who certainly did not form any kind of guild or social group) had inherited their crowns. In fact the lines of many ancient crown-wearers have died out or become forgotten. Young men told me that they would not accept a *kondo* if they were offered one, so tiresome were the ritual restrictions that went with it. In recent years at least one heir to a *kondo* had declined his inheritance and returned the crown to the king. None had been bestowed for many years, the last recipient having been an ex-county chief, H. K. Karubanga, M.B.E. (the author of *Bukya Nibwira*), who was a very old man when I was in Bunyoro in the 1950s,

PLATE 3

Group of 'Crown Wearers' (Bajwara Kondo): c. 1936

and who has since died. Despite the provisions in the two Bunyoro Agreements, it does not seem likely that *makondo* would have continued to be awarded, even if the kingdom had survived, as a kind of Bunyoro Kingdom honours list. The institution was evidently obsolescent, if not obsolete. Bikunya, writing in 1927 (pp. 51–2), gave the names and titles of fifty-one *bajwara kondo* (of whom thirteen were Babito). Nyakatura, in a work published twenty years later, listed forty-four (pp. 231–5). A list of surviving crown-wearers prepared by the Native Government in 1950 contained only fifteen names. These included, as well as a number of 'mothers' brothers' of former kings, several hereditary palace officials. Only two or three past or present official chiefs in the Bunyoro kingdom were listed.

The Nyoro institution of *kujwara kondo* expressed the close traditional association in Nyoro thought between the grant to a particularly favoured chief or other important person of some part of the ritual quality of the kingship itself, and the grant to him of enhanced political (i.e. territorial) authority. In states like traditional Bunyoro, the former was an essential aspect of the latter.

Further, the award of a *kondo* was not a one-way matter: the recipient was required to present the Mukama with a white bull and eighteen bundles of cowries, together with such other gifts as he might see fit to make. Mauss's classic analysis of prestation is as relevant to the gift of political authority as it is to other kinds of gifts: here as in other cases the thing given is not 'inert', but 'retains a magical and religious hold over the recipient' (Mauss 1954, p. 10). Political authority in traditional Bunyoro implied ritual obligation, even ritual danger, for its possessor, as well as the power to govern, and the institution of *kujwara kondo* expressed both of these aspects.

I conclude, then, that much Nyoro royal ritual, and especially the association of a special ritual potency (*mahano*) with the kingship, may be regarded as a symbolic expression of political relationships. I said above that such ritual potency is associated with many other objects and situations besides political authority. But if one of the functions of ritual is to express symbolically important social values, it is not surprising that in Bunyoro, where notions of superordination and subordination, and the hierarchical social system with which these notions were

associated, were paramount social values, the kingship should be a central focus of such ritual. In this chapter I have given some account of the kingship primarily from this point of view; in the next chapter I discuss the Mukama's secular relationships with the various categories of persons who make up his kingdom.

6

THE TRADITIONAL STATE

Iɴ the last chapter I discussed the king's relationships with certain categories of relatives and other persons whose statuses were at least in some respects symbolically significant. Thus the *Okwiri* had the secular responsibility of representing the princes' interests, but he also symbolized Bito values in contradistinction to those of the kingship. Similarly, although the Kalyota represented the princesses, at the same time she was a symbolic expression of the female aspect of the *Obukama*. The king's mother's office was ritual, not executive, and the crown-wearers, although as great chiefs they possessed high executive authority, were, as *bajwara kondo*, participants in the royal mystique, in the *mahano* of kingship itself. It would be arbitrary to attempt to lay down a hard-and-fast distinction between ritual and secular authority in the context of a traditional kingdom like Bunyoro; the difference is one of aspect, and of degree and emphasis, rather than of kind. But the kinds of people whose relationships with the king I now discuss all occupied roles which were seen and defined primarily in secular or 'practical' terms, even though they had some symbolic importance as well. First I describe the various categories of the king's palace officials, regalia keepers, domestic staff, informal advisers, and the royal bodyguard. I then consider the role of the traditional chiefs and the Mukama's relationship with them. Finally, I say something of his relations with his people as a whole, to whom traditionally he was the ultimate source of power, and from whom, directly or indirectly, and at various times, he exacted fealty, services, and tribute. I leave until Chapter 7 consideration of his relationship with his chiefs during the colonial period, and with the Protectorate administration. But we shall see that many traditional relationships and values survived, more or less modified, into modern times, and some of them played a significant part in the

changing scene with which we shall be concerned in the next
chapter.

As we noted, traditionally the Mukama was surrounded by
numerous ritual and household officials, responsible both for the
performance of various domestic duties, and for the care of
specific items of his extensive regalia. There was still a substantial
number of such persons in the 1950s; the palace payroll contained more than a hundred names and twelve of the persons
named were senior holders of traditional palace offices. As well
as these, there were numerous unsalaried ceremonial officials,
whose services were required only on important occasions; these
received gifts from the Mukama from time to time. Collectively,
all these people were known as *banyamirwa*, 'those who are concerned with customary matters'. The following were some of the
more important of them:

> *Mugema* was the custodian of the royal tombs, most of which
> lie in the Buyaga and Bugangaizi counties of the Mubende
> district, the 'Lost Counties', reincorporated in Bunyoro in
> 1964.

> *Mujaguzi* (literally 'he who rejoices') was the head regalia-
> man, and he was responsible for overseeing all the other
> regalia-men. These were collectively called *bakuru b'ebik-
> wato*, 'the elders of the regalia'. He was also responsible for
> the more important of the royal drums, and had the right
> to beat the first drum at the biennial *Mpango* ceremony.
> He should be a member of the Basita clan.

> *Owakahimba* looked after the important spear *Wakaitantahi*,
> and was sometimes called 'the great wife of the palace'
> (*omugo wa karuzika*).

> *Owamugarra* looked after the Mukama's personal drum, which
> was specially made for him on his accession.

> *Owanyamugoya* (the verb *kugoya* means 'to mix, to stir things
> together') looked after a special rake-like item of the
> regalia, the significance of which is that all counties are
> drawn together under the Mukama.

> *Muhesera* (*kuhesa* means 'to work in iron') should be a member
> of the Bayaga clan. His ancestor was said to have come
> from Bukidi (the homeland of the Babito) and to have
> brought with him an ironsmith's hammer, together with

a bow and a quiver full of arrows (Banyoro do not use the bow). He has the task of attiring the king in one of his ceremonial crowns on special occasions.

Mwokya, the king's head cook, might be from any clan, and he had numerous assistants. The *Bokya* (pl. of *Mwokya*) had the right to milk the king's sacred *nkorogi* herd of cows, whose milk could be drunk only by the king.

Muswata built the reed shelters in the palace grounds which were used by the king on ceremonial occasions.

Mwambukya (*kwambuka* means 'to cross a river or stream') was responsible for the Mukama's ablutions; he was in charge of the royal wells, and supervised the palace water-carriers.

Mukonda, the chief diviner, had custody of a special stick, *ruhimbo* (*kuhimba* means 'to lift') and Mukonda's ancestor was said to have parted the waters of the Nile to enable the Babito to pass into Bunyoro when they came to take over the kingdom.

Other important dignitaries were the leaders of the Mukama's corps of court musicians (the horn-players [*Bamakondere*], the flautists [*Basegu*], and the drummers), the king's special potters, barkcloth-makers, and smiths (the three most important of Bunyoro's few specialist occupations); his chief herdsman, beer-brewer, door-keeper (*Mukumirizi*), and so on, and the custodians of the Mukama's throne (*Owanyamyarro*), and of various other spears, shields, crowns, and other items.[1]

Several of these offices were vested in certain clans, though this requirement was being decreasingly observed in the 1950s. Also, many of the holders had several assistants (for example, there was a considerable number of cooks), and the duties of most of them were not demanding, for the care of a particular artefact, or attendance on the Mukama on certain ceremonial occasions, could occupy only a small part of a man's time. None the less, most of the *Banyamirwa* were required to live in or near the royal enclosure.

Clearly, this large and complex domestic establishment was far in excess of what was needed for purely practical purposes;

---

[1] There is a detailed account of the regalia (both of Cwezi and Bito origin) in K. W. 1937*b*.

neither in ancient nor in recent times could it be regarded as having been either economical or efficient. A large part of its significance, like that of the regalia themselves, was symbolic. Nevertheless, by means of it the considerable task of running the royal establishment did get done. Further, sociologically regarded, it served as a means of integrating the kingship with the Nyoro people as a whole. For it involved a great many different individuals and, even more important, several different categories of individuals, in a common interest in the palace, and so in the kingship itself. All of Bunyoro's traditional craft specializations were represented, as also were a considerable number of Bunyoro's numerous clans. This last point is of particular importance, for the clan system, as the focus of local rather than nationwide loyalties, may be regarded as having stood, at least in traditional times, in some measure of opposition to the kingship. The vesting of particular palace offices in particular clans went some way to negate this opposition, by integrating the clan system with the palace organization, and so with the kingship. Further, the honour of a palace appointment was not limited to its holder: not only his near agnates, but all the members of his clan, shone in his reflected glory. Thus, although the importance of clan membership, like the importance of the kingship itself, had declined in modern times, traditionally the palace was, as it continued to be in some degree until the end, the locus of a large and widely representative cross-section of the Nyoro people.

When I was in Bunyoro, the hereditary tenure of such an office still conferred much prestige, even when it was part-time and unpaid. A young man who held the office of Muhesera, and who had been acting as my part-time assistant, turned down an offer of lucrative employment in Buganda because he did not want to give up his hereditary position in the palace. I have heard of similar cases.

At least prior to the 1955 Agreement, which deprived the Mukama of his power to appoint and dismiss his chiefs without consulting his council, there was a further attraction about such appointments. In traditional times a man who had given good service as a *munyamirwa*, if he gained the Mukama's personal favour, might expect to be granted a small estate (*kibanja*) somewhere in the kingdom. He would thereby acquire political

rights over the peasant occupants of the area, and would become in effect a minor chief. Grants of this kind continued to be made until the 1950s, though in recent times they tended to take the form of appointment to a minor chiefship or village headmanship. As in Norman England, personal service to the king might be richly rewarded. This manner of recruiting chiefs was clearly not wholly appropriate to the modern, civil-service type of administration which the British had been trying to inculcate for more than half a century, and educated Banyoro were not slow to point this out. We shall return to this topic in the next chapter.

In addition to the *banyamirwa*, there was a smaller category of informal advisers and retainers known as *basekura*. These men occupied no formal status, but were defined simply as 'old men who sit and talk with the Mukama'. The word *kusegura* (or *kusekura*) means 'to talk familiarly, intimately, and frankly with someone'. In the 1950s there were said to be about twenty of these men who visited the Mukama from time to time, and two or three of them were said to be particularly influential. It was asserted that if an official chief wished to approach the king informally he would be dependent on the good offices—available for a consideration—of one of these men. For they were 'near to the Mukama' (*haihi n'Omukama*) in a way in which the official chiefs were not. They were said to 'rule' (*kulema*) the other palace officials, including the *banyamirwa*.

The *basekura* included some selected members of the *banyamirwa* (in the 1950s the man who held the office of *Owamugarra* was said to be one of the two or three men closest to the king), but they also included persons without formal office, who had attached themselves to the royal household as dependants. Traditionally in Bunyoro a man who had lost his cattle or his wife, or who had otherwise become poor and unfortunate, could approach the Mukama (or a major chief) and attach himself to him as a kind of servant–retainer or client. Such a man might receive a special name, like Rwehikya ('he who brought himself'). *Basekura* might be selected from among the more intelligent of such people in the palace.

The *basekura*, then, were the king's privileged familiars and private advisers, and like the court jesters of medieval Europe they could say 'shameful things' (*by'orwanju* or *by'ensoni*) to him

with impunity.[1] An informant gave as examples such rebukes as 'you eat too much!' and 'you are too fat!' He added that they could use impolite words like *mazi* (ordure) when talking to the king, unthinkable for others. It is also said that they could contradict the Mukama, something which would be impossible for his official chiefs, whose relations with him were dominated by what we have called, following Maquet, the 'premise of inequality'. Like the *banyamirwa*, specially favoured *basekura* might be awarded estates or minor chiefships, as well as occasional gifts.

Among the Mukama's attendants and servants should also be included his executioners (*babogora*) and, at least in Kabarega's time, his bodyguard or standing army (*barusura*). These two categories seem to have overlapped, and like some other palace officials, their members were for the most part persons (often strangers from neighbouring countries) who had attached themselves to the king as client–servants. As well as serving as what Roscoe not inappropriately called 'special police', they appear also to have acted as messengers and attendants (Roscoe 1923, p. 86). Like other similar kingdoms, Bunyoro did not traditionally have a permanent standing army; in time of war (usually against Buganda) the chiefs, who sometimes themselves acted as military leaders, would call up all available able-bodied men in their areas. Some chiefs gained high reputations as war leaders, and crowns (*makondo*) have been awarded to successful generals. Only during Kabarega's reign did the *barusura* evolve into an effective military force (there is a brief account of them in Casati, chap. 4), and it was gradually dispersed during the long-drawn-out campaign against him in the 1890s.

I turn now to consider the traditional system of territorial administration of which the king was the head: who became chiefs in traditional times, what did they do, and what was the nature of their relationship to the Mukama? There is not enough evidence to reconstruct in detail the pre-European system of chiefship in Bunyoro, but certain statements may nevertheless be made about it with reasonable certainty. First, and most important, as we noted in Chapter 2, there is no doubt that

[1] The comparison with medieval court jesters is more than mere analogy, for some of the *basekura* appear to have played just this role. A former palace official told me that some *basekura* knew how to skin small animals, like the serval cat (*mondo*), in such a way that by putting a hand inside the skin they could make it nod and shake its head as though it were alive, thus causing great merriment.

chiefship, as far back as we have any account of it, was explicitly
territorial; a chief of whatever rank was a person to whom the
Mukama had granted rights over a specific named territory and
its peasant inhabitants. Accounts even of the earliest times contained in Bunyoro's traditional history describe the allocation
of political authority in territorial terms.

It would not be necessary to lay so much emphasis on this
point were it not for the erroneous impression conveyed by
Roscoe, already referred to (and still widely accepted) that
traditionally Bunyoro was ruled by a class of 'pastoral nomads'.
As we have already noted, he was mistaken in supposing that
Bunyoro's ruling dynasty was composed of pastoral Bahuma,
though it is true that Bahuma women were favoured brides for
Babito princes, so that kings were often of Huma descent on
their mother's side. Bahuma cattle-men claimed and were
accorded high status in Bunyoro, and some of them were
appointed as chiefs, but *qua* Bahuma they were not rulers but
herdsmen, who characteristically attached themselves to the
great chiefs as custodians of their herds.

The following extracts from three earlier books relating to the
Banyoro (there is little evidence in Roscoe's work that he was
acquainted with them) make it quite clear that traditional
chiefship in Bunyoro was explicitly territorial, and that whatever the chiefs were they were not nomadic cattle-herders.
First, Baker wrote in 1874:

The order and organization of Unyoro were a great contrast to
the want of cohesion of the northern tribes. Every district throughout
the country was governed by a chief, who was responsible to the king
for the state of his province. This system was extended to sub-govern-
ment and a series of lower officials in every district, who were bound
to obey the orders of the lord-lieutenant. Thus every province had
a responsible head, that could be at once cut off should disloyalty or
other signs of bad government appear in a certain district. In the
event of war, every governor could appear, together with his con-
tingent of armed men, at short notice. These were the rules of government that had been established for many generations throughout
Unyoro (1874, pp. 212–13).

Emin Pasha, writing a few years later, gives a similar picture:

The whole of Unyóro is divided into large districts, over each
of which a *makúngo* [*mukungu*], temporarily appointed by the king,

presides, whose duty it is to collect the contributions of cattle, corn, &c., due to the sovereign, and to administer justice. . . . A *makúngo* is dependent for provisions for himself and those belonging to him on the district he administers, in which he cultivates large tracts by means of his men slaves, and has his own herds. . . . They are bound to present themselves from time to time at the king's court with presents. Each *makúngo* appoints a number of *matóngali* [*batongole*] who administer sub-divisions of the district on the same principles. A *makúngo* usually retains all the *matóngalis* he finds in power on taking office, and hence this dignity is far more permanent than the other, often indeed it has become hereditary (1888, p. 89).

This account is further confirmed by Emin's assistant, Casati:

The King of Unyoro rules this extensive territory by means of governors appointed over every single district. The *magnoro* [*banyoro*], as these administrators are called, are the chiefs of the various jurisdictions, which they govern in the name of the king, supply soldiers in time of war, and pay tribute in ivory, animals, iron and food. To these are subject the so-called *matungoli*, who have a limited power over some divisions of the territory. The provinces must always be represented at the Sovereign's residence, either by the chiefs invested with their government or by their representatives, who have the title of *makongo* [*bakungu*] (1891, p. 49).

To these clear statements may be added an extract from a memorandum prepared by the Mukama in 1948:

Government and People of Bunyoro in Olden Days. The Mukama was . . . the ruler of the people of Bunyoro . . . Below him he had chiefs of various grades. He appointed saza chiefs to rule over different areas in his kingdom. Whenever he wished to discuss something he called together these chiefs who came to the capital. . . . Saza [county] chiefs had below them smaller chiefs like Endabaraba, Abatongole, Abakungu, etc.

A further memorandum in the Hoima district records, probably also written by the Mukama, states that:

Under the Mukama were the chiefs, who were chosen by the Mukama. Under the chiefs were the petty chiefs, who were chosen by the chiefs. . . . Chiefs were chosen from three classes, (1) Princes (of the Mukama's clan), (2) Shepherds (Bahima), (3) peasants.

Thus, although in pre-European times there was nothing like the formal four-tiered pyramid of official, salaried chiefs, which

will be described in Chapter 9 (and which was largely a British creation), it is abundantly plain that there was at least a loosely organized hierarchy of territorial rulers who were very far from being 'pastoral nomads'.

The different terms by which the chiefs are referred to in these accounts may give rise to some confusion, especially as there have been some changes in usage since Baker's and Emin's day. It appears that in traditional times there was a limited number of great chiefs called *bakungu* (Casati calls them *magnoro*, that is, *banyoro*), roughly equivalent in status to the *saza* (county) chiefs of the colonial period. These men ruled over large areas, and were directly responsible to the king. Below them were lesser chiefs, traditionally called *batongole*, who had more limited powers and controlled smaller areas. These sometimes had assistants, variously called *ndabaraba*, *ndyamuki*, and by various other terms. More is said of them in Chapter 9.

Confusion may arise from two sources. The first is that the term *mukungu* later became devalued, so that in this century it has been applied not to the senior grade of official chiefs, then called *saza* chiefs on the Ganda model, but to the lowest grade of salaried chiefs, the village headmen, who, however, continued also to be called *batongole*. The second source of confusion is the ambiguity of the term *munyoro*, which as well as meaning any member of the Banyoro people, also meant, and still means, 'great chief, lord, master' (Davis, p. 110). At the present day it is used as a polite term of reference, as we might use 'Mr.' or 'Esquire'. Roscoe was mistaken in thinking that the *Banyoro* were a separate group of 'free-men', who had been 'raised from serfdom', and were distinguished from the other two 'classes' by a distinct group of totems (1923, pp. 10–18). The fact seems to have been that in the nineteenth century, as in the twentieth, *banyoro* were not a separate class, distinguished both from the 'pastoral people' and the 'serfs'; the term was simply applied to any important person, and 'importance' in traditional times would have implied the possession of political authority. Roscoe's over-formal and indeed mistaken representation of the matter was no doubt due to his lack of understanding of the traditional political process. He is correct in saying (pp. 10–11) that 'any man who showed ability and rendered special service to the king was rewarded by being

made a . . . *Munyoro*'. But he is in error in translating *munyoro*
as 'free-man', and supposing that *banyoro* composed a separate,
hereditary class. We noted above that the Mukama could, and
did, reward his household officials with grants of minor political
authority, i.e. make them chiefs, and he could, and did, so
reward anyone upon whom he wished to confer special favour.
This is all there is to it. The persistence of this mode of
appointment to political office is further considered in the next
chapter.

It is not clear from these early sources exactly what the
relationship of these lower chiefs (*batongole*) was, both to the
great *bakungu*, and to the Mukama himself. Emin states quite
explicitly that they held their appointments directly from the
great chiefs, not from the king, and Baker's and Casati's statements are consistent with this. We shall see in the next chapter
that an unanticipated effect of European overrule was, paradoxically, to strengthen rather than weaken the king's power
over his chiefs, so it might perhaps be thought than Emin was
right, and that traditionally political power was very much more
decentralized than it is now asserted was the case, and was not
after all seen as a royal monopoly. But this was firmly denied
by all Banyoro whom I consulted on the matter. They stressed
that throughout Nyoro history all political authority has been
regarded as belonging to, and allocable by, the Mukama alone.
It seems to me reasonably certain that even though the great
chiefs no doubt nominated some of their subordinate chiefs,
even these appointments would have had to receive at least
formal confirmation by the king or by his representative from
the palace. No doubt here as elsewhere in political affairs theory
and practice sometimes diverged, but it is likely that at least in
principle the *batongole* held their authority nominally from the
Mukama and were seen as so holding it. Nevertheless they were
evidently subordinate to the powerful *bakungu* in whose areas
they were, whether, as no doubt was sometimes the case, they
owed their appointments to him, and so stood to him in a kind
of client–patron relationship, or whether they held their local
authority as a direct gift from the king. Their exact status no
doubt depended both on the number of their dependants and
on the nature of their relationship both to the Mukama and to
the local *mukungu* chief. In any event, Nyoro tradition is quite

explicit that accession to all positions of political authority always required the Mukama's validation.

Below the level of the dozen or so *bakungu* chiefs, each of whom had a special title,[1] the lesser chiefs were not ranked in any formal hierarchy, though no doubt they were informally ranked in terms of the areas of their jurisdiction, their seniority, and the extent of their importance and influence.

Little can be said of the chief–subject relationship in traditional times, before the complexities of modern administration imposed upon chiefs a multiplicity of specialist tasks (discussed in Chapter 9). As persons of local power and influence, they ruled over people who were their dependent clients rather than the subjects of an impersonal administration, and the relationship between chiefs and their people was expressed through service (including military service), tribute, and personal attachment on the part of the subjects; protection, patronage, and economic assistance on that of the chief. But one aspect of the traditional chief's role should be mentioned here, and that is his part in dispute settlement. No doubt in traditional times, as today, minor disputes between fellow-villagers were settled within the community, without recourse to the chiefs, the 'Mukama's spears'. But major issues, notably homicide and sorcery (a form of homicide) seem at least in some cases to have been of concern to the chiefs. The case of homicide is particularly instructive. It is said that in ancient Bunyoro the blood feud (*kuhora nzigu*) could be carried out by the fellow clansmen of a person killed, without reference to higher authority, the matter being considered closed when the murderer or one of his close agnates had been killed in return. The right of private vengeance is referred to by Emin (p. 86), though he states also that the relatives of the murdered man may, for a price, call upon the chief to take action. Roscoe also asserts that a murderer 'caught red-handed' could be killed on the spot, otherwise the matter would be taken to the 'head of the clan', who could, if necessary, appeal to the king for assistance (1923, p. 64). I was told that, at least for many generations past, local chiefs would have exercised strict

---

[1] The traditional titles were replaced, after the conquest of Bunyoro, by Ganda ones, and in the 1950s the four county chiefs were called *Mukwenda*, *Kaigo*, *Kimbugwe*, and *Sekibobo*, on the Ganda model. In the last years of the kingdom the old Nyoro titles were, however, restored.

control in their areas over the pursuit of private vengeance by injured parties. In this context, as in others, Nyoro practice seems to have represented a compromise between the usages of 'acephalous' lineage-based societies like the Nuer, and those characteristic of more highly centralized states, where everybody is 'a king's (or a chief's) man', and his life—or death—a matter of more than merely private concern.

To the question who could become a chief in traditional Bunyoro, the shortest and simplest answer is 'anyone whom the Mukama wished to make one'. Chiefship was not restricted to any particular class or category of persons; Babito, Bahuma, and commoners were equally eligible, though a member of the last category appointed to a major chiefship would probably belong to a distinguished family, 'known to the Mukama'. It seems probable that in traditional times Babito were better represented among the lesser (*batongole*) chiefs than their representation among the lower grades of chiefs in recent years would suggest.[1] Where succession to supreme authority is based on unilineal descent, a ruler's sons and brothers are always a potential threat to him, and in Bunyoro this threat was met, at least partially and at some periods, by giving chiefships to the royal agnates. It is said that Kabarega gave many of his sons, and some of his brothers, small chiefships or 'estates' (*butaka*), allocating major chiefships (as far as the Babito were concerned) only to his father's brothers, who could no longer be regarded as a threat to his security. As we saw in Chapter 5, the king's official brother and sister (*Okwiri* and *Kalyota*), the heads of the princes and princesses respectively, also possessed large estates *ex officio*, whose peasant occupants they ruled over as chiefs. Kabarega used to give his wives (*bago*) small areas to administer after they had passed child-bearing age.

But the main ground for the award of territorial chiefship was not relationship, either by kinship or by affinity, with the Mukama, but rather that the recipient had earned the king's approbation and favour, either by service or by gift. The crown-wearers, if they were not major chiefs already, received on appointment large areas to rule over. Outstanding military service might traditionally be rewarded by a grant of territorial

---

[1] For details of this low representation and possible reasons for it see pp. 203-5 below.

authority, and chiefship could also be granted in return for gifts of cattle or women to the king. And, as we noted earlier, loyal service in one of the numerous palace offices was often rewarded by a minor chiefship.

In principle, chiefship was not hereditary, in the sense that a chief's authority passed automatically to his heir. Chiefs were indeed sometimes succeeded by their sons, but often they were not; in theory every chief was individually appointed, or his appointment was confirmed, by the Mukama. Like everything else in the kingdom, all political authority was thought of as in the last resort the king's personal possession, and at his disposal: the word *Mukama* means 'master' or 'owner'. Subordinate political authority is the Mukama's gift, and like all gifts it is not given unconditionally. Whether a chief had inherited his position or not, he held it at the king's pleasure, and retained it only on conditions of service and homage to him. If the Mukama wished, he could dismiss a chief summarily, and he sometimes did.

An able commoner who attached himself to a major chief or to the king himself could rise to a high position, but naturally a chief's son stood a better chance of acquiring a chiefship—all other things being equal—than a peasant's son. As a member of a well-known family he might be personally known to the king; he would be familiar with the obligations and circumstances of chiefly office, and he would be a likely candidate for appointment to a palace post, often the first step towards a chiefship. This tendency towards the establishment of a chiefly class was reinforced by the custom, continued until recent times, of sending the sons of distinguished families to be brought up by relatives in the Mwenge area (south of present-day Bunyoro and now part of Toro district), for it is said that traditional Nyoro good manners (*makune*), and the most superior accent and fashion of speaking, were specially characteristic of this area, which lay near the heart of the ancient Kitara empire.

But whatever the grounds of a chief's appointment, his political authority had to be conferred upon him by the Mukama in person or, in the case of some lesser appointments, by the Mukama's deputy (*mukwenda*). The king could select anyone he liked for the job of *mukwenda*; often he would send some poor dependant whom he wished to benefit by enabling him to receive

the gifts of food, beer, or (in recent times) money customarily made on such occasions. For whether the appointment was confirmed by the Mukama himself or by his representative, the person appointed would be expected to reciprocate with a gift 'to thank him' (*kumusima*). In theory, this confirmation was supposed to take place in all cases where positions of territorial authority were being filled; succession to clan or lineage headship, as well as to the proprietorship of large estates or *bibanja*, equally required the king's sanction, for all involved the acquisition of authority over the people who occupied particular territories, and so the grant of a kind of 'chiefship'.

We noted in Chapter 5 that the delegation of territorial authority was not a merely secular matter; it also had a ritual quality. Something of the royal 'essence' (*mahano*) was communicated at the same time. This was expressed in the traditional rite, referred to earlier, of 'drinking milk' with the Mukama. In former times the king may actually have given milk to his major chiefs to drink on their appointment, as Roscoe asserts (1923, p. 299), but it appears that at least in recent generations the milk has been replaced by dried coffee-beans, which the king ceremonially handed to the person being vested with authority.[1] In either case the symbolism is plain. The king's special *nkorogi* cows and their milk were traditionally intimately linked with his and his country's well-being; and dried coffee-beans, often handed to guests to chew on formal occasions, were used also in the ceremony of making a blood pact (*mukago*), a bond which involves a relationship of intense mutual support and solidarity.[2] The fact that the two segments of which a coffee-bean is composed are closely united within the same pod makes it a specially apt symbol for any relationship involving a particularly close attachment. The person to whom a part of the royal authority has been delegated in this way then kisses the Mukama's hand, thereby expressing his profound obligation and attachment.

This ritual exchange set the seal on the real transfer of delegated political authority and its associated privileges, in

[1] Roscoe states that coffee was used only in the case of ordinary pastoral people who were not chiefs but simply heirs to property (1923, p. 302). It seems, however, likely that at least some political authority (i.e. rights over people in specified territories) was involved.

[2] For some account of it see Beattie 1958b.

exchange for loyalty, homage, and service to the king. It initiated what was thought of as an enduring personal relationship between the Mukama and his subordinate political authorities. Chiefs had to provide the king with periodic gifts of beer, grain, and cattle, as well as ivory and other goods, and they had to supply men for work at the palace, and for military service, when called upon to do so. Of course the weight of these exactions ultimately fell on the peasant population, who in return looked for protection, occasional feasts, and help in time of need from their chiefs. Relations between chiefs and people are discussed in Chapter 8, but it may be noted here that although a chief's authority derived from above him, that is from the Mukama, his material reward came from below, that is directly from his people. It was thus in a chief's interest to rule justly and well, for disaffected peasants could always move elsewhere, and offer their goods and services to another chief.

So traditional Nyoro chiefs were not in the least like modern civil servants, drawing salaries from a central authority and committed to specific administrative rules (though of course there were norms of government in Bunyoro as elsewhere): they were 'the Mukama's spears' (*macumu g'Omukama*), bound to their ruler by ties of dependence, obligation, and personal loyalty. In Max Weber's terms, the traditional Nyoro state was a patrimonial one; it was neither patriarchal nor 'feudal'. I return to this point later.

The close bond between the Mukama and his major chiefs was also practically expressed by the requirement that they should maintain houses at or near the capital, as well as in the areas allotted to them, and by the fact that they were required to attend on the king constantly. A chief who failed to do so would render himself open to suspicion of rebellion, and would be in danger of dismissal (Roscoe 1923, p. 52). When a chief left the capital he had to leave behind him a deputy (*musigire*) who assumed all his titles, and took his place in attendance on the king. It could almost be said that the deputy *became* the chief, during the latter's absence. In the same way, when the chief was at the palace he would be represented by a deputy in his own area. So in theory the senior chiefs were permanently in attendance on the Mukama, while at the same time they were always serving as the king's territorial administrators. Thus the

musigire system enabled the senior chiefs to perform, or at least to appear to perform, two barely compatible roles. On the one hand, as a 'king's man', a chief had constantly to express, by frequent attendance at the palace, his personal devotion to and dependence upon the Mukama. Rebellions did sometimes occur, but this arrangement must have served, at least in some degree, as a check to centrifugal tendencies. On the other hand, as a territorial ruler a chief had to assume, and to be seen by his personal presence to assume, responsibility for order and good government in his area. It may be noted, also, that an effect of this system was to provide the king with a powerful and more or less permanent cadre of advisers (the group would have included a number of the 'crown-wearers', who were also senior territorial chiefs), over and above the more limited and essentially private group of the *basekura*. In polities like Bunyoro there was no need for a separate royal council or secretariat, for the same individuals could serve both as royal counsellors and as administrators.

The king's control over his chiefs was further strengthened by the fact that he did not spend all his time at his capital. Like William I of England, he frequently made long tours around his kingdom, accompanied by a numerous retinue of palace officials and hangers-on, and stayed for days or weeks at or near the headquarters of one or other of his chiefs. The chief thus favoured would be required to provide the king and his followers with the necessary accommodation (a group of wattle-and-grass houses would have to be built, laid out on the model of the royal palace itself, but of course very much smaller), and ample supplies of food and drink would have to be provided. Of course these demands fell on the chief's subjects, and in return the king was traditionally expected to provide a great feast of meat and beer for them. Though it was said that no such feasts had been given for many years, royal tours were still being carried out in considerable state when I was in Bunyoro. In October 1952 the Mukama paid a formal visit to a place called Rwengabi, a few miles from my camp in Kihoko, in southern Banyoro; Rwengabi was said to have been the site of a former palace. This necessitated several weeks' work by a substantial levy of local men; ceremonial reed arches were erected along the route the Mukama's procession would follow (there is a picture of one

PLATE 4

Ceremonial arch erected for Mukama's visit to Rwengabi, 1953

of them in Plate 4), and a large audience hall and a number
of houses were built, most of them within an enclosing reed
fence (*rugo*). Each day during his visit the Mukama held
audience in the rectangular hall, the floor of which was strewn
with fresh, sweet-smelling lemon-grass (*tete*). In the latter years
of the Protectorate these royal tours were rather frowned upon
by the European district officials, who held that the Mukama
used them as a means of economizing on his palace expenses.
They were also growing increasingly unpopular with the people,
who were required to contribute labour and foodstuffs to support them, and saw little or no return for their efforts. But they
were important traditionally, both in enabling the Mukama to
keep an eye on the activities of his chiefs of all ranks in their
areas, and also in keeping him in touch with trends in public
opinion throughout the country.

Something is said in the next chapter of the king's relations
with his chiefs in recent years, and in Chapter 9 relations
between chiefs and subjects are discussed. I now go on to
consider the king's relations with his ordinary people, both in
traditional and in modern times.

Just as the Mukama was traditionally seen as the source of all
authority in the Bunyoro kingdom, so also he was the pivot of
its economic life, the centre from, and to, which all good things
unceasingly flowed. In fact his political aspect and his economic
aspect were inseparable, for each was an indispensable expression of the other. His role as supreme giver and supreme
receiver was equally strongly stressed in both contexts.

I have already said that traditionally anyone who received or
expected to receive a favour from the Mukama should make a
return, or an anticipatory, gift. Even in the 1950s, after half
a century of European administration, territorial chiefship was
still regarded by many as a royal gift, for which a reciprocal gift
was expected and often made. But it was not only on appointment that chiefs were expected to give gifts to the Mukama;
further gifts were expected from time to time. Nor was such
gift-giving restricted to persons appointed to or confirmed in
positions of authority. Everybody should give to the king.
Numerous sayings express the Mukama's aspect as supreme
receiver in the kingdom. 'What is given to the king does not
return' (*ebigenda hali Omukama tibigaruka*), Banyoro say; once a

thing is given to the Mukama, the donor cannot change his mind and ask for it back (this is not to say that he does not look for some eventual return for his offering). Again, one of the Mukama's drums, beaten at his accession ceremony and at the two-yearly *Mpango* ('refresher') rites, was called Tomunju. This name is a pun, the reply to a riddle which asks 'What does the Mukama's big drum say?' The verb *kutoma*, when used of the royal drums, means 'to sound'. But the word can also be construed as *to mu'nju*, 'put (the things) in the house', the things referred to being the heap of offerings presented to the king on ceremonial occasions. These offerings are called *birabuko*, from the verb *kurabuka*, 'to bring gifts to a superior'.

One occasion on which such offerings were made was the *Mpango* celebration. At a certain point in the proceedings a basket was put on a table, and all present were expected to put money in it, according to their means and—sometimes—their expectations. The names of the contributors and the amounts of their contributions, which might be anything from a few cents to several shillings (the East African shilling is divided into 100 cents), were recorded by a clerk, and the proceeds, together with the list, were handed to the Mukama for his personal disposal. Similar collections took place when the Mukama paid formal visits to his county and sub-county chiefs' headquarters.

I spoke above of the king's ceremonial visits to different parts of his kingdom, and of the exactions of food and labour that these visits entailed. During his visit to Rwengabi in 1952 every householder in the area was obliged to provide gifts in kind (called *bitereke*): a bunch of bananas, a basket of millet, a chicken, or some such offering. This obligation was widely felt to be onerous and was evaded when possible; strenuous efforts and a good deal of threatening by the local 'parish' (*miruka*) chiefs and village headmen were required to produce what was considered a barely adequate response. I heard many complaints that the reciprocal feasts traditionally provided by the Mukama on such occasions were either quite inadequate or were not given at all; instead the *bitereke* were loaded on to the royal lorry and taken to the palace.

Gifts, often quite large ones and in recent times mainly (though not exclusively) cash, could be given to the Mukama not only by men wishing to become chiefs or by chiefs desiring

promotion, or by persons wishing to obtain the grant of large tenanted estates (*bibanja*), but also by people with no immediate ambitions, but who might some day find themselves dependent on the king's good will. Such gifts could vary from a shilling or two to very much larger amounts; figures as high as one and two thousand shillings have been reported to me, though naturally it is not easy to obtain confirmation of such reports. In one well-authenticated case, however, a man well known to me, who had left Bunyoro as a boy in the early 1900s, had made a substantial fortune in the liquor trade in Nairobi. He had returned to Bunyoro as an elderly man a few years before I met him, and one of his first acts on arrival was to make a substantial gift to the Mukama, said to have been in excess of 2,000 shillings, thereby 'making himself known' (*kweranga*) to the king. Since that time he had acquired from the kingdom government a valuable beer-club licence concession in the area, and he had obtained a very desirable piece of land (*kibanja*) near Hoima, on which he had built a substantial house of modern design.

Such gifts as this both expressed solidarity and attachment, and at the same time provided a kind of insurance against future need. In former times a dependant of the Mukama who had lost all his cattle through raids or disease, or whose wife had left him and who lacked means of procuring another, could expect a gift of a few cows, or a woman, from the Mukama, so that he could start a new household, always provided that he had earlier taken the precaution of 'making himself known' to the king by appropriate gifts. Traditionally, the Mukama was expected both to 'like' (*kugonza*) his subjects, and to give generously to them, both as gifts to individuals and in the form of great public feasts. Such expectations survived up to the last years of the kingdom, although they were decreasingly satisfied.

We noted in Chapter 5 that some of the Mukama's special titles expressed his role as giver. Thus *Agutamba*, part of his official title, means 'the medicine that cures, or wards off, poverty' (*omubazi ogutamba bunaku*), and *Mwebingwa* means 'he to whom people run for help when in need'. The title of the ruler of the neighbouring kingdom of Ankole, *Mugabe*, 'giver or divider out (of cattle)' expressed the same notion.

Evidently it is quite consistent with traditional Nyoro political ideas, and particularly with the essentially personal nature of

the political bond, that gifts should pass constantly, in both directions, between the ruler and his subordinates. At least until 1955, when a new Agreement drastically curtailing the Mukama's powers to appoint and dismiss his chiefs was signed, the king's personal favour was an indispensable condition of political advancement. Personal loyalty and attachment to him counted for very much more than conformity to the bureaucratic, civil-service norms of efficiency and incorruptibility. We shall see in the next chapter that in the 1950s and even earlier increasing numbers of educated Banyoro had actively opposed this undoubtedly unsatisfactory and anachronistic state of affairs. But to condemn the kinds of transactions it involved as mere corruption would be to overlook the vital part played by the interpersonal exchange of goods and services in traditional polities of the Nyoro type. It should be added, also, that in traditional Bunyoro to have the dependants and the resources needed to make handsome gifts to the king was itself an indication of fitness for authority; in pre-European times there was no need for the specialist training and knowledge, especially literacy, which are indispensable to a modern administrator. What was important was that chiefs should be 'king's men'; in the Nyoro idiom, 'the Mukama's spears' (*macumu g'Omukama*). To be a person of wealth and influence, to be well known to the king, and to be personally loyal to him, were the essential qualifications for office.

There remains one aspect of the Mukama's traditional role as giver and receiver which may appropriately be considered here, and that is his central position as receiver and distributor of women. Traditionally, the king did not marry (*kuswera*) as ordinary people did. In theory all the women in the country, like everything else in it, were already his. Also, it would be inconceivable for him to assume the subordinate status of son-in-law (*muko*) to his wife's father (*isezara*), or to engage in disputes about bridewealth with a commoner.[1] He obtained his wives (*bago*, sing. *mugo*) in two ways. First, he received them as gifts from his chiefs and subjects, especially girls whom they had

---

[1] Bakama's wives were predominantly from non-royal clans. Nyakatura (chap. 3) lists the clans of the mothers of eighteen Bito kings; only two of them were Babito. For an account of the markedly inferior status of men *vis-à-vis* their brides' families (especially the father-in-law) see Beattie 1958*a*.

captured in war. Secondly, he might select them himself, or
have them chosen for him by his officials. In the second case,
if the Mukama wished to take a particularly attractive young
girl as a wife, he would cause a special bead necklace to be
placed around her neck, either putting it there himself, or
sending a messenger to do so. This act of betrothal was called
kuligira, and although such a girl, if she were very young, might
be left with her parents until she reached puberty, she was from
that time onward known as *mugo*, and was bound to the king
and unavailable to anyone else. There was no ceremony of
marriage and no formal payment of bridewealth, though gifts
of cattle, slaves, and other goods would be made to the girl's
father. To be selected by the Mukama in this way was traditionally regarded as a great honour, and might lead to wealth
and high position for the girl's parents, especially if their
daughter should have the good fortune to become the mother
of a future king. But sometimes the girl might remain in the
palace for only a few months or even weeks, and as Roscoe
rightly observes, not all parents were anxious for the honour
(1923, pp. 150–1). Certainly in recent times it has not been
much coveted. On a visit to the remote Lake Albert village of
Tonya in 1955 I was told that on a recent tour the Mukama had
been much taken by a very pretty girl among those dancing for
him, and had indicated through his chief minister that he would
like to acquire her. The girl, however, was warned, and being
unwilling she quickly left the area. I was assured that had she
been attired in the special necklace she would have been unable
to refuse, and would have had to go to the palace, even if only
for a short time.

It is impossible to say how many royal wives there might have
been at the palace at any one time, but the number of some
earlier kings' accredited offspring suggests that they must have
run into scores, if not hundreds. Mukama Kabarega is said to
have had 140 children, many of whom (besides the last king)
were still alive in Bunyoro in the 1950s (Bikunya, pp. 75–6).
Traditionally one of his wives, who had been in the palace for
a long time, had had children, and was especially favoured by
the king, would be appointed chief wife (*mugo mukuru*), and
would have authority over her fellow *bago* in domestic matters.
Her parents would be rewarded with generous gifts of cattle and

other goods. In recent reigns there has been only one Mugo, married by the king in Christian marriage early in his reign.

As well as the *bago*, there was in traditional times a further category of women in the palace called *baranga* (sing. *muranga*). These were maidservants (*bazana*) to the *bago*, and appear to have been considerably less restricted in their movements than their mistresses. They are said to have been readily available as concubines to palace officials, and indeed to anyone who pleased them. These are the women referred to by Emin Pasha as 'a great number of girls [who] live as servants to his [King Kabarega's] wives. They are usually good dancers', he goes on, 'or distinguished by corporeal advantages, and enjoy unlimited freedom at night. They are called *vranga* [i.e. *baranga*]' (1888, p. 87). Emin not unreasonably describes them as prostitutes. Roscoe appears to have been mistaken in thinking that 'Mulanga' (*muranga*) was a special female official appointed to select the king's women (1923, pp. 149–53); *baranga* were handmaids in the royal household (Davis [p. 110] defines *muranga* as 'handmaid, female servant of chief or king, concubine'), and although it is likely that these women may sometimes have introduced other girls into the palace, I could find no evidence that there was ever an official post of the kind Roscoe describes.

There can be little doubt that in pre-European times the complex and continuing network of exchanges, both between the king and his chiefs and between king and people, served to counteract in some measure the powerful divisive forces in traditional Nyoro social structure. We saw in Chapter 1 that Banyoro explicitly oppose 'state' and 'community'. And within the 'state' itself (*bukama* or *bulemi*) the territorial chiefs were both intrinsic to the kingship and at the same time a potential— sometimes actual—threat to it. The various kinds of exchanges just considered served more or (sometimes) less effectively to bind the chiefs to the king, and the common people to both.

It is understandable, then, that with the advent of the European rulers, from whom (rather than ultimately from his people, as in traditional times) the Mukama thenceforward held his authority as a native ruler, and especially with the introduction of a civil-service type of administration, a cash economy, and taxation instead of tribute, these old bonds should quickly weaken. I said that in the 1950s there were constant complaints

that the Mukama did not give feasts (*kwinura*) for his dependants and subjects as his father and grandfather had done. People asserted that nowadays he only helped a narrow circle of friends. It was not always realized that the political and social changes of the preceding half-century had radically altered the traditional situation. For the king no longer received such quantities of foodstuffs and beer from his subjects as his predecessors had; peasants were now growing cash crops as well as foodstuffs, and they could sell their surpluses of the latter for cash, which was needed to pay taxes and school fees, and to purchase desired consumer goods in the shops. Also, the decline of Bunyoro's herds to a point where few families owned cattle, and these mostly in a single corner of the district, meant that the provision of great feasts of meat on the traditional pattern was no longer practicable.

We should recall, too, that many of the gifts which had formerly been of services and foodstuffs were now commuted to money payments. Unlike cattle, grain, and beer, cash does not have to be returned to the people who provided it in the form of feasts and gifts. It can be retained inconspicuously and indefinitely, and is convertible into a wide range of desirable objects not available in traditional times, such as permanent buildings, expensive education for one's children, motor cars, and other imported goods. In Bunyoro, as in some other similar kingdoms, the economic aspect of kingship was strongly stressed. Thus it was inevitable that the traditional view of the king and his chiefs as centres for the collection and redistribution of goods, and the modern pattern of bureaucratic administration introduced by the European administration, should have conflicted, and that this should have led to frustration and misunderstanding. Nor is it surprising that the nature of these stresses was not always fully understood by those, both Banyoro and British, most closely concerned with them.

I have elsewhere referred (though with some qualifications) to the traditional Nyoro polity as 'feudal' (e.g. Beattie 1960a, p. 39). After the brief review given in this chapter of the king's relations with his chiefs and people in pre-European times, it may be useful to take a closer look at this feudal analogy. Obviously much depends on what one means by the term 'feudalism'. As Goody has recently noted in a useful article

(1963), some authors have written as though any society with a ruler, a rough hierarchy of chiefs, and a subordinated peasantry were *ipso facto* feudal. Many earlier anthropologists, especially in Africa, took such a view. So regarded, a vast number of African states, both traditional and modern, are 'feudal'. But so vague and all-inclusive a formulation is evidently of little value, for it provides us with no criteria for distinguishing some kinds of such states from others. Somewhat more useful (and etymologically more legitimate) is the definition of feudalism by reference to a particular form of land holding. Thus defined, a polity is 'feudal' when it is based on the relation of vassal and superior arising from the holding of land 'in feud', that is, in consideration of service and homage from vassal to lord. Though this definition selects only one element in the complex of medieval European feudal institutions, and that one not always regarded as essential, it does point to the reciprocal, contractual element in feudalism, and so to the essentially personal nature of the relationships involved, with their stress on the bond of personal loyalty between inferior and superior. Thus Maquet, who regards traditional Ruanda as a feudal state, stresses the personal bond between two persons unequal in power, involving protection on the one hand, fealty and service on the other (chap. 6 and *passim*). These criteria do conveniently, if rather broadly, distinguish such polities from those in which specialized political authority is either lacking altogether or is distributed on impersonal, bureaucratic, 'rational–legal' grounds. Such simple, single-criterion characterizations have some descriptive value, but they tend to obscure the fact that certain important features of European feudalism are quite lacking in states like Bunyoro.

A clear statement of the central characteristics of European feudalism is Marc Bloch's, quoted by Goody in his article just referred to. Bloch (p. 466) specified five fundamentals. These were (1) the fief, usually but not essentially land; (2) the personal nature of the bond of political dependence; (3) the dispersal of authority; rulers have to delegate, and they have to make loyalty worth while. These three criteria fit many African kingdoms, including Bunyoro, well enough. But Bloch adds two more: (4) a reference to a specialized military class, something that is not found in Bunyoro (the royal bodyguard, *barusura*, could hardly be so described) or in many of the African polities

which have been called feudal; and (5) the reference to the survival in some form of the idea of the State.

The importance of this last point is that in African kingdoms like Bunyoro there is no idea that the polity was ever more centralized, more state-like, than it is now. The beginnings of European feudalism involved the weakening of the State, even its breakdown, and the distribution of formerly centralized powers among private individuals. But in most African states there has been no such breakdown, indeed an exactly opposite process seems to have taken place, for many, if not most, of the polities which have been described in feudal terms represent a trend towards increased centralization, not away from it (Goody, p. 8). Often they represent the first beginnings of a centralized political control, not its dissolution. Thus, for example, among the Nilotic Alur of north-western Uganda, hitherto chiefless communities have in historical times come of their own free will under the dominion of chiefly lines (Southall, chap. 8). And it is probable that in the case of at least some of the interlacustrine Bantu kingdoms minorities from elsewhere imposed more or less centralized forms of government on hitherto 'acephalous' and segmentary communities.

European feudalism and African states like Bunyoro also differ significantly in regard to the categories of persons who are linked as superordinate and subordinate. In Europe the characteristic feudal bond was between the tenant or fief-holder and a nearby chief or lord. The tenant held his fief from his lord, owed loyalty and obeisance to him, and looked to him for protection. He was not directly linked in any way with the king, with whom his relationship was only of secondary importance, if it existed at all. But in kingdoms like Bunyoro the case was very different. Although the great chiefs were powerful men, and presented a constant threat of revolt, loyalty to and dependence upon the person of the king himself were explicit and universal values, constantly expressed. I have stressed that all subordinate political authority in Bunyoro was held, and was seen to be held, as the direct gift of the king himself, and at his pleasure. In Bunyoro, the polity sometimes described (for example by Roscoe) in feudal terms was really a means to creating and sustaining a centralized system of government; in no sense was it the result of the breakdown of such a system.

Bunyoro, then, and states like it, differ in some important respects from the feudal states of medieval Europe, and however we restrict or modify our definition of feudalism the indiscriminate use of the feudal analogy must tend to discount these differences. But this is not to deny that where there *are* resemblances between African and medieval European polities it is legitimate, and may even be illuminating, to point them out. The social anthropologist studying a traditional African kingdom is bound to be interested in asking how other small-scale societies, in other times and places, have dealt with problems of government and of territorial administration. Simple technology, a dispersed population, poor communications, and widespread illiteracy are features which were shared by both traditional African and medieval European societies, and the means by which a central authority can maintain some kind of political control in such conditions are not unlimited.

Evidently what it is most useful to compare are not whole societies, but rather particular institutions, after each has been adequately understood in its own proper context. If, as is certainly the case, early kingships in Europe are comparable in at least some respects with those studied by social anthropologists in Africa and elsewhere, there is no reason why such comparisons should not be investigated, due account being taken of the usually very different social and cultural contexts of the institutions being compared. Certainly such comparisons may be useful to the anthropologist, in suggesting new interests and approaches in his own study. They may even be of interest to the historian for the same reason. A crucial difference between social history and social anthropology is that while the historian can, and must, make use of written sources, he cannot know and talk to the people whose institutions he writes about. The social anthropologist, on the other hand, cannot make use of documents (or at least only to a very limited—though increasing— degree), but he can get to know the people whose society he is investigating, and so observe their institutions in action, in the rounded context of daily life. The political anthropology of small-scale societies may provide interested historians with working examples of kinds of political institutions which they can know only from documents. It is perhaps not inconceivable that this may contribute to their understanding of them.

7

THE MODERN KINGSHIP

THE history of the Nyoro kingship during the present century records the decline of the Mukama's traditional power, his eventual reduction to the status merely of constitutional head of state, and, finally, the dissolution of his kingdom. But the process was not just one of gradual diminution in his personal authority with the increasing democratization of local government. In fact, as we shall see, in one important respect the Bunyoro Agreement of 1933 represented a step in exactly the opposite direction.

Before the signing of the 1933 Agreement, administration in Bunyoro showed few of the characteristics of 'indirect rule'. It will be remembered that in the early years of the century territorial administration was largely in the hands of imported Ganda chiefs, and the young king Duhaga, appointed in 1902, was not a man of very forceful character. At least during the early years of his reign he was overshadowed by his senior chiefs (especially by Byabacwezi, a former general of Kabarega's who had co-operated with the British after Kabarega's defeat, and the Muganda James Miti) and he was much influenced by the Anglican Church Missionary Society, whose protégé he was. But he was by no means merely a mouthpiece of the British administration, and an early Bunyoro district handing-over report (1921) describes him and the Katikiro, Petro Bikunya (author of *Ky' Abakama ba Bunyoro*), as 'very prone to settle matters on their own without consulting others or even informing them of their decisions. The chiefs do not', the report goes on, 'except Jemusi [the last Muganda chief] and the Pokino [the senior county chief] stand up and give their opinions as freely as they should if they clash with the Mukama. He likes to have his own way whatever others want. The Katikiro supports him.' We shall see that practically the same words could be (and were) used of Duhaga's successor thirty years later.

In pre-Agreement days the Mukama had little say in the choice of his territorial chiefs. In the handing-over report just referred to, the then district commissioner gave a frank statement of the procedure adopted. 'New chiefs', he wrote, 'are selected from a list of three submitted by the Mukama and Lukiko [Luganda for 'council']. This list need not be and in fact is not generally followed. The list of chiefs compiled from observation on tour is the one I prefer to follow, though if the chiefs whose names are submitted by the Lukiko appear better they could be selected. I prefer that the selection of chiefs should rest with the D.C. rather than the Native Government as there is less intrigue if this policy is followed.'

But by the 1920s the days for direct rule on this benevolently autocratic pattern were over. During that decade and in the early 1930s, pressures began to build up for an Agreement for Bunyoro comparable with those which already determined the relations of the Ganda, Ankole, and Toro kingdoms with the Protectorate Government. By 1930 the Banyoro had co-operated peacefully with the European administration for more than twenty years, and the king and his chiefs, as well as the European administrators of the period, felt that it was time that the kingdom was granted a status comparable with those of the neighbouring kingdoms. The Nyoro king, in particular, was anxious to acquire control over the appointment, promotion, and dismissal of his chiefs at all levels: during the drafting of the 1933 Agreement, a district commissioner reported that the Mukama 'set great store' by what was alleged to be his traditional power to nominate his own chiefs. It was in any case becoming plain to the Protectorate administration that the time had come to formulate a clear statutory basis for the powers and duties of the native ruler and his government. And, not least important, an official inquiry into what appeared to be abuses in Bunyoro's curious system of land tenure had resulted in a series of firm recommendations for its reform.[1] It was thought that statutory force could be given to these recommendations by incorporating them in the new Agreement.

So in 1933 the first Bunyoro Agreement was concluded between the Uganda Protectorate Government and the Mukama

[1] Rubie and Thomas, 1932. Bunyoro's system of *kibanja* land tenure and its political implications are discussed in the next chapter.

of Bunyoro and his chiefs. This instrument, which as Lord Hailey has pointed out was 'a declaration of government policy rather than having the character of a treaty' (1950, p. 46), required the Mukama 'to loyally co-operate with the Governor and to follow his advice in all matters relating to the administration of the *Obukama bwa Bunyoro-Kitara* [the Bunyoro kingdom] and the welfare of its inhabitants' (section 3). Like the rest of Uganda, Bunyoro was subject to Protectorate legislation; new measures affecting the interests of the people of Bunyoro were to be brought to the notice of the Mukama 'provided time and circumstance permit' (section 4). The Mukama was to be assisted by a Native Council (Rukurato) of prescribed composition. Originally no provision was made for the popular election of councillors at any level, but by the early 1950s fifty-two of the seventy-five members of the council were native government officials or the Mukama's nominees. The remainder were elected commoners, mostly chosen by the 'electoral college' method from the lower councils (there were chiefs' advisory councils down to the level of the parish chiefs).[1] The Agreement also provided, in accordance with the Rubie and Thomas Report recommendations, for the reforming of Bunyoro's system of *kibanja* land tenure; all land was to be held 'by the Governor for the use of the inhabitants of the *Obukama bwa Bunyoro-Kitara*', subject to rights already recognized and the government's right to appropriate land for public purposes. Certificates of occupancy, not of ownership, might be granted by the Native Government to the persons who lived upon and cultivated the areas designated in the certificate (sections 25–7).

The reasons for these provisions relating to Bunyoro's land, and their consequences, are discussed in the next chapter; what is of particular interest in the present context are the provisions made by the Agreement for the appointment and dismissal of the Mukama's chiefs and officials. I quote the relevant sections of the Agreement in full:

14. Ministers, Saza and Gombolola Chiefs [i.e. county and sub-county chiefs] shall be appointed and dismissed by the Mukama subject to the approval of the Governor whose decision shall be final. The Mukama may consult the Rukurato and shall discuss his proposals with the District Commissioner, who will forward them with

[1] The council system is discussed in Chapter 9.

his comments to the Provincial Commissioner, who will in turn submit them for the final decision of the Governor. Provided that the Governor may delegate his powers of approval in the case of Gombolola Chiefs to the Provincial Commissioner.

15. Muluka Chiefs and Bakungu [i.e. parish chiefs and village headmen] shall be appointed and dismissed by the Mukama. Such appointments and dismissals may be discussed with the Rukurato but shall not be subject to the approval of the Governor.

These provisions meant that the Mukama could appoint and dismiss his ministers, his county chiefs, and his sub-county chiefs subject only to the approval of the Governor (for practical purposes this meant the approval of the district commissioner of Bunyoro), 'whose decision shall be final'. Thus in regard to these appointments he was subject only to a check from outside the traditional political system, not from within it. In the case of the two lower grades, the 'parish' chiefs and the village headmen, even this check was removed; the Mukama could appoint and dismiss these officials without reference either to his own council or to the Protectorate Government. In regard to all of these appointments and dismissals the Agreement provided that the Mukama 'may' consult his official council (*Rukurato*), but it did not require him to do so. Still less did it require him to pay any attention to such advice as his council might give him.

So although an intention of the Agreement was to restore an appropriate degree of autonomy to the traditional native authority, in accordance with the principles of indirect rule then current,[1] its effect was to put back rather than to advance the development of democratic local government in Bunyoro. The personal powers it gave to the Mukama were certainly greater than any he could have enjoyed traditionally. Although the king had always been seen as the sole source of political authority, in fact, as we have noted, his power was traditionally a good deal less than absolute. In matters of appointments to major chiefships he would have been required to consult his crown-wearers and other senior chiefs, and consistently to have ridden roughshod over their advice would have been to risk revolt. We may recall the popular story of the legendary king Isaza, whose contempt for the advice of his elders almost killed him. So, by the terms of the 1933 Agreement, chiefship again

[1] Cameron's *Native Authority Ordinance* had been enacted in Tanganyika in 1927.

became, to an even greater extent than it had been traditionally, the Mukama's personal gift, a benefit which, if he wanted to, he could bestow solely in his own private interest. If he so wished, he could completely disregard the views of his council, which was anyway advisory only. As for the Protectorate Government, represented in Bunyoro by the district commissioner, it effectively possessed only a power of veto; it could not compel the Mukama to appoint a minister or chief whom he did not want. And it was usually not difficult for the Mukama to make a convincing case for the dismissal of a chief whom he wished to get rid of.

These aspects of the Agreement were plain enough to most of the senior chiefs, and some of them at least signed the Agreement without enthusiasm.[1] That they were apparently rather less plain to the Protectorate officials responsible for drafting the Agreement was no doubt partly due to the fact that in the 1930s Bunyoro had been under direct British rule for more than a quarter of a century. During that time the Mukama's traditional though not very clearly specified obligation to consult his senior chiefs and advisers in matters of chiefly appointments had of course been in abeyance, since chiefs had been for the most part directly appointed by British officers. In the circumstances the European administrators can hardly be blamed for having been unaware of the traditional checks on the Mukama's power. Also, during the early part of this century the emphasis in colonial administrative thinking was on firm rule and good government, rather than on the development of democratic institutions. There are many cases in Uganda and elsewhere in Africa in which the implementation of the principles of indirect rule involved the devolution upon African rulers of wider and more nearly absolute powers than they had traditionally possessed.

Not surprisingly the Mukama took considerable personal advantage of his new powers, which he thought very rightly and properly his; he would have been more than human if he had not. It is not surprising either that during the years from 1933 to 1955 (in which a new Agreement was enacted) dissatisfaction with these new powers and with the ways in which they were being used was increasingly expressed. Complaints came mainly

[1] See Dunbar, p. 148.

from the growing class of educated Bunyoro, which included some officials in the Mukama's own government as well as school-teachers, Protectorate Government employees, and others. Indeed during this period the king's relations with some of his senior chiefs, especially with those who showed independence and criticized or opposed him in any way, were sometimes extremely bad. Some of the conflicts that arose at this time no doubt reflected the sort of palace intrigues that are inseparable from personally oriented systems of authority of the Nyoro type, but some of them were evidently expressions of the developing struggle for power between the king and his senior chiefs.

Thus in 1938 the influential and independent-minded county chief Pokino was dismissed by the Mukama, on the ostensible ground that he had one night deliberately speared and killed a special bull of the king, named Rubamba. It is said that this bull was a considerable public nuisance, wandering unchecked about the capital, damaging crops, and knocking people off their bicycles. The chief asserted that he had encountered it one night in his gardens, and when he tried to drive it off it charged him. He thereupon speared it, thinking that it was some kind of wild animal. The Mukama, however, insisted that the act had been done from spite, and demanded a prosecution. In the ensuing Central Native Court case the accused chief was fined 200 shillings, and required to pay a further 200 shillings as compensation to the Mukama. The Protectorate Government, who considered the Pokino an exceptionally able and energetic chief, pressed the Mukama to reinstate him, but he flatly refused, as he was perfectly entitled to do under the terms of the 1933 Agreement. It is said that the government then told him (using its powers under section 14 of the Agreement) that he could have either this man or nobody as Pokino. The Mukama settled for the second alternative, whereupon the title of Pokino was abolished, and his county, called Buhaguzi, was absorbed into the neighbouring and larger Bugahya county. It is likely that there were also administrative reasons for this change, but it was widely believed in Bunyoro fifteen years later that the precipitating cause was the Pokino's offence. The Mukama's advisers in this affair were no doubt his unofficial rather than his official counsellors; I was told that among the Pokino's more

vociferous opponents were the senior princesses (Babitokati), who argued that killing the bull Rubamba was tantamount to attempting to kill the Mukama himself, and that to allow the culprit to continue in a senior chiefship could only bring disaster. Whatever the facts of the case, the affair provided the Mukama with a welcome opportunity to get rid of a powerful and strong-willed chief.

A year later, the ex-Pokino was having tea with the Mukama on some formal occasion when he suddenly cried out that he had been poisoned. He recovered after a drink of milk. It is not recorded how this tea-party ended.

In 1948 long-standing enmity between the Mukama and another of his senior chiefs (a Mubito, grandson of Kabarega's hated rival Ruyonga, with whom Sir Samuel Baker had made the blood pact in 1872) came to a head. This chief was charged in Bunyoro's Central Native Court with what the Mukama not unreasonably called 'rather terrible and offensive' conduct towards him. This included his remarking publicly that the sight of the Mukama made him sick, and that if he (the Mukama) went to England (as he was at that time about to do), he would 'return with a black mark against him'. The offending chief, whom the British district commissioner of the time described as 'an extremely capable and energetic man' (though he went on to say that he was 'unfortunately soured by the fact that he did not attain the Mukamaship of Bunyoro'—which he could not anyway have done as he was not the son of a Mukama), was convicted and fined 100 shillings. The conviction was later quashed by the district commissioner (it is not clear on what grounds), but the offender was dismissed from his county chiefship and was never reinstated.

The Mukama's relations with his chief minister (Katikiro) were also frequently strained during this period. In 1950 his hostility to his Katikiro at that time, a highly educated Munyoro who had spent some time in America and England and had many European friends, and who was accordingly suspected by the Mukama's informal advisers of being pro-European and of wishing to oust the Bito dynasty and 'sell the country to the Europeans', led to that official's resignation. He was replaced (after an acting appointment whose holder later became Bunyoro's chief justice) by a county chief who was regarded by the

Provincial Administration at the time as the least suitable of the four candidates considered; as a chief he had been officially described as 'shifty and weak'. He was, however, believed to be devoted to the Mukama, who anticipated no difficulty in dominating him. In fact not very long afterwards he went over to the side of the Mukama's critics.

Other examples could be quoted of chiefs said to have been either dismissed or demoted, regardless of their seniority, efficiency, or popularity, because they had in some way or another personally offended the Mukama. Certainly when I was in Bunyoro I was impressed by the number of ex-chiefs of high rank, still able and energetic men in the prime of life, who had left their posts under mysterious circumstances, and most of whom were then making substantial incomes as private individuals, from agriculture or commerce.

Correspondingly, it was widely asserted during the early 1950s that incapable and unpopular men had been appointed as chiefs, and incompetent chiefs promoted, simply because they had by one means or another found personal favour with the Mukama. I was told that many relatively educated and enlightened men were unwilling to become chiefs under the system as it then existed. A clerk in the central Native Government office wrote:

It is a general opinion that Bunyoro has the poorest type of chiefs. The chiefs of this type appointed under such machinery [the 1933 Agreement] failed deliberately to apprehend the principles, I say deliberately because many of them knew the wishes of the power that appointed them [i.e. the Mukama] and so wished to satisfy those wishes.

It was noted in the last chapter that even in recent times loyal service in the palace was an important means of acquiring such favour, as also was the making of substantial gifts, in cash or kind, to the Mukama through one or other of his unofficial counsellors. These were usually members of his palace retinue of *banyamirwa* or *basekura*, without formal administrative positions, but it was widely said that they were 'nearer to the Mukama' than any of his official advisers were. Two of them in particular were known to be specially influential (the chief minister mentioned above had once remarked that there were

three Katikiros in Bunyoro, himself and these two men), and one of them had a considerable reputation as a diviner and magician. These men acted as go-betweens between the king and his 'clients', especially in the matter of the making of gifts to the king in connection with the appointment, promotion, and dismissal of chiefs and other officials in the Native Government. I learned from a former private secretary to the Mukama, who had been dismissed for 'insubordination', something of the order of the prestations involved; his information was amply corroborated by others concerned. Thus in three recent instances promotion to a county chiefship had involved payments, through one or other of the unofficial advisers mentioned above, of sums of up to 200 shillings (in addition, in one case, to a pressure lamp), and several promotions to sub-county chiefships had involved lesser gifts both in cash and in kind. Before we condemn such practices as corruption (and in the 1950s many educated Banyoro, as well as European officials and missionaries, did so), we must recall that, as was stressed in the last chapter, traditional political relations in Bunyoro were essentially personal: it is not only in the political context that the change-over to a money economy has radically altered relationships traditionally based on, and even conceived in terms of, the mutual exchange of goods and services.

People frequently remarked to me that in the old days, prior to the 1933 Agreement, chiefs had been much stronger and more able than they were in the 1940s and 1950s, when most of the best posts went to 'yes-men' and sycophants. It is said that this was because in pre-European times the Mukama could not so easily get rid of a chief he disliked, as he would have to take some account of his senior chiefs' advice in such matters. And we noted above that in the earlier days of the British administration the Mukama had little say in the appointment of chiefs, who were selected on merit by the district commissioner.

A major point of criticism by chief and ex-chiefs was the Mukama's virtual by-passing of the Bunyoro Central Council (the Rukurato) in local administration affairs. In a memorandum submitted to the Protectorate Government towards the end of this period an ex-county chief wrote:

. . . In all these articles [i.e. by the terms of the 1933 Agreement] one finds that whatever Government [i.e. the Protectorate Government] wishes to do [the district commissioner] just takes up the

matter with the Mukama, discuss and finish it, and then order the people what to do. . . . He is not bound at all by the Rukurato. In front of this Agreement we have no Rukurato at all—our Mukama—the Ruler, is our Government, and that is all.

Criticisms of the Mukama and his administration were sometimes made (usually by literate Banyoro, often disappointed chiefs or ex-chiefs) in the form of anonymous letters addressed to the district commissioner or other officials, and sometimes more widely circulated. The following are extracts translated from an anonymous letter written in Runyoro in 1948, and posted to the Katikiro and others from the Mubende district:

Winyi [the Mukama] and his chiefs sold the nation by signing the 1933 Agreement. We have not found a single thing in that Agreement which benefits the people of Bunyoro; it is the Agreement of Gafabusa [the Mukama] and his princes only. . . . Gafabusa has done away with the Bunyoro *rukurato*. The country is not wanting in men of the quality of the late Bikunya [Bunyoro's first Katikiro and the author of *Ky'Abakama ba Bunyoro*]. But Gafabusa has made Bunyoro his personal estate (*akagifora kibanja kye ky'obwesengeza*). He chooses his katikiro for his qualities as a personal servant, as someone fitted to run his errands.

The writers continue rhetorically:

In this whole country of Bunyoro if there is any chief who serves the nation rather than his stomach, tell us who is he? If he was appointed for his ability rather than because of his friendship to Mukama Winyi Gafabusa, tell us who is he? If he was appointed chief without first bribing the Mukama, tell us who is he? Oh, how Winyi has eaten up this nation to the finish! He is hiding himself from his people, a thing that was never done by any of his ancestors. And we, the ancient masters of the land (*abakama b'ensi*) fear him like God!

Another anonymous letter addressed to the Mukama himself in 1949 (the principal author was suspected to be a respected senior chief), accused him of filling his palace with uneducated diviners and sorcerers, instead of with eminent and respected men of chiefly family. 'It is such people of the former kind that tell you what to do, who shout at you, and who choose the chiefs for this country, from the katikiro to the *muruka* chief of Mutanda [a remote 'parish'].' The writers, who were evidently

persons of some political sophistication, went on to formulate some specific demands. These were:

(1) The country should be allowed to choose the katikiro (prime minister) every three years.

(2) County chiefs should be chosen by the Rukurato, not by the Mukama, who would have to approve the Rukurato's choice.

(3) The Katikiro should work closely with the Provincial Administration, without interference from the Mukama.

(4) Neither the Mukama nor the Katikiro should make or implement any decisions without the Rukurato's consent.

(5) All the county chiefs should be given crowns (makondo). [A curious reversion to traditional symbols in this context.]

(6) No member of the royal clan (Babito) should be appointed a chief.

(7) The Bunyoro Agreement should be revised, as it was not made with the country but with the Mukama personally.

(8) The job of choosing clerks, porters and messengers for the native government should be left to the Katikiro; the Mukama should not concern himself with such minor matters.

The letter was signed 'Committee of Citizens of Kitara'. Needless to say, the recommendations it contained did not appeal to the Mukama, either then or later.

Some of the allegations contained in these letters may have been exaggerated, but they were symptomatic of the increasingly articulate opposition to the Mukama's 'personalized' form of government. More and more complaints were made about the unsuitability, incompetence, and corruption of the chiefs he selected, and about the way in which he exercised his power of summary dismissal, one means by which he effectively prevented any free expression of opinion by the majority of official Rukurato members. Most of the younger men I talked to, including my research assistants, expressed lively dissatisfaction with the Native Government as it then was. My best assistant, the late Mr. Perezi Mpuru, told me that his father, a sub-county chief highly regarded by the Protectorate administration, had been refused a deserved promotion because he was not prepared to offer the expected gift to the Mukama through his palace advisers. I heard many similar stories.

The substance of these complaints was not so much, or at least not only, that the Mukama's personal style of government was morally wrong; it was rather that it was an anachronism; that it was, in the circumstances of the time, a bad government. In the five years or so preceding 1955 there had been some progress towards the democratization of the District Council, on which both the Native Government and the Protectorate administration were represented. In 1949 the number of popular representatives on this council was increased from four to ten, and in 1952 to twenty. But this had entailed no weakening of the Mukama's personal power. Although the Katikiro was the chairman of the Rukurato, the Mukama was the chairman of the Standing Committee of the District Council, as well as of the finance and other sub-committees of his own government. In 1953 he agreed to resign his chairmanship of the Standing Committee, and to establish an appointments committee to deal with chiefly appointments, dismissals, and promotions. But, to begin with, he was chairman of this committee, and he expressed his opinions before anyone else. Not surprisingly, these opinions were then endorsed by the other members of the committee. All these committees, the district commissioner wrote in a government memorandum, 'were but reflections of the Mukama's will, and exercised little independent judgment'. As the district commissioner remarked in an official letter to the Mukama himself, 'it is difficult to see how a committee over which you yourself preside could be described as advisory to you'. All of these committees could only discuss such matters as were referred to them by the Mukama, and he exercised further censorship by deciding which of the resolutions reached should go forward for the Governor's approval.

By 1953–4, opinion in the district was turning steadily against the Mukama. The process of democratization gained momentum when in August 1954, a committee of fourteen educated Banyoro, elected by the District Council, met Sir Keith Hancock, who was at that time visiting Uganda to advise on constitutional reforms in Buganda, to discuss with him possible reforms in Bunyoro. Most of the members of this committee were progressives who were opposed to the Mukama's autocratic ways; they included his chief justice (*Muramuzi*), some senior chiefs, and Central Government officials, and a few

PLATE 5

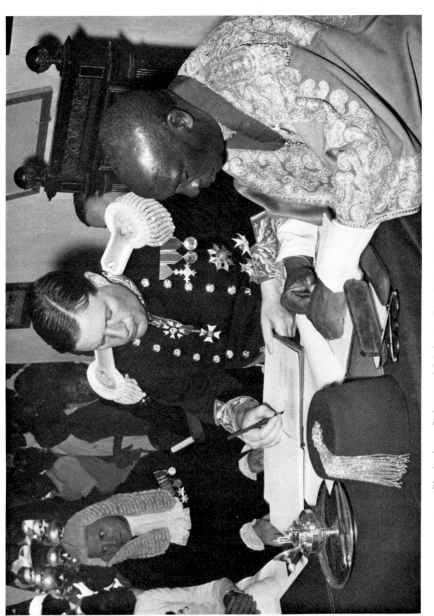

Sir Andrew Cohen and Mukama Tito Winyi signing 1955 Agreement

educated and influential laymen, as well as, surprisingly, the Katikiro himself, who had been the Mukama's choice as his chief minister three years earlier, but who had since become estranged from his master owing, it is said, to the latter's constant interference in minor administrative matters. At first the Mukama raised no objection to the proposed discussions, but he later became alarmed, and protested to the district commissioner that the meeting was 'unconstitutional' and should not be allowed to take place. He was overruled.

Much of the credit for the reforms which were so soon to be effected was due to the district commissioner at the time, the late Mr. K. P. Gower, whose firm but patient efforts to win over the king were eventually successful, though understandably the Mukama continued to regard the attempt to deprive him of his authority without enthusiasm, and opposed it for as long as he could. He was unconvinced by Professor Hancock's argument that his statutory withdrawal from the burden of personal responsibility for appointments and dismissals would protect him from the danger of unseemly involvement in political disputes and disagreements, and he sought to the end to retain at least some control over chiefly appointments, and over the deliberations of his councils.

But all educated Banyoro, including his own chiefs, were now strongly and openly in favour of strengthening the executive authority of the Rukurato, and depriving the king of the exclusive and personal powers conferred on him by the 1933 Agreement. As the district commissioner wrote in an official report, 'the chiefs at all levels wish to see the power of the Mukama in respect of appointment and dismissal transferred to a less capricious body'. The Mukama, at last, knew that he was beaten. Increasing popular support for the Hancock Committee's recommendations, the falling away of many of his former friends and supporters, strong administrative pressure, combined, no doubt, with the timely award to him of a knighthood in June 1955, led him in the end to capitulate. On 3 September 1955 the new Bunyoro Agreement, which effectively reduced the Mukama to the status of a constitutional ruler, was signed by him and by the Governor of Uganda, Sir Andrew Cohen, at a public ceremony at Hoima. The terms of the new Agreement, with regard to the appointment and

dismissal of chiefs, were clear and unambiguous. The old sections 14 and 15 (see pp. 151–2 above) were replaced by the following:

18. The Katikiro shall be elected by the Rukurato and shall be appointed by the Omukama, subject to the approval of the Governor.

19. The other Ministers, Executive Officers, county and sub-county chiefs shall be appointed by the Omukama in conformity with the advice of the Appointments Committee, whose advice shall be subject to the approval of the Governor or in the case of county and sub-county chiefs the Provincial Commissioner.

20. Muluka ['parish'] chiefs shall be appointed by the Omukama in conformity with the advice of an appointments committee of the county council of the county in which a vacancy exists. Bakungu [village headmen] shall be elected by the people of the muluka in which a vacancy exists, and shall likewise be appointed by the Omukama.

. . . 22. (1) Officers and chiefs appointed by the Omukama shall be subject to dismissal and disciplinary action by the Omukama in conformity with the advice of the Appointments Committee. . . .

The Mukama continued to exercise considerable, though diminishing personal influence even after the signing of the Agreement, but from that time onward chiefship was no longer, as it had hitherto been, his personal gift. Though chiefs continued to be formally appointed by him, they were now chosen by a committee whose recommendations he was obliged to accept. The reforms so long and so persistently sought, both by the Protectorate administration and by a growing body of Banyoro themselves, had at last been achieved.

It would be a mistake to suppose that the Mukama's resistance to the inevitable democratization of his kingdom's administration was motivated entirely by self-interest. He genuinely believed that he knew what was best for his kingdom; he was not a young man, and he preferred old-fashioned ways. Like most of the older generation of Banyoro he was deeply committed to the past, and, as I showed in the last chapter, the giving and receiving of gifts in the context of political relations was the traditional norm. He was not alone among traditional rulers in resisting processes of change which he neither sympathized with nor wholly understood, and it would have been

PLATE 6

Part of audience at signing of 1955 Agreement: the acting Katikiro is at the microphone

remarkable if he had shown any inclination to co-operate in these unwanted processes.

Bunyoro's territorial administration in the 1940s and 1950s, then, was a strange mixture of traditional and modern 'civil-service' values; here as in other contexts social and political change had not proceeded evenly on all fronts. Traditional values, though they had been much eroded by social and economic change, and especially by the advent of a cash economy, continued to be very much more important than was always recognized. Lord Hailey was rather wide of the mark when he wrote in 1950, discussing the Agreement districts of Bunyoro, Ankole, and Toro:

> The Ruling Chief, . . . [though] formally recognized as supreme and his status declared as hereditary, . . . no longer presides over chiefs who are bound to him by any traditional ties. He is the head of a cadre of official chiefs whose duties are prescribed by the Protectorate Government, and who exercise an authority derived from and defined by a Protectorate Ordinance (p. 56).

At the time when Lord Hailey was writing, chiefs were still bound to the Mukama of Bunyoro by ties which were conceived and expressed in traditional, rather than in modern, bureaucratic terms. The chiefs' authority was still seen by most Banyoro as deriving from and as defined by their personal link with the Mukama, rather than as based on the Uganda Local Government Ordinance, a piece of legislation which was resented and as far as possible ignored by the Mukama, and which few chiefs below the highest ranks knew anything about. Most of the lower grades of chiefs still saw themselves, as most of their subjects saw them, as 'the Mukama's spears', deriving their authority not from an ordinance passed by the Government in Entebbe, but from the favour of the Mukama himself.

Even during the 1950s most Banyoro, certainly most peasant Banyoro, thought of their kingdom's government not as a kind of instrument or branch of the central Protectorate administration, with which they were anyway little concerned, but rather as a quite separate and self-contained polity. Interaction between the Protectorate Government and the Bunyoro Native Government took place mostly at the higher levels; most official contacts were with the Mukama and his ministers, and with the

upper grades of chiefs. Though some European district commissioners in Bunyoro knew the people and the country well, there had always been less communication between the provincial administration and the people at the grass-roots level than had been common in other areas of East Africa. This was partly due to the problem of language, a problem which was much less acute in Kenya and Tanganyika, where Swahili provided a lingua franca available to officials and people alike. All British Government officials in Uganda spoke some Swahili and many spoke Luganda, but it was exceptional for one to know Runyoro. Like their people, lower chiefs in Bunyoro for the most part spoke no other language than their own, and communication between them and European officials had generally to be carried out through interpreters. An effect of this was to sustain for the ordinary people, for longer perhaps than might otherwise have been the case, the importance of the Kingdom Government and its officials, as against that of the Protectorate administration. Certainly, when I was in Bunyoro, I was struck by the fact that the district commissioner's office in Hoima was not constantly besieged by members of the public with a multiplicity of minor complaints, as such offices were, during the colonial period, in most other parts of East Africa.

8

THE *KIBANJA* SYSTEM: THE CHIEFS
AND THE LAND

I N the Bunyoro kingdom political authority was indissolubly
related, both in thought and in practice, with specific and
proprietary personal rights over particular pieces of land.
Nyoro chiefship cannot be understood without some knowledge
of Nyoro land-holding, in particular of the development and
continuing importance of its characteristic system of land
tenure, the *kibanja* system. For the 'owners' or 'masters' (*bakama*)
of the often quite extensive populated estates (*bibanja*) in which
much of the country was (and probably still is) taken up were
themselves a kind of chief, indeed before the 1933 Agreement
they had composed the lowest rank of government chiefs, then
known as *bakungu*. Up to the 1950s, if an official chief did not
already possess a *kibanja* on appointment to office, he quickly
acquired one. Traditionally in Bunyoro, a chief should have his
own personal dependants, and this role was not filled by those
officially subject to his jurisdiction. Also, relationships between
the official government chiefs and the *bakama b'ebibanja*, and
between both of these categories of persons and the ordinary
people, played an important part in Nyoro affairs. In this
chapter I give some account of the origins, growth, and social
importance of the *kibanja* system. I then describe the kinds of
people who were *kibanja* proprietors during my time in Bunyoro,
the kind of authority they possessed, and their relationship with
their peasant occupiers. And finally I consider the relationship
between these persons and the hierarchy of official, salaried
chiefs (discussed in more detail in the next chapter), and the
degree to which these two categories tended to become assimilated to one another.

It seems that during the reign of Mukama Kabarega, the last
independent Nyoro king, rights in land were held by four categories of persons. First, the whole country and everything in it

were thought of as belonging to the Mukama, the 'Master' or 'Owner' of the country. This right derived from tradition, and as we saw in Chapter 3 it was validated by myth. In virtue of it the king could, and did, allot specified territories to specially favoured persons, over the inhabitants of which they exercised political control, under the Mukama's overriding authority. It is tempting to call the rights so held 'feudal' or 'fief-holding', since they entailed the holding of estates in land 'on condition of homage and service to a superior lord' (*Shorter Oxford English Dictionary*, definition of 'feudal'). But although the Mukama's chiefs in traditional times were comparable in some respects with the feudal lords of medieval Europe they were certainly very different from them in others, and as we noted at the end of Chapter 6 the analogy between the institutions of European feudalism and those of African polities like Bunyoro must be used with caution.

This necessary delegation of the royal authority gave rise to the second category of rights, those of the territorial chiefs of various ranks. All of these, however limited the areas of their jurisdiction, held their authority at least in theory directly from the king, and all of them were responsible to him, either directly or through a superior chief, for the good administration of their areas. From their peasant subjects they received tribute in food-stuffs, beer, and labour, and a part of this, together with a proportion of the herds (if any) in their areas, had to be passed on from time to time to the Mukama. He, in his turn, was expected to reciprocate with periodic feasts and gifts for his chiefs and people. In effect these chiefly rights were over people rather than over land, but they were none the less explicitly territorial, since they were over people only so long as they occupied specified territories. As we have noted, they also involved the right to a portion of the agricultural produce of the land. As well as tribute and service, chiefs claimed and were accorded homage and respect by their subjects, who in turn looked to their local rulers for justice and protection. If a peasant was dissatisfied he could always move to the jurisdiction of another chief, and in fact movements from one area to another were frequent.

The third category of rights in land in the traditional system comprised those vested in the heads of the more or less localized

agnatic groups of clansmen into which Banyoro are said to have been territorially organized in pre-European times. These authorities, the *bakuru b'enganda* (sing. *mukuru w'oruganda*, literally 'the senior man of the clan') were the heads of localized lineages rather than of clans—since Nyoro clans were dispersed and had no single heads—and their territorial authority was restricted to the actual allocation of cultivation rights. In the 1950s Banyoro still said, somewhat anachronistically, 'The Mukama rules the people [i.e. through his chiefs], the clans rule the land'. It is widely believed in Bunyoro that before the widespread disturbances and population movements caused by the Kabarega wars, 'clans' were localized to a much greater extent than they were afterwards, although even then each group of clansmen is said to have occupied its territory by the Mukama's grace. Thus Banyoro claim that formerly one clan (*ruganda*, pl. *nganda*; the term is used for a group of agnates, of whatever size) occupied one *mugongo*. This last term means 'back' or 'ridge', and in this context it denotes the raised, habitable portion of land between swamps or streams, which are numerous in Bunyoro. On the higher parts of these areas, which might be of several square miles in extent, were clustered anything from half a dozen to fifty or more homesteads and their gardens. One such area is illustrated in Plate 1. Many, probably most, *migongo* are still named after one or other of Bunyoro's hundred or more clans, which may suggest rather higher local concentrations of fellow clansmen in the past than are found today.[1] Whatever its size, such a group had its head, the *mukuru w'oruganda*, one of whose responsibilities was the allocation of land for occupation and cultivation, usually to members of his own group, but sometimes to affines and other non-agnates who wished to live or cultivate on the *mugongo*. By the 1950s, however, the *bakuru b'enganda* had long ceased to have any important function, indeed they were hardly recognized at all. Certainly they no longer had much to do with the allocation of land for residence and cultivation, a task which by that time was entirely in the hands of the lower grades of the Mukama's official chiefs.[2]

---

[1] For a brief account of Nyoro clans and lineages and their relation to territory see Beattie 1957a, pp. 319–25.

[2] The few and isolated fishing villages on the Lake Albert shore were an exception to this (most have since been dispersed by the rise in the level of the lake during the past decade). In them substantial residential groups still lived in compact

The fourth category of rights in land were those held by individual householders themselves. These rights included the right to build a house (in traditional times a day's work for a group of neighbours), to cultivate the soil, and to graze stock, and to pass these rights on to an heir. They could only be abrogated if the occupier abandoned his plot or neglected to cultivate it over a long period, or if he were driven out of the area for being a sorcerer, a habitual thief, or otherwise undesirable.

Evidently none of these rights (except, perhaps, the Mukama's overriding 'ownership' of the whole country and everything in it) amounted to a permanent, indefeasible right to a specific piece of land; all were held conditionally, either on the king's favour (in the case of the chiefs), or on productive occupation and acceptable behaviour (in the case of the peasants). The notion of permanent, unconditional rights in land of a kind approximating to what we understand by freehold did not develop until after the capture of Mukama Kabarega, the institution of a British administration, and in particular the land settlement in Buganda under the terms of the Uganda Agreement of 1900. This Agreement provided (among other things) for the grant of some 9,000 square miles of land to about 3,700 Ganda princes, chiefs, and other notables. These allocations, or *mailo*, as they came to be called, were of individual estates, held on what virtually amounted to freehold tenure. This settlement was in fact based on a misunderstanding of the existing system (in Buganda, as in Bunyoro, rights in land had traditionally been conditional, not absolute), and its effect was to establish, as Meek put it, 'a small landed aristocracy who became quasi-freehold proprietors of practically the whole of the settled areas of the country' (p. 133). In fact, as Meek pointed out, the original division of land gave way in time, through sale and inheritance, to 'peasant proprietorship on a widespread scale'. In 1952 the original 3,700 allotments had increased to 52,000 registered properties, and approximately 8,000 whose claims had not yet been investigated (Hailey 1957, p. 787). Only very minor grants were made in two of the other kingdoms (and none at all in Bunyoro), but the advantages of freehold tenure were

communities structured in terms of unilineal descent. But they were quite atypical of Bunyoro as a whole.

at once evident to members of ruling classes far beyond Buganda. Constant but unsuccessful requests for such grants in Bunyoro were made by the Mukama and his chiefs during the first half of this century.

None the less a system of land tenure having many of the features of freehold developed in Bunyoro. When after several years of political turmoil orderly government through a system of chiefs (the system was based on the Ganda model and, as we noted in Chapter 4, many of the early chiefs were Baganda) was reintroduced at the beginning of the present century, it was natural that the area administered by a chief should be regarded, as it had been in traditional times, as a kind of official 'estate', from the inhabitants of which he could properly exact service and tribute. In the early 1900s these obligations were commuted to a cash payment called *busuru*. This change was in itself bound to alter the basis of the traditional relationship between chiefs and subjects. For with the growing availability of consumer goods, money, unlike services, and tribute in kind, could be converted into a variety of private satisfactions; it did not have to be as it were ploughed back into the community, in the form of feasts and gifts. Thus the process of 'depersonalizing' the traditional relationship between rulers and people began, and as we shall see it was by no means complete even in the 1950s.

The *busuru* payment, originally 4 shillings, was increased in 1914 to 7 shillings per adult male, 1 shilling being passed on to the *muruka* or 'parish' chief, at that time the lowest grade of formally recognized administrative officials. Until the reforms of 1933, discussed below, this payment was the official chiefs' main source of revenue, and it was quite enough to make the position a sought-after one. But as soon as a chief relinquished office through retirement or otherwise this emolument ceased, and with the gradual change-over to a cash economy it became necessary to make some provision for the support of retired chiefs. This was done by cutting bits off the 'official' estates (*bwesengeze*) which all chiefs held in virtue of their office, and allotting these to the retiring officials to serve as places of residence, and (through the *busuru* paid by their peasant occupants) sources of income for them. These personal estates quickly came to be regarded as the private and devisable

possessions of their holders (Rubie and Thomas, p. 20). So, early in the century, there was created for the first time a distinction between a chief's 'official' domain, his rights over which terminated with his appointment, and his private estate, which was his personal property and could be passed on to his heirs. This distinction was no doubt more obvious to the chiefs than it was to the peasants who occupied these estates, for their obligations were much the same in either case. The private estates thus founded came to be known by the term *kibanja* (pl. *bibanja*), a word which traditionally referred only to an actual homestead site—in Buganda it still applies only to a peasant small-holding.

In course of time, especially after the introduction of fixed salaries for chiefs in 1933, the notion of purely 'official' holdings gradually died out, but the private, unofficial *kibanja* estate became an established feature of Nyoro social and political life. In the early years of the century the Mukama had begun to give such private estates to members of the royal family (the Babito 'princes' and 'princesses') for their personal use and profit, as well as to retiring chiefs. But as early as 1907 they were being granted, with full *busuru* rights, to certain other persons who were neither ex-chiefs nor Babito. These persons included serving chiefs of various ranks, domestic and ritual functionaries of the Mukama's extensive palace, and other 'people of standing who were well known', and who 'though they may not be doing government work, are looked on as dignitaries by the people', as a later instruction from the Protectorate Government expressed it. These persons, described in 1932 as 'better class natives' (Rubie and Thomas, p. 19), were precisely the same kind of people as those who had received *mailo* grants in the Buganda settlement of 1900.

During the quarter of a century from 1907, Mukama Duhaga and his successor, who themselves possessed substantial private holdings, continued increasingly to make such grants, and an official inquiry in 1931 revealed that all of the best of the occupied lands in the country were taken up either as official *bwesengeze* estates or as *bibanja*.[1] In that year approximately

[1] The Report of the inquiry was published as Rubie and Thomas 1932. But ten years earlier it was possible for a European administrator to write (in district handing-over notes dated 1921): 'I would oppose all grants of land to natives

18,000 out of 22,000 taxpayers were paying *busuru*, about 12,000 to serving chiefs on their official estates, and the other 6,000 to private individuals on their unofficial *bibanja*. These private *bibanja* estates varied in size from about five acres to several square miles, and the number of *busuru*-paying tenants on them varied from two or three to eighty or more, with an average of about six per *kibanja*. Thus in 1931, 84 per cent of the people lived as *busuru*-paying tenants on one or other of these two kinds of estates. But, and this was a crucial point, private *bibanja* holdings were steadily increasing at the expense of the official estates. For it was to a chief's interest to attract people from his official to his private estate, where they would continue to be a source of revenue to him after his retirement. The transfer of revenue from official to private hands which this involved was a feature of the situation which particularly disturbed Rubie and Thomas (p. 20).

Thus over a period of about half a century there developed in Bunyoro a mode of land-holding which differed significantly from what may be supposed to have been the traditional system. Though chiefs still held, from the king, rights over the people who occupied the areas allotted to and administered by them, so did many people who were not official chiefs. Further, these *kibanja* rights were thought of as permanent rights to specific areas of land *qua* land, and their peasant occupants were required to pay a fixed sum of money annually (no longer tribute in kind), as long as they occupied their holdings.

This development into what was beginning to look remarkably like a system of landlord proprietors and rent-paying tenants (though it still differed significantly from this) had been accelerated by two factors. First, in Bunyoro as elsewhere in Africa, with the introduction of a money economy and of cash crops (cotton, and later coffee and tobacco), the basis of land-holding tended (as Lord Hailey, following Sir Henry Maine, put it) to change from community and custom to individualism and contract, the new conception of 'ownership' gradually replacing traditional notions of usufruct and 'fiefhold' (Hailey

personally. This is not native custom. Land is all communal in Bunyoro.' Nothing of course could have been further from the truth, but the fact that, as the writer says elsewhere in his report, he had 'never interfered with this question and allowed the Mukama and his chiefs to settle the matter himself' (*sic*), no doubt explains his misinformation on this point.

1946, p. v). Banyoro chiefs early demanded some form of security of tenure (and they continued to do so through the 1950s), on the ground that this was essential for the proper development of their land and, especially, so that they could borrow money on the security of their land, for investment in improved buildings and agricultural equipment. It is, however, fair to say that up to the 1950s the large *kibanja* holders had, with very few exceptions, shown little disposition to develop their holdings on progressive agricultural lines. Before the 1933 Agreement did away with the *busuru* payments, the opportunity to collect rent was undoubtedly a more important attraction than the potentialities for agricultural development. But we shall see that this financial motive was by no means the only ground for the attraction of large *bibanja*.

The second factor which accelerated the development of a system of quasi-freehold estates in Bunyoro, the Uganda Agreement of 1900, has already been mentioned. We noted that this Agreement provided a large number of chiefs and other important people in Buganda with estates (*mailo*) on what was virtually freehold tenure. Banyoro constantly asked the Protectorate Government for the allocation of freehold estates in their country on the Ganda model, and in 1921 the Secretary of State in London had expressed his willingness to sanction such grants. But by this time the Uganda Government, having learned from the Buganda case, were firmly opposed to them, and although the Banyoro chiefs continued to hope up to the time of Independence, no such grants were made. This was a continuing source of grievance; Banyoro considered it unfair that such grants should have been approved in Buganda, and subsequently allowed on a lesser scale in Ankole and Toro, but withheld in Bunyoro, despite earlier intimations that they would be considered (Rubie and Thomas, p. 15).

The situation revealed by the official inquiry was naturally unacceptable to the Protectorate Government, which could hardly contemplate with equanimity a state of affairs which involved the rapid growth of a class of landlords or 'squireens', performing no economic function in return for the share of produce they received, and exacting a cash rent from a community of peasant cultivators who themselves possessed no guaranteed security of tenure. Something evidently had to be

done, and the government accepted the detailed recommendations for the reform of Bunyoro's *kibanja* system which were set
out in Part IV of the Rubie and Thomas Report.

The authors of the Report recommended the total abolition
of the landlord–tenant system which the development of large
tenanted estates implied, and its replacement by a system of
tenure, and a method of providing emoluments for chiefs, more
in conformity with enlightened modern ideas. The payment of
tribute in cash (*busuru*) on both official and unofficial estates
was to be abolished, and replaced by a consolidated tax payable
to the Native Treasury. Chiefs were to receive fixed salaries
according to rank. Compensation would be paid to all those
land-holders under the old system who stood to lose by the
reform. On the principle that 'every man is entitled to the free
and undisturbed occupancy of the land which he cultivates',
the Committee recommended the issue of certificates of occupancy to actual cultivators. These certificates guaranteed to the
holder 'undisturbed occupancy, subject to necessary conditions,
of the land, of whatever extent, of which he is actually making
use, with the right to dispose of the results of his labour upon
that land to his heir or by sale to another native' (Rubie and
Thomas, p. 31). Arbitrary grants on the old model were to be
abolished, and the only title to land was to be its actual occupation and cultivation. Even retired chiefs would not be allowed
to retain their private estates; they would receive either pensions
or gratuities, and if they wanted to they could take out certificates of occupancy over their residential plots, like everybody
else. The Committee supposed that 'the national collection of
tribute and its allocation to tribal purposes' would remove
'almost the only attraction of the private ownership of large
tenanted areas'.[1] Despite the careful and thorough investigation
upon which they had based their recommendations, events
proved that their supposition was mistaken.

The Protectorate Government accepted these recommendations in all essentials; provision for their implementation was included in the 1933 Agreement, and the appropriate instructions

---

[1] Rubie and Thomas, p. 32: 'Our recommendations will, indeed, normally
preclude any person from deriving an income from the tribute or rent of others.
For such a result we make no apologies and have no regrets. If, as the outcome,
there is evolved a nation of small farmers, we shall be well content.'

were duly conveyed to the Mukama's government, which
received them without enthusiasm. Directions are on record
laying down the form of procedure for obtaining certificates,
and providing that the *gombolola* (sub-county) chief must visit
the area applied for, confirm in writing that the applicant is
actually occupying and cultivating it, and mark out boundaries.
The area marked out was to be 'slightly over twice the area
which the applicant is cultivating or can cultivate', according
to a contemporary instruction. Provision was made for the
inspection of holdings and the checking of boundaries by the
head land clerk of the Native Government, and for periodic
inspections by chiefs and administrative officers. No limit (other
than that just mentioned) was laid down regarding the extent
of the area appropriate for grant under the certificate of occupancy; in fact all reference to areas and acreages was officially
discouraged, lest any suggested figure should become standard-
ized and claimed by applicants as of right. The boundaries of
the *kibanja* were recorded on the back of the certificate of
occupancy simply by naming the species of the trees (usually
four) which formed its corners—a fig tree, a euphorbia, a
Uganda coral tree, and so on. Official English translations of
the form of certificate of occupancy, and of the form of application for a certificate, are included as Appendix 1 and Appendix
2 to this chapter (pp. 197–9).

By these means the Protectorate Government hoped to arrest
the process which had been gathering momentum since the
beginning of the century, and to replace the large tenanted
bibanja by cultivated small-holdings. These holdings were not
mailos; they were not held in freehold, but on condition of
continuous occupancy and cultivation. The land itself was held
by the Governor for the occupation and use of the inhabitants
of the *Obukama bwa Bunyoro-Kitara*, subject to the conditions laid
down in the 1933 Agreement. A certificate conveyed rights of
occupancy only, and it was valid only so long as the certificate
holder himself occupied and cultivated the land specified in it.

But by 1933 the system of landed estates for chiefs and other
important people was too deeply ingrained to be so easily
eradicated. The reform did achieve the important ends of
abolishing the old official (*bwesengeze*) estates, and of placing the
chiefs on a salaried and (above the *muruka* or 'parish' level)

Land reform

pensionable basis. These were indeed significant achievements. But it did not achieve its major purposes of eradicating the *kibanja* system of large private and populated holdings in land. Though the cash payment of *busuru* to the proprietors of these estates by their peasant occupiers was stamped out (despite one or two abortive attempts to revive it), large tenanted *bibanja* continued to exist, and in 1953 they seemed to have lost little of their attractiveness. I consider below why this should have been so.

During the period of my field-work in Bunyoro, the *kibanja* system had again become a matter of major concern to the Administration, and, with the Native Government's co-operation, I made detailed inquiries into its development over the twenty years since 1933. It soon became plain that many of the 600 or so grants of *bibanja* over large populated estates which had been made before 1933 had been confirmed, not withdrawn, when the new system was initiated. In most cases the old private estates had continued to exist in the hands of their original 'owners' or their heirs, undiminished or only slightly diminished in size. Certificates of occupancy under the new regulations had been issued in respect of these estates, the essential provision that the holder's rights depended on his occupation and cultivation of the designated land being conveniently disregarded. The certificates were taken as conveying rights of proprietorship over the often considerable areas of populated land involved, and indeed some of the less sophisticated *kibanja* holders took the registration fee of 5 shillings to be the purchase price for the land. The verb *kugura* ('to buy') was constantly used by both officials and applicants in the context of *kibanja* applications. It was clear, also, that many more rights to large, tenanted *bibanja* had been granted by the Mukama since 1933; ample unalienated land had become available with the abolition of the official estates. The only substantial difference between the pre- and post-1933 tenure of such estates was that *busuru* could no longer be collected from the peasants who lived on them.

Up to the year 1953, about 5,000 certificates of occupancy had been issued by the Bunyoro Native Government. Of course, not all of these were over large *bibanja* with dependent households on them; most of them were over plots of a few acres, occupied and cultivated by the certificate holder and his family

in strict accordance with the terms laid down in the certificate. But between a fifth and a quarter of them at least, probably more, were held in respect of *bibanja* containing one household or more besides that of the certificate-holder himself. In this matter it was not possible to obtain exact information: the Native Government land registers contained no references at all to the sizes of the *bibanja* they recorded, nor to the numbers of households and persons resident on them, and no district-wide survey of *bibanja* holdings had—or has—ever been made. However, what I believe to be a fairly representative picture emerged from a survey which I undertook in 1953, by means of a questionnaire circulated to all of the twenty-five sub-county chiefs in the kingdom. The figures thus obtained are unlikely to be completely accurate, but they probably underestimate rather than exaggerate the total number of tenanted *bibanja* and the numbers of households on them. It was by this time generally known that the Protectorate Government did not favour large tenanted estates, and, as we shall see later, the chiefs themselves were among the most numerous proprietors of such estates. Again, I could only use the data submitted from ten of the twenty-five sub-counties (the others sent in either no returns or incomplete ones). These ten were, however, fairly evenly scattered throughout the kingdom and there was reason to believe that they were reasonably representative.[1]

At the time of my inquiry the total number of taxpayers (which may be taken as approximately the same as the total number of householders)[2] in these ten sub-counties was 12,083, and the total number of *bibanja* registered in them was 1,981. So in this sample, just over 16 out of every 100 householders

[1] These ten sub-counties were: Musale, Mutuba I, II, III, and V in Bugahya county; Mumyoka, Sabairu, and Sabawali in Bujenje county; and Sabairu and Musale in Buruli county (see Map 2).

[2] In three village house-to-house surveys, covering a total of 132 households in widely separated parts of Bunyoro, I found the number of persons per household (taking a self-contained domestic unit as a household) to average 4·3. The number of persons represented by each taxpayer (assuming that the estimated total number of taxpayers, 29,149, and the estimated total population, 108,380, were approximately correct) was 3·7. These two figures represent a variation of only 0·3 on either side of four. Some households, for example those containing only women or the very old, had no taxpayers, but equally, some taxpayers, such as young men still living at home, had no households of their own. So in the present context the equation one householder equals one taxpayer may be taken as approximately correct.

were registered *kibanja* holders. This figure is consistent with the proportion for the whole district, that is, 5,000 certificate-holders out of a taxpaying population of 29,149; which is just 17 per cent.

According to the sub-county chiefs' returns, there was a total of 4,567 households on these 1,981 *bibanja*. On the generally, though not invariably, valid assumption that the proprietor of a *kibanja* maintains a household on it, 1,409 of these *bibanja* had only one household per *kibanja*. Thus the remaining 572 *bibanja* (approximately 29 per cent of the total number of *bibanja* in the sample area) had a total of 3,158 households on them. So for all 1,981 *bibanja* the average number of households per *kibanja* was approximately 2·3, while the average number of households on each of the 572 'populated' *bibanja* (by 'populated' I mean containing one or more households in addition to the proprietor's) was 5·5. The following figures indicate the distribution of households on the 'populated' *bibanja* in the sample:[1]

		Percentage of total
Bibanja with only two households		22
Bibanja with three or more households		78
„ „ four „ „		57
„ „ five „ „		40
„ „ ten „ „		13
„ „ twenty „ „		3

Thus while the average number of 'dependent' households (that is, households *additional* to those of the *kibanja* holders themselves) on all the *bibanja* in the sample was just over one, the number of such households on the 572 *bibanja* which actually had dependent households on them was 4·5. In other words, nearly 70 per cent of the households occupied only 29 per cent of the *bibanja*.

Two facts of particular interest in the present context emerge from this brief analysis. First, it shows that of the 4,567

---

[1] These figures are remarkably similar to the pre-1933 ones. In a sample of 365 pre-1933 tenanted *bibanja* listed by the Bunyoro Native Government for the purpose of assessing compensation, 53 per cent contained less than 5 tenant householders, 36 per cent more than 5 but less than 10, and 11 per cent more than 10 (Bunyoro Native Government files).

householders who occupied the 1,981 *bibanja* in our sample at least 2,586 did not live on their own *bibanja*, or even on 'free' unallocated land, but as dependants on the *bibanja* of others. If this figure is expressed as a percentage of the 12,083 taxpayers (approximately equivalent to the number of householders) in the sample areas, it appears that at least 21 per cent of the population, and probably more, were living as 'tenants' in *bibanja* 'owned' by other people. Expressed in terms of the total population of the Bunyoro district, it appears likely (if, as I believe, the sample was reasonably representative) that, in 1953, out of Bunyoro's taxpaying (= householder) population of approximately 29,000, while about 5,000 possessed *bibanja*, something over 6,000 (representing about 25,000 persons) were living as 'tenants' on other people's land. These dependent householders, who represented a fifth of the total population (possibly considerably more), could never themselves take out certificates of occupancy over the areas they lived on and cultivated, for the rights granted by the certificates had already been conferred on the proprietors of the *bibanja* in which they lived as 'tenants'. Evidently this state of affairs was not at all what the authors of the 1933 reforms had intended.

The second significant conclusion to be drawn from these figures (the obverse of the first one) is that 572 of the 1,981 *bibanja* holders in the sample area (about 29 per cent of the total) possessed rights not only over their own households and gardens, but over land occupied by other householders as well, the average number of such dependent households per populated *kibanja* being between four and five. This suggests that of the district total of 5,000 *kibanja* holders, something like 1,500 were proprietors of populated *bibanja*, some of them of several square miles in extent, and each containing on the average four or five dependent households, sometimes considerably more. In other words, at least 20 per cent of Bunyoro's population were living as 'tenant' occupants of land held by less than 5 per cent. These 'landed proprietors' claimed and were accorded quasi-chiefly status, and indeed in a sense they were, and were regarded as, a kind of 'chief' (*munyoro*). The political and social implications of this state of affairs will be plainer after we have considered in more detail the relationship of the 'masters' or 'owners' (*bakama*) of these populated *bibanja*

to their dependent householders, and equally important, to the official chiefs.[1]

A brief description of a typical larger-type *kibanja* which was well known to me will provide a convenient starting-point for a discussion of these relationships. Mr. Zekeri (this is not his real name) was the proprietor of a *kibanja* which covered a little less than a square mile; it was extremely fertile, and was situated a few miles from Hoima on the main road to Masindi. The area is more densely populated than parts of the country further away from either of Bunyoro's two towns, but in 1953 at least a third of the *kibanja* was unoccupied or fallow land covered by elephant grass and bush. Early in the present century it had been allocated by Mukama Duhaga to a princess (Mubitokati) distantly related to him; at that time it was about half its present size. When she died she left it to her daughter, who on leaving the country passed it to her brother. He was a sub-county chief and so a person of some importance, and in 1938 (five years *after* the 1933 reforms) he managed to have the area of his *kibanja* doubled. Mr. Zekeri, who was a young man in his twenties when I knew him, was his heir. When the *kibanja* had been first granted there had been ten dependent householders on it, and I was told that most of them were servants or dependants of the original Mubitokati owner. This may or may not have been so; almost all of the original tenants had long since died or departed, so it was impossible to reconstruct the original settlement pattern. In 1953 there were eighteen separate households on the *kibanja*: the proprietor did not live on it himself, as he had a house a mile or two nearer to Hoima, where he was employed.

One of the households belonged to an old man, a classificatory 'grandmother' of Mr. Zekeri (i.e. a member of his father's mother's clan), who had lived there since the time of the first owner more than forty years earlier. Another old inhabitant had been the local representative or agent (*musigire*) of the Mubitokati proprietor. Neither he nor any of the remaining occupants was related in any way to the present owner. All the others had

[1] Though any *kibanja* holder could call himself a *mukama w'ekibanja*, it would be thought pretentious for a certificate-holder to do so unless he had at least one dependent household on his *kibanja*. In fact the term was usually restricted to the proprietors of *bibanja* which contained several 'tenant' householders.

come to settle there at various times, to live near relatives or friends, to be near their work in the town, or just because they liked the place. Four were members of one clan (though not closely related); two were 'brothers' in another clan, and two more were classificatory 'sister's sons' to the last two.[1] The rest were unrelated to anyone else on the *kibanja*. Five new house-holders had moved in during the previous five years.

Two points may be noted here. First, the householders who lived as tenants on the *kibanja* were not linked to the *kibanja* head by close, or indeed for the most part by any, genealogical ties: Bunyoro's *bibanja* lands were not at all comparable (as Banyoro sometimes claimed) with the *butaka* or 'clan lands' of the Baganda. *Kibanja* membership was not correlated with member-ship in any kind of kinship group. Nor were the tenant occupiers in recent times servants or retainers of the *mukama w'ekibanja*; they were just people who happened, or had chosen, to live there. Often they were people who had lived there before the area was made over as a *kibanja*, usually over their heads.

The second point is that in spite of this, and even though the *mukama w'ekibanja* might sometimes be an absentee or semi-absentee, the community which resided on the *kibanja* did possess a kind of social unity. In the case just considered this centred round the young 'master', who although he did not live on his *kibanja* often visited it. Not only were there (in this case) not the slightest signs of resentment on the part of any of the tenants, but in fact the older ones, particularly the two old men referred to above, identified themselves with the *kibanja*, regard-ing themselves (in a sense quite compatible with the *mukama w'ekibanja*'s proprietorship) as the 'owners' of the land it com-prised. 'We are the owners of the soil' (*'itwe abakama b'eitaka'*) they told me. It was plain that they felt a real personal stake in the land, and this feeling was shared by most of the other residents on the *kibanja*. In the event of any misdemeanour, such as a breach of proper respect or propriety, by any member of the *kibanja* community, these old men, together with (or even without) the young *mukama w'ekibanja* and any householder on the *kibanja* who wished to be present, would together sit in judgement on the case and could impose a penalty in meat or

---

[1] That is, their mothers were members of the clan to which the two 'brothers' belonged.

beer.[1] When I asked these old men what would happen if the present owner 'sold' his *kibanja* to someone else, they replied unanimously 'he could not sell the land outside his family; he would be ashamed'. In fact during my time in Bunyoro the sale of *kibanja* land was common, even though it was prohibited by the regulations. But it was in conformity with the values and attitudes associated with the *kibanja* system that when it was being discussed this fact should be either ignored or denied.

We may conclude, then, that in the 1950s a *kibanja* was not merely a topographic or even an economic unit; it was also a social unit. And the status of its head in relation to the *kibanja* community was very much more like that of a chief than that of a landlord. These points will become clearer when we consider in more detail what, in the 1950s, the heads of populated *bibanja* did, and how they were regarded.

The rights which the holder of a *kibanja* certificate held by law, stated in the certificate of occupancy itself, were very different from the rights which he held by custom. His certificate entitled him to undisturbed occupation of his *kibanja* so long as he continued to occupy and cultivate it, unless the land or any part of it were required for any work 'for the good of the country', in which case he was to be compensated for any damage to his crops or other improvements. The certificate conferred on him absolute ownership of all the buildings he erected, and all the trees and crops he planted. He could sell these to another native of Bunyoro, but he could not sell, transfer, or sublet any portion of the land itself. He could leave by will to another member of the tribe his rights under the certificate, and any improvements to the land. In the absence of a will, his heir by native custom was to succeed him. He could not collect any tribute or similar impost from any native living on the land, and the rights conferred by the certificate were to be cancelled by a discontinuation of occupation or cultivation by the certificate holder or his successor.

These were his legal rights. But by custom and general acknowledgement he possessed far more extensive rights over his land and the people on it, many of which were quite inconsistent with those he possessed by law. It was because of these

[1] The nature and functioning of informal tribunals of this type are discussed in Beattie 1957*b*.

rights, not because of the legal ones, that large tenanted *bibanja* continued to exist, and even increased both in number and size, after the 1933 reforms. The following were the more important of them. First I list the *kibanja* holder's rights *in rem*, over the land itself, as against other persons, and second, his rights *in personam*, over the people who occupied his land.

First, he had the right to retain his *kibanja* even though he neither occupied it nor cultivated any part of it. He believed that this right derived from purchase, and ultimately from the Mukama's gift either to him or to his predecessor; whatever the certificate said, it did not derive from his personal occupation and cultivation. If he wished, he could allow others to build and cultivate in his *kibanja*, and if he wanted to live elsewhere he could (though he need not) leave an agent (*musigire*) to look after his interests there. He might indeed leave it completely untenanted and uncultivated for years, though if he did so he would be wise to stake his claim by planting a few permanent trees, usually barkcloth trees (*mitoma*, a species of fig; *antiaris africana*). In the 1950s a number of *bibanja* were held in this way by men who were employed in far-away parts of the Protectorate, and they had no doubt that their claims would be admitted on their return.

Second, the *mukama w'ekibanja* had the right to sell his *kibanja* if he wanted to. Despite the conditions of tenure laid down in the certificate, few *kibanja* proprietors distinguished between the sale of the improvements on the land and the sale of the land itself. I noted above that the registration fee of 5 shillings was commonly taken to be the purchase price of the land. In this connection Banyoro almost invariably spoke of 'buying' (*kugura*) a *kibanja*. Practically all Nyoro writings, both official and unofficial, relating to the registration and transfer of *bibanja* use the language of sale and purchase; thus a county chief would minute on a recommended application '*aikirizibwe akigule*' ('he may be permitted to buy it'). In fact during the 1950s *bibanja*, especially in the neighbourhood of Hoima and Masindi, were changing hands for sums of from 500 to 2,000 shillings and more, though these transactions were usually kept secret.

Third, the *mukama w'ekibanja* claimed a right of ownership over all termite mounds, thatching grass, and timber on his *kibanja* (though he might allow his tenants to make use of them),

and he claimed, also, a front leg of any game animal killed on his land. He also regarded any deposit of potter's clay or building sand as his property (though in the 1950s this claim was beginning to be challenged in the courts), and other people could be refused or have to pay him for access to them.

So much for the *mukama w'ekibanja*'s rights over the land itself: what of his rights over the people who lived on it? First, he had the right to accept or refuse peasants from elsewhere who wished to settle or cultivate on his *kibanja*. In the event of all or most cultivable land in Bunyoro becoming absorbed into *bibanja*, this might well have become a source of considerable profit to the *bakama b'ebibanja*. But except in the neighbourhood of the two main towns there was—and still is—no real shortage of land in Bunyoro, and I heard of no instance where money or goods had been demanded from prospective tenants, though occasional gifts would certainly be expected. There were nevertheless many *kibanja* holders who although they had more land than they could use themselves, none the less refused to allow other people to cultivate it.

Second, the *kibanja* holder had the right to expel a settler from his *kibanja*. But public opinion would not have approved such expulsion unless good cause were shown, for example being a particularly troublesome person like a thief or (the most usual ground) a sorcerer (*murogo*). If the settler and his ancestors had been settled on the land for many years, perhaps, as was frequently the case, before the present *kibanja* holder obtained his rights over it, it would be a good deal more difficult to evict him on any ground except sorcery. None the less such evictions sometimes took place.

Third, he had the right to impose conditions on his tenants with regard to the type of building which they might erect on their holdings in his *kibanja*. Many *kibanja* holders refused to allow their tenants to build permanent houses with corrugated-iron roofs, as to do this might be taken as implying a claim to permanency of tenure and also, in some cases, to a superiority of status which might come into conflict with that of the *kibanja* holder himself. Not all *kibanja* holders imposed this condition, but at least in the 1950s many did, and most tenants accepted it without protest. A tenant might also be forbidden to plant

a permanent crop such as coffee, or even a banana plantation, on his holding, for the same reason.

Fourth, the *mukama w'ekibanja* had a somewhat undefined right to certain goods and services from his tenants. Although he could no longer exact *busuru* (commuted tribute) from the people on his *kibanja*, as he could before 1933, he still received from them presents of bunches of bananas, jars of beer, and other goods, including a bowl of edible termites during the swarming season. Banyoro sometimes stressed to me that these gifts were voluntary; they were brought 'because of friendship'. No doubt they were often regarded in this way. But it is significant that they should be made, and that they should have become in some measure institutionalized. It should be added that since gift-giving usually implies some past or future return, these transactions involved the recognition that the tenants themselves had certain claims on their *mukama w'ekibanja*. I return to this theme below. No doubt, also, the giving of gifts from time to time contributed to the social cohesion which bound the *kibanja* head or his representative and his tenant settlers into a single community. The peasant occupiers of a *kibanja* might even cultivate a field for their *mukama w'ekibanja*; they said that if they did so they would receive food or beer in recompense for their labour. But they did not cultivate because of the food or beer, but, quite explicitly, because the field was the *mukama w'ekibanja*'s.

Fifth (and now the close connection between land-holding and the possession and exercise of political authority begins to become plain), the proprietor of a populated *kibanja* had a right to be respected and obeyed by the people who lived on his *kibanja*. As a *mukama w'ekibanja* he was a person of importance, and as such he claimed a superior and authoritarian status. His claim was generally acknowledged by the community at large, and it was often emphatically expressed by himself. One large *kibanja* owner (significantly a Mubito) wrote in 1948 to the district commissioner, in response to a complaint that he was oppressing his tenants: 'I do not want trouble with them; they can continue digging provided that they understand that we are the owners of the *kibanja*, and consequently they should co-operate with us.' The occupants of a *kibanja* should 'hear' or 'listen to' (*kuhurra*) their *mukama w'ekibanja*, just as a subject

should 'listen' to his chief; they were 'his' people, and were so referred to both in casual conversation and in official correspondence. In a court case heard in 1953 (Nyoro Central Court Case No. 34/53), a *kibanja* owner was charged by one of his tenants with (literally) 'buying' him, together with others, in his *kibanja* without their knowledge, and then forbidding them to cultivate.[1] The court's judgement, which was in favour of the *kibanja* holder, included the words 'and he is instructed to obey the orders of the *mukama w'ekibanja*'.[2] No specific orders were referred to; it was not implied that the tenant should follow the *kibanja* holder's orders only in respect of cultivation, rather that he should do so in all matters.

In another case (Central Court Case No. 18/47) a tenant, who was ordered to uproot a banana plantation in a *kibanja* which was the property of a man who was both a Mubito and a county chief, argued that he had owned and cultivated this plot since long before it was allocated as a *kibanja*. This was not disputed, and the plaintiff won his case (since if the *mukama w'ekibanja* wished the bananas removed he should have brought the matter of his tenant's disobedience to a lower court, rather than take the law into his own hands). But he was none the less ordered not to replant his bananas in the disputed area, and told that in future he should 'obey the orders of the *mukama w'ekibanja*'. Not unnaturally he wished to appeal, on the ground that to be refused permission to cultivate was tantamount to being expelled from the *kibanja*. But as he had 'won' the case there was nothing he could do about it. In these as in most Nyoro social contexts the superordination–subordination relationship was diffuse, rather than specific. The *mukama w'ekibanja* was seen as a superior; he was a kind of chief, a *munyoro*, and his tenant was *ipso facto* a subject. In such a relationship an attitude of respect and obedience in all contexts was appropriate and expected.

Sixth and finally, the *mukama w'ekibanja* had the right, and indeed the duty, to act with other householders in his *kibanja* as arbitrator and judge in the settlement of disputes between his peasant occupants. Even major matters would be taken to him

---

[1] In Runyoro, '*okumugurra omu kibanja hamu n'abandi omunsita, kandi natutanga kulima*'.

[2] '*Kandi naragirwa okuhondera ebiragiro bya mukama w'ekibanja.*'

before being passed on to the nearest official chief, for he was the 'ruler' (*mulemi*) of the *kibanja*. The sort of matters which he would take the major part in settling would include cases of fighting, theft, adultery, accusations of sorcery, and trespass by goats or fowls. The tribunals which he convened could apportion guilt and impose a penalty. Of course he would not sit in judgement alone (though he could take administrative action without consultation); he sat with other householders of the *kibanja*, perhaps even with a prominent outsider, such as the head of a neighbouring *kibanja*. He could himself accuse any tenant who cursed him or behaved rudely or abusively in his presence; anyone who was a rude, lawless person, a *muhole*. Such an offender might be 'fined' a goat and four large pots of beer; this was the standard penalty but it was often reduced.[1] At an appointed time the goat would be slaughtered and eaten, and the beer drunk, by as many members of the *kibanja* community as wished to attend, in particular by the offender himself (who acted as host) and by the other persons most directly concerned. These usages stressed not only the high value placed on the cohesion of the *kibanja* community as a social unit, but equally the obligation on the part of the tenants to 'hear' and obey the *kibanja* head. He and his tenants saw their relationship as being of the same kind as the traditional relationship between a chief and his subjects.

The ways in which, in the middle of the twentieth century, owners of large *bibanja* justified their continued possession of the authority implied in being a *mukama w'ekibanja* (which the more educated of them knew well has no legal basis), are revealing. Sometimes, and typically, they laid claim to a traditional right to rule over others, a right founded in their membership of a ruling class. 'We are the proper governors of the country, and it is right that we should continue to rule', a Mubito land-owner (not an official chief) told me. It is noteworthy that in this context he spoke of the status of *mukama w'ekibanja* in terms of 'ruling' rather than of ownership; like other proprietors of populated *bibanja* he saw himself as a kind of chief. Sometimes

---

[1] I referred above to the informal tribunals of which this is one type. The payment exacted is only very inaccurately described as a 'fine', since it was consumed and enjoyed by all concerned, and the aim was to rehabilitate rather than to punish. See Beattie 1957*b*.

it was said that it was best for ignorant cultivators to have 'masters' to take care of them, and to look after their true interests: without the supervision, guidance, and control of the *bakama b'ebibanja*, it was suggested, these unenlightened peasants would quickly ruin their land by bad cultivation. I asked a chief who obtained a *kibanja* in 1930, with three homesteads already established on it, what these people thought of their sudden change of status from independent cultivators to dependent settlers on another man's land. He replied: 'I didn't know them and they didn't know me. But they were very happy to get a *mukama w'ekibanja* to rule over them.'

Some *kibanja* holders claimed that the majority of their tenants were old family servants or retainers. In fact this was rarely, if ever, the case, but it is significant that many people should still have thought of the situation in these terms. Others, even less plausibly, attempted to assimilate the *kibanja* system to a presumed earlier system of clan or lineage tenure. The original localized lineages were broken up, they said, during the wars with Kabarega at the end of the last century, and their members were scattered widely over the country and beyond it. After peace was restored, those who returned found that their patrimonial lands had been occupied by others, so they sought, and were granted, new allocations as *bibanja*. There is no evidence that anything of this kind occurred, though it is possible that something like it may have taken place in a few cases. The *kibanja* system of land-holding, like the notions of 'chiefship' and 'government' with which it was so closely associated, stood in clear opposition to any system of clan or lineage tenure.

Despite the evident disabilities of peasant tenantship, in the 1950s only a minority of the tenants of occupied *bibanja* thought of themselves as being oppressed or ill-treated. There were complaints, as we have seen, but these referred to particular abuses, not to the system itself, and they were surprisingly infrequent. For the tenant, too, had his acknowledged rights. He had, to begin with, a right to reasonable security of tenure, provided that he was not a sorcerer or otherwise undesirable, and he could pass on this right to his heir. And he could, of course, move elsewhere if he wanted to. He might even become a *kibanja* holder himself (though unless he were an influential

and important person he would be unlikely to obtain a large tenanted *kibanja*), if he could find a piece of available uncertificated land elsewhere, pay the registration fee of 5 shillings, and make a few small presents to the local chiefs through whom his application for a certificate would be submitted. He had, of course, no right to take out a certificate of occupancy over land which he cultivated in the *kibanja* of another, even though he and his forebears had occupied this land for generations. This fact occasionally gave rise to complaint and even to litigation, for as we have noted, it frequently happened that a wealthy or important person was given a *kibanja* in which peasant cultivators were already settled, without any consultation with these persons. Peasants were not always as complaisant as the chief's remark quoted above might suggest, though they usually were. If one of them had himself been contemplating taking out a right of occupancy over his plot, his right to do so was, of course, permanently negatived by the grant of an overriding right to another.

But there were some counterbalancing advantages in tenantship. In the past, at least, tenants looked for the protection of their *mukama w'ekibanja* from the exactions in service and tribute of other powerful persons, in more recent times of the government chiefs. Such demands could be for labour on roads or public buildings, for provisions for visiting dignitaries such as senior chiefs or government officials, and for certain other services, and the occupants of a *kibanja* expected their *kibanja* head to see that these burdens fell on them as lightly and fairly as possible. In 1931 a government officer reported that powerful chiefs almost universally shielded their private tenants from labour and other demands, a procedure which evidently imposed a heavier burden on those who were protected by less influential masters. These obligations were, of course, less regarded in the 1950s than they were when chiefs were dependent for practically the whole of their income on the *busuru* they collected on their private and public estates. But the *kibanja* head still functioned in many situations as an intermediary between the people on his *kibanja* and the lower grades of government chiefs. Government instructions affecting his people were ordinarily conveyed through him, and he summoned the people on his *kibanja* to hear and discuss them.

In the 1950s most Banyoro saw the relationship between the *kibanja* holder and the people settled on his *kibanja* as one of mutual though asymmetrical interdependence. The relationship was a personal one; it was more like that between members of a large household than like a purely economic landlord–tenant relationship. 'The *mukama w'ekibanja* is like a household head' ('*omukama w'ekibanja nka nyineka*'), Banyoro told me; and just as a household must have a head, so must the *kibanja* community. Like the members of a household, the occupants of the *kibanja* regarded themselves, at any rate in theory, as bound together by mutual loyalty and common interest. Certainly in many *bibanja* known to me they composed a group very conscious of its unity and identity.

It should be said, too, that at least in the 1950s few Nyoro peasants were individualists in the Western sense; there was no feeling that because some people were *bakama b'ebibanja* therefore everybody ought to be. The most important thing was to occupy a proper and recognized place, at whatever level, in one's local community, and the occupants of a *kibanja*, together with its *mukama*, were seen as composing such a group, at least ideally. Every group has to have a leader, especially in Bunyoro, and for most people the natural leader of the inhabitants of a *kibanja* was its *mukama*.

The *mukama w'ekibanja*, then, was more like a chief than a landlord. In fact he *was* a sort of chief; no less than the official chiefs he possessed authority over people, and indeed in some respects he conformed more closely to the traditional Nyoro idea of what a chief should be than the official chiefs did. For one thing, as an 'unofficial' he was not required, during the Protectorate period, to conform to Western, bureaucratic standards of efficiency and political morality, a requirement which, as we shall see in the next chapter, gave rise to serious problems for the official chiefs. And, paradoxically, the larger *bakama b'ebibanja* were often, indeed usually, more rather than less 'chiefly' in the traditional sense than members of the lower ranks of paid government chiefs, the village headmen or *batongole*. A man who possessed a large *kibanja* of, say, ten or more households usually did so either because he was a member of the ruling Bito family or closely related to it, or of another chiefly family with a tradition of ruling, or because he was sufficiently

important, wealthy, and well-connected to lay claim to such high status. Such a person thought of himself, and was generally regarded, as altogether superior to a *mutongole* chief who might have no *kibanja* or only a small one, and who received only a tiny salary (about 25 or 30 shillings a month in the 1950s).These officials, who were generally extremely hard-working and conscientious, and were responsible for the day-to-day administration of settled areas containing up to 200 households, sometimes more, tended to be looked down upon as persons of small importance equally by the old élites of Babito and other 'landed' families, and by the new one, of clerks, school-teachers, shopkeepers, and so on. Certainly they were not regarded as chiefs (*banyoro*) of equivalent standing to the large *kibanja* owners. I return in Chapter 9 to some of the problems raised by this state of affairs from the chiefs' point of view.

A further advantage which the *mukama w'ekibanja* enjoyed *vis-à-vis* the official chiefs was that he was not 'transferable', as the government chiefs were: he was (or was thought to be) bound to the people on his *kibanja* by permanent links of social and political interest, expressed through both a personal stake in the land, and a close personal relationship with every one of his peasant occupiers.

So in the 1950s the *mukama w'ekibanja* played a role in socially stratified Bunyoro which was not wholly filled by the lowest grade of government chiefs. In fact he sometimes found himself in opposition to these officials. The relatively assured status and 'squirearchal' prestige of the large unofficial *kibanja* proprietors was sometimes resented by the salaried government chiefs, especially those of the lower ranks who possessed no or only small *bibanja*. This feeling of inferiority was reinforced by the growth of the idea of private property in land, for it was thought that if a system of freehold tenure should be introduced the large *kibanja* holders would be the main beneficiaries. It was widely held (and not only by the *bakama b'ebibanja*) that it was inappropriate for government chiefs to exercise direct authority over peasants living in the *bibanja* of others; the proper authorities in the *bibanja* were the 'masters' of these *bibanja*. Interference by government chiefs in the internal affairs of the *bibanja* was often thought to be an unwarrantable intrusion.

The central fact is this. In traditional Nyoro thought everyone who possessed personal rights over land and over the people who live on that land was *ipso facto* a chief, and conversely everyone who was a chief possessed, or should possess, such rights. So what the development of the *kibanja* system over the first fifty years of this century implied was not simply a proliferation of land rights, of estates and 'landlords'; it was rather, and primarily, a proliferation of chiefs. I noted that the first *bibanja* were private estates given to serving or retired official chiefs for their comfort and support. These chiefs were no less 'chiefs' on their private estates than they were, or had formerly been, on their official estates. Indeed their authority on these private lands was in some ways greater than it was on their official estates, for they saw themselves as holding it permanently and as the Mukama's gift, to be enjoyed by themselves and their descendants for ever, and not (as in the case of their official estates) temporarily and *ex officio*. When grants of *kibanja* land began increasingly to be made to persons who were not chiefs or ex-chiefs, but who were rather friends, retainers, or ex-servants of the Mukama, or other 'important persons who were well known', what was being dispensed was not just a parcel of land rights, it was rather the status of *munyoro* or chief. What the process involved was on the one hand an increasing individualization of the land-holding of chiefs *qua* chiefs, and on the other hand an immense accession to the chiefly class. In 1933 an administrative officer recorded that the number of *bakungu* (minor chiefs) was far too large, and was continually increasing with the increasing grants of *bibanja*.[1] 'Every *kibanja* holder and every *kibanja* headman', he wrote, 'is a *mukungu*, even if there is only one other tenant.'[2] What was emerging was not a distinction between chiefs and landlords; it was rather a distinction between two different kinds of chiefs, the salaried official ones, and the proprietors of tenanted *bibanja*.

[1] The term *bakungu* had now come to be applied, as it still was in the 1950s, to the lowest grade of recognized chiefs, the *batongole* or village headmen, and not, as in traditional times, to the great county chiefs.

[2] A. I. Richards describes a similar 'extraordinary multiplication of minor officials' in Buganda. The statement of one of her elderly informants that 'a man always likes to have some people under him, even if they are only a few' (Richards 1966, p. 61) would have found a heartfelt echo in Bunyoro.

An obvious solution to this awkward dualism was to merge the two categories of chiefs in one, and the pre-1933 proliferation of minor official chiefs (*bakungu*) evidently represented an attempt to find a solution along these lines. But the uneconomic multiplication of minor chiefs was an anomaly in the new, salaried, African 'civil service' the development of which was official administrative policy. It was, accordingly, sharply checked by the 1933 Agreement, which provided that chiefs should receive salaries, not tribute, and which provided for drastic reductions in their numbers.

The tendency towards assimilation none the less continued, though in the opposite direction. Even though *kibanja*-holders could no longer claim to be, *ipso facto*, official chiefs, official chiefs could, and did, seek to acquire the prestige-conferring status of *kibanja* holder. From 1933 onward, when a man was appointed to an official chiefship one of the first things he did was to seek to acquire a populated *kibanja* if he did not already possess one, and to extend the boundaries of his present one, if he did possess one. Without a *kibanja* he was not in the fullest sense a chief. The figures which follow show a close relationship between the holding of political office and *kibanja* proprietorship. They derive in part from information submitted in 1953 by the chiefs themselves about themselves, in reply to a questionnaire dealing mainly with their career-histories, and partly from the information gained in respect of the broad sample of populated *bibanja* referred to earlier in this chapter.

Even from the first of these sources, the chiefs' response to questions about their own holdings, it was plain that the great majority of official chiefs at all levels possessed populated *bibanja*. It was also evident that in most cases these were obtained, or their extent increased, after their recipient's appointment to political office or promotion to higher rank. Predictably, however, the figures relating to the populations on their *bibanja* submitted by those chiefs who replied to the questionnaire were understated. Most of the senior chiefs were by this time well aware of the government's concern about the proliferation of tenanted estates, and they saw no point in drawing attention to the extent of their own holdings. On the basis of figures later obtained it became plain that in some cases they had denied

possessing a *kibanja* at all, in others they had omitted to enter the numbers of their dependent households, and in yet others they had greatly understated them. The second set of returns, in respect of all the *bibanja* in the sample areas, were considerably more accurate, though still probably underestimated. They were submitted mainly by the lower grades of chiefs (i.e. 'parish' chiefs and village headmen), in respect of all the *bibanja* in their areas. These *bibanja* often included those of senior chiefs serving in other parts of the country, which the lower chiefs concerned had no vested interest in concealing. Further, their own personal *bibanja*, where they possessed any, were often outside their official areas, and so were reported on by somebody else. In any case, the lower chiefs' holdings were very much smaller than those of the two higher grades of chiefs (the sub-county and county chiefs), and so they felt less reluctance in disclosing them: also, they were less sensitive than the higher and better educated chiefs to official misgivings about these 'estates'.

Considering, first, the chiefs' personal returns, these showed that in 1953 at least 22 of the 25 sub-county chiefs possessed *bibanja*. According to these returns, the average number of dependent households per *kibanja* was 7, but the second set of returns referred to above showed that this figure (which is the one I gave in an earlier publication on the *kibanja* system)[1] was approximately half of the correct one.[2] Of 42 'parish' chiefs (*miruka*) who submitted information on their careers, 34, that is, just over 80 per cent, possessed *bibanja*, the average number of tenant householders per *kibanja*-holding *muruka* chief being just over 6. Out of a smaller but still fairly representative sample of 15 *batongole* or *bakungu* chiefs (paid village headmen, the

---

[1] In Beattie 1954*b*.

[2] It may be useful to tabulate the two sets of figures together for easy comparison:

Chiefs' personal returns (earlier figures)

Out of 25 sub-county chiefs, 22 owned *bibanja*, with an average of 7 tenant households.

	42 'parish' chiefs,	34	,,	,,	,,	,,	6	,,
,,	15 village headmen,	9	,,	,,	,,	,,	5	,,

Populated bibanja *returns* (later figures)

3 *bibanja* owned by county chiefs had an average of 54 tenant households.

12	,,	,,	,, sub-county ,,	,,	,,	,,	,, 15	,,	,,
24	,,	,,	,, 'parish'	,,	,,	,,	,, 7	,,	,,
61	,,	,,	,, village headmen ,,	,,	,,	,,	,, 6	,,	,,

lowest category of official chiefs) 9 possessed *bibanja*, with an average of 5 dependent households on each.

Turning now to the second set of returns submitted by the lower chiefs in respect of all the *bibanja* in their areas, out of 369 populated *bibanja*,[1] 113 (just over 30 per cent) were shown as having been allotted to serving or retired official chiefs of one or other rank. This was the largest specified category of recipients of populated *bibanja*.[2] Also, government chiefs received *bibanja* with the largest resident populations. Thus for the 100 chiefs for whom detailed information was available the average number of tenant households per populated *kibanja* was 9; for all the other categories of recipients combined it was 5·5. The figures are, moreover, sharply graded according to chiefly rank:

Rank of chief	Number in sample	Average number of dependent households per kibanja
County	3	54
Sub-county	12	15
'Parish'	24	7
Village headmen	61	6

There was thus a striking difference between the sizes of the *bibanja* held by *saza* and *gombolola* chiefs, and the sizes of those held by the *miruka* and *batongole* chiefs. This is correlated with other important differences between these grades of chiefs, which I discuss in the next chapter; here I need only say that the difference is associated with a marked difference in social status between the two higher and the two lower grades.

Another significant finding was that the populations of the *bibanja* acquired by the county and sub-county chiefs had decreased since they had received them, while the populations of the *bibanja* acquired by the two lower grades of chiefs had

[1] Returns were submitted in respect of 572 populated *bibanja* (p. 177 above), but details regarding the status of the original recipient were given for only 369 of them. Hence the smaller sample used here.

[2] The (very much smaller) proportions of some other categories of recipient are of interest. Apart from a large and unspecified residual category comprising Bito, prominent cultivators, and other 'persons of importance' (totalling 43 per cent), ex-servants or ex-retainers of the Mukama accounted for 9 per cent; independent traders, craftsmen, etc., 8 per cent; members of various government departments, 6 per cent; and school-teachers, 4 per cent.

increased since they had received them.[1] This strongly suggests
that the higher grades of chiefs tended to receive *bibanja* which
already contained substantial populations, while the lower
grades received *bibanja* with few (in some cases probably no)
dependent households, to which they then proceeded to attract
settlers.

Though complete accuracy cannot be claimed for any of
these figures, they do, I believe, show a significant correlation
between the holding of political office and the proprietorship of
populated *bibanja*. In 1953 approximately 17 per cent of the
total tax-paying population of Bunyoro were *kibanja* holders
(and a still smaller proportion held populated *bibanja*). But no
less than 70 per cent of the sample of chiefs for whom information was available possessed *bibanja*. And they owned at least
30 per cent of the populated *bibanja* in the country. It is plain,
also, that the higher a chief's rank the more likely he was to
possess a *kibanja*, and the more dependent 'settlers' he was likely
to have. The identity, in Nyoro thinking, between political
office on the one hand, and the possession of private and personal rights over an area of land and its peasant occupants on
the other, is clearly demonstrated by the history of the beginnings and development in Bunyoro of the *kibanja* system.

I conclude this chapter by asking why, although the 1933
reforms succeeded in some of their aims, they quite failed to
achieve their primary objective of securing for every cultivator
the free and undisturbed occupancy of the land he cultivated, and
the right to obtain a certificate confirming this. The answer,
which is largely implicit in what has already been said, is four-
fold. First, the system of populated landed estates for the ruling
classes and their associates, which was historically based in the
traditional identity between political authority and the holding
of personal rights in land, and which supported the privilege

[1] The figures deriving from my second sample are as follows:

Rank of chief	No. in sample	Total dependent households when acquired	Total dependent households in 1955	Approximate increase or decrease
County and sub-county	15	347	276	20% decrease
'Parish' and village headmen	85	546	711	30% increase

and prestige of an aristocracy whose rights had not yet begun
to be seriously questioned, was evidently too deeply ingrained
in Nyoro thought to be eradicated simply by promulgating a
new and very different set of rules. Second, the hope had been
held out to the Nyoro chiefs for many years that freehold tenure
might some day be approved, as it had been in Buganda. If this
should happen, it was thought that the possession of a large
kibanja would create a prescriptive right to freehold over the
same area. Third, the persons who were entrusted with the task
of introducing and implementing the new system, necessarily
with only limited supervision, were the Mukama and his chiefs,
and they were the very people who had the greatest vested
interest in the old system of landed estates, which they regarded
as their proper right and prerogative. The 'landed gentry' were
in effect asked to dispossess themselves, and it can hardly be
a matter for surprise that instead of doing so they attempted to
mould the new system to fit the old pattern. Finally, and not
least important, at least up to the 1950s the people of Bunyoro
as a whole, peasants as well as proprietors, acquiesced in the
kibanja system: there were complaints but, as we saw, these were
of individual abuses rather than against the system itself. And
no legislation is likely to be effective, at least in the absence of
any effective means of enforcing it, unless a considerable proportion of the people it concerns have some interest in seeing
that the rules deriving from it are obeyed.

APPENDIX I

UGANDA   No. ......

BUNYORO-KITARA

CERTIFICATE OF RIGHT OF OCCUPANCY
OF A NATIVE OF BUNYORO

WITH the approval of His Excellency the Governor the Native Government of Bunyoro recognises the right of .... to the occupancy of the garden cultivated by him at

.... Kibanja (Garden).

.... Omugongo.

.... Gombolola.

.... Saza.

This certificate is granted subject to the following conditions:

(1) The person named above, or his successor, is entitled to the undisturbed enjoyment of the land described above, subject to the requirements of condition (7) below.

(2) The person named above, or his successor, is the absolute owner of all buildings erected by him, all trees planted by him, and all crops cultivated by him on the land.

(3) No tribute or similar impost may be collected from any native living on the land.

(4) The person named above, or his successor, cannot sell, transfer or sub-let any portion of the land; but on giving up his tenancy he may, upon giving notice of his intention to the Native Government of Bunyoro, sell the buildings, trees and crops which are his property, to another native of Bunyoro.

(5) The person named above, or his successor, may leave by will to another member of the tribe his rights under this certificate and any other improvements, or, in the absence of a will, his heir by native custom will be entitled to succeed him.

(6) The person named above, or his successor, shall pay to the Native Government of Bunyoro when due, such taxes, dues, and other charges for which he may by law or with the consent of the Governor be held responsible.

(7) The person named above, or his successor, may be disturbed in his occupancy, if necessary to allow of the construction of any works for the good of the country (for example, roads, railways, schools, dispensaries) in which case the person named above, or his successor, will be compensated for all damage to his garden.

(8) The rights conferred by this certificate will be cancelled by a discontinuance of cultivation or occupation of the land by the person named above or his successor.

SIGNED on behalf of the Native Government of Bunyoro.

....

Two members

....

Signed   ....
            District Commissioner

Date   ....   Paid Shs.   ....

APPENDIX 2

APPLICATION FORM   *Land Form No. 1.*

Application for issue of a certificate of occupancy.

Name of applicant (in capitals) ....

Description of holding applied for ....

        Ekyalo...   Mutala...

        Gombolola..   Saza.......................................

                  Signature or mark of applicant

Date ....

Recommendation of Gombolola Chief.

    I have examined the area and I certify that the above applicant
is cultivating the land applied for.

                    Signed...

Date ....   Title   ....

Recommendation of Saza Chief.

                    Signed...

Date ....   Title   ....

Katikiro's Remarks   Signed...

Date ....   KATIKIRO WA BUNYORO–
                    KITARA.

To District Commissioner,

    Approved.   Signed...

Date ....   OMUKAMA WA BUNYORO–
                    KITARA.

Number and date of Certificate ....

    Passed to Omukama

Date ....

                          Signature of D.C.

9

THE MODERN TERRITORIAL CHIEFSHIP

IN Chapter 6 I gave some account of traditional chiefship in Bunyoro, and in the last chapter I discussed the identification, in Nyoro thought, of political authority with proprietory rights over land, and the enduring significance of this identification. I now go on to consider in more detail the Nyoro chiefly hierarchy as it was when I was in Bunyoro: in this chapter I discuss the kinds of men who became chiefs, in the next I describe the kind of work they did, and the ways in which they were regarded both by their Banyoro subjects and by their European masters.

We noted in Chapter 2 that in 1953 there were four grades of official territorial chiefs; 4 county (*saza*) chiefs, 25 sub-county (*gombolola*) chiefs, 65 'parish' chiefs (*miruka*), and about 161 village headmen (*batongole* or *bakungu*).[1] Each of these last officials was in charge of an area of about two or three square miles, which might contain anything up to forty or fifty scattered households, and a hundred or so people.

The pyramid of Nyoro native government administration sixteen years ago is represented in Fig. 2. Bugahya county was larger than any of the others, and it contained almost half of Bunyoro's total population (it will be recalled that the former Buhaguzi county had been absorbed into it in 1938).

Territorial chiefship in Bunyoro has not in recent years been hereditary, at least in principle, though it is said that in traditional times a great *mukungu* chief (then the equivalent of a

---

[1] The four vernacular terms were adopted from Luganda; as used in everyday (as opposed to official) Runyoro they are *bamasaza* (sing. *omwe'isaza*), *bamabohorra* (sing. *omwe'ibohorra*), *bemiruka* (sing. *owomuruka*), and *batongole* or *bakungu* (sing. *mutongole* or *mukungu*). The conventional English translations of these terms which I use here are by no means exact; in particular, 'parishes' have nothing to do with churches, being simply administrative divisions of sub-counties, and the area under the control of a 'village headman' is a scattered area of settlement, not a 'village' in the sense of a compact group of dwellings. But the official English usage had become well established, and I adopt it here.

modern county chief, and not, as in later times, the lowest rank of official chief) would have expected a son to succeed him. And the titled 'crown-wearers' (*bajwara kondo*) passed on their crowns to their heirs, together with (at least in some cases) the populated 'estates' that went with them. During the colonial period chiefship certainly tended to run in families, especially at the senior grades; a young man who had grown up in a county or sub-county chief's home would already know something about the job, and, no less important, he would be personally known to other senior chiefs, perhaps even to the Mukama himself and his advisers.

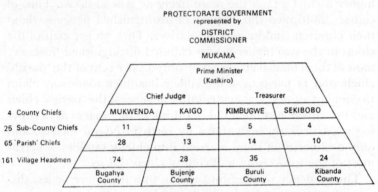

FIG. 2. The pyramid of local government in 1953.

It was plain from an inquiry into the backgrounds and career histories of chiefs which I carried out in 1952–3[1] that most chiefs were in fact sons or other close relatives of former chiefs or other 'important persons'. In this connection it should be remembered that the word *munyoro*, which I translate 'chief', applied in a general sense to any eminent person, for example to a ritual or domestic functionary in the king's palace, or to the proprietor of a populated *kibanja*; in its everyday use it was not restricted

[1] In association with similar research being undertaken at that time among some other East African peoples, under the aegis of the East African Institute of Social Research at Makerere College. For the detailed results of these inquiries, see Beattie 1960*b*. Questionnaires were distributed to all the chiefs, and I received detailed responses from all the county and sub-county chiefs, from 41 'parish' chiefs (that is, from 65 per cent of them), and from 18 village headmen (11 per cent). Many of these were followed up by interviews. Though the samples are less than adequate in respect, at least, of the village headmen, many of whom were scarcely literate, I believe that some valid conclusions can be drawn from them.

to the official chiefs.[1] Also a significant number of chiefs were related by marriage to chiefs or other distinguished persons. But there was a marked difference in these respects between the two upper ranks of chiefs, the county and sub-county chiefs, and the two lower grades of 'parish' chiefs and village headmen (we shall see that they differ significantly in other ways too). In fact all of the county chiefs and over 80 per cent of the sub-county chiefs claimed chiefs or other distinguished relatives among their paternal kin, while only 61 per cent of the 'parish' chiefs and 55 per cent of the village headmen did so.[2]

Again, chiefs tended to marry into chiefly families, and the higher a chief's rank the more likely he was to do so. This, of course, multiplied the number of distinguished persons whom their children could claim as relatives. Thus 76 per cent of the chiefs in the two higher grades claimed distinguished 'in-laws', most of them official chiefs, while only 44 per cent of the 'parish' chiefs and 11 per cent of the village headmen made any claim to eminent affines. It is evident that in general the 'parish' chiefs and the village headmen did not think of themselves as occupying a particularly high status by birth in Nyoro society, and only a minority of them married into chiefly families, whereas most of the sub-county and county chiefs did so.

The tendency of chiefships to run in a few more or less distinguished families can be illustrated by reference to the genealogies of ex-county chief Petero Rwakaikara of the Bamwoli clan, county chief Ezekieri Mucwa of the Bapina clan and, at a rather lower level, 'parish' chief Yosiya Baligonzaki of the Bakurungu clan. Rwakaikara was a son of Paulo Byabacwezi, a very well known chief and a man of strong personality, who remained in Bunyoro and was taken by the Baganda when Mukama Kabarega fled to Lango district in the late 1890s.[3] He (Byabacwezi)

---

[1] See p. 131 above. Even more generally, the term Munyoro is of course applied to any member of the Nyoro people.

[2] The percentages given here and later in this chapter are percentages of my sample which, as noted above, was complete in respect of the county and sub-county chiefs, but not in the case of the two lower grades.

[3] As Mr. Rwakaikara explained to me, 'if some chiefs hadn't stayed behind in Bunyoro the country would have been destroyed'. It almost was anyway, as we saw in Chapter 4. Byabacwezi is said to have dominated the young king Anderea Duhaga during the early years of his reign, lording it in the palace and riding around on a horse while Duhaga occupied inferior accommodation elsewhere. There is a photograph of him facing p. 195 in Fisher.

afterwards acted as regent, and later as chief adviser to Mukama Kitehimbwa and his successor Duhaga. Of Petero Rwakaikara's eight patrilateral half-brothers two were also county chiefs (Anderea Buterre and Zakayo Jawe), one was a sub-county chief, and a fourth was a 'parish' chief. Two of his paternal uncles had been sub-county chiefs and one a 'parish' chief in the early years of the century. His paternal grandfather, Nyakamatura, had been a county chief under Kabarega, and his paternal great-grandfather Mwijoro had been a military leader under Kabarega's predecessor, Kamurasi.

Ezekieri Mucwa, the county chief of Bugahya in 1953, was a full brother of Zerubaberi Mukidi, who was a sub-county chief at the same time. Their father Zedekiya Rwakaikara had served as a chief in Lango and Karamoja districts, and two patrilateral second cousins had held senior chiefships in Bunyoro and Lango. Two of Mr. Mucwa's mother's patrilateral half-brothers had been county chiefs in Bunyoro; his mother's full brother had been a village headman. His wife was the daughter of a 'parish' chief.

Yosiya Baligonzaki, a 'parish' chief in Bugahya county, was the son of a 'parish' chief and his father's brothers were both village headmen. Two of his father's patrilateral first cousins had also been minor chiefs. Two of his paternal great-uncles had also been chiefs (at roughly the equivalent of sub-county chiefdom level) in Kabarega's time. His maternal grandfather had been a county chief in Masindi, Bunyoro, and two of his maternal great-uncles had held minor posts in the Mukama's palace. Yosiya's family was by no means as eminent as those of Rwakaikara or Mucwa, who belonged to two of the most outstanding chiefly families in the country apart from the Babito. But it was moderately distinguished none the less, and at least some of its members would be known to the senior chiefs, possibly to the Mukama himself.

I referred in Chapter 5 to Bito representation in the ranks of the official chiefs, and remarked that there were fewer Bito chiefs than one might have expected, in view of their numbers and eminence. In fact they were hardly more strongly represented in proportion to their numbers than several other clans. In 1953 one county chief (an elderly man on the verge of retirement) was a Mubito, actually a son of Mukama Kabarega and

a half-brother of the reigning Mukama, and there were four Babito among the twenty-five sub-county chiefs, all of whom claimed actual genealogical relationship with the king within the past four generations. In my sample of forty-one 'parish' chiefs there were two Babito, neither of them with any known genealogical connection with the ruling line. I knew of no Mubito among the village headmen. These relationships are indicated in Fig. 3.

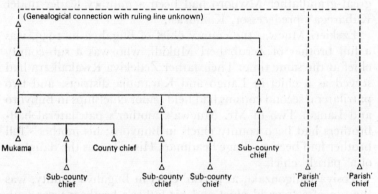

FIG. 3. Representation of Babito in Bunyoro Native Government, 1953.

In fact, among the county and sub-county chiefs taken together there were slightly more Bito chiefs than there were chiefs of any other single clan (and there had been a number of important Bito chiefs in the past),[1] but this was probably partly due to the fact that there were slightly more educated Babito available for appointment to the higher chiefships than there were members of other clans.[2] All of the five Babito in the two higher grades of chiefships had had some secondary education, comparing favourably in this respect with the average for these grades. There was no evidence of any tendency to appoint Babito to higher chiefships just because they were Babito. We

[1] For example H. K. Karubanga (the author of *Bukya Nibwira*), whom I knew as a very old man, had been a county chief for many years. He was the great-great-grandson of former Mukama Nyamutukura, and the reigning Mukama's fourth cousin. Another Mubito ex-chief was Kosiya Labwoni, grandson of Kabarega's *bête noire* Ruyonga (Baker's Rionga), also a fourth cousin of Mukama Tito Winyi.

[2] There was certainly a substantial number of princes and sons of princes in Bunyoro: Mukama Kamurasi is said to have had about fifteen sons, Kabarega no fewer than seventy-eight, and in the 1950s many of these and their descendants were still living.

have seen that traditionally accession to high office in Bunyoro was based not on agnatic kinship with the ruler, but on the royal favour, founded in the subject's attachment, service, and devotion to the king's person, as well as on ability and merit. Also, as we noted in Chapter 5, even in the 1950s Babito, at any rate those Babito who were 'near to the throne', did not see themselves as fitting into a hierarchical political structure anywhere except at or near the top. 'A Mubito's word should be a command', I was told, and no Mubito would willingly accept a position in which he might have to take orders from a commoner. A non-Mubito informant told me that 'it is considered to be a great come-down for Babito to be chiefs'.

During the Protectorate years chiefs, even at the lowest level (that of the village headmen), were required to be literate at least in some degree. In 1953, 3 out of the 4 county chiefs had had secondary education, as had 12 of the 25 sub-county chiefs; the others had all had some primary education. At the levels of the 'parish' chiefs and village headmen standards were considerably lower. Of 41 'parish' chiefs only 6 (15 per cent) had had any secondary education, 33 (80 per cent) had had some primary education, and 2 had had no formal schooling at all. Of a small sample of 15 village headmen none had had secondary education; no one with education above primary standard six would consider taking so humble a position as that of a *mutongole* chief. Twelve had had some primary education; three had no schooling at all.

A man had little chance of being appointed as a sub-county chief (otherwise than by promotion from a 'parish' chiefship) without secondary education. At the time of my survey 10 of the 25 sub-county chiefs had been directly appointed from outside the service, and only one of them lacked secondary schooling. The other 15 had been promoted, after varying terms of service, from *miruka* chiefships.

Evidently, then, to become an official chief in Bunyoro in European times some degree of formal education was required, but at the lowest levels it was sufficient to be barely literate. This of course represented a major departure from traditional norms of political appointment. But we have noted that even in the 1950s (at least up to 1955) appointment and promotion in the Mukama's government probably depended as much on

his personal favour as on administrative experience, efficiency, or literacy.

Almost all of the chiefs had been engaged in other paid employment (or, in a few cases, had been self-employed) before they were first appointed as chiefs. Thus only 1 out of the 4 county chiefs, 2 of the 25 sub-county chiefs, 4 out of 41 'parish' chiefs, and 1 out of 16 village headmen had *not* had some other job before they were appointed at some level in the chiefly service. Let us now consider the kinds of employment from which chiefs were recruited, and, in conjunction with this, the rank of chiefship to which appointments from outside the service were made.

Of the 4 county chiefs, the 3 who had previously been employed had all been clerks in the Bunyoro Native Government service, and had started their careers as chiefs at the sub-county level; the fourth had started at the 'parish' level. Of the 10 sub-county chiefs who had been appointed from outside the service (that is, *not* by promotion from 'parish' level), 4 had been Native Government clerks, 3 had been teachers, 2 had been nursing orderlies in government hospitals, and 1 had been a clerk in the Protectorate administration. As noted above, all of these had had secondary education except one, and he had had five years of primary schooling. Of the other 15 sub-county chiefs, 13 had been first appointed as 'parish' chiefs; only 2 had risen from the ranks of village headmanship.

A fairly typical sub-county chief's career history may be briefly given, by way of illustration. Erifazi Matongole did not come of a particularly distinguished family, but his father had been a 'parish' chief and his father's brother had been a village headman, so they were at least 'known' to the senior chiefs. Erifazi had been born before the turn of the century in Bugungu, north-west Bunyoro. He had had three years of secondary schooling (so about nine years at school altogether) at King's School, Budo, in Buganda. After leaving school he had held a temporary job as cotton-buyer for an Indian trader, and had then served briefly as a police clerk in Masindi. He then took a post as a nursing orderly at Mulago Hospital, Kampala. He held this job for about ten years, until he was, as he put it, 'called by the Mukama' to take a sub-county chiefship—as an educated man he would not have entered the service at a lower

level. From 1933 to 1953 he had served in five sub-counties in three different counties. In 1953 he had two wives, his first and 'ring' wife (that is, married in church in Christian marriage), and a younger one; two other wives had died. He owned four *bibanja*, one inherited and the other three 'purchased' since he had become a chief; on all combined there was a total of twenty-three households. So Erifazi's status as a sub-county chief was augmented by his unofficial status as an important *mukama w'ekibanja*.

Taking the 13 sub-county chiefs who had started as 'parish' chiefs, together with the other appointees at *muruka* chief level (14 still serving as 'parish' chiefs at that time, and one county chief), we have a sample of 28 men who had been appointed to 'parish' chiefships from other jobs. Some of course had held more than one job before appointment as a chief; I here record the employment last held before appointment. Once again by far the largest category of previous employer was the Native Government; 9 of the 28 had been Native Government clerks when they were made 'parish' chiefs, 2 had been office and court messengers (*askari*). Next came employment in clerical or other capacities by private firms (5), by the Protectorate Government (4), as primary school teachers, and as domestic servants to Europeans (3 each). Only one of our sample had been appointed directly from the Mukama's household (a break with traditional times, when service in the palace often led to a minor territorial chiefship), though about half a dozen others had held jobs in the palace at one time or another.[1]

Here is a brief career history of the 'parish' chief who had been appointed directly from service in the palace. Eriya Rwese-mereza had spent fifteen years in the Mukama's establishment as a domestic servant; he started as a table boy, serving food at the Mukama's meals, and was eventually promoted to be head of all the table servants. When he wished to get married to a 'ring' wife, the Mukama paid the bridewealth money for him, and the cost of a marriage feast. He then offered him a 'parish' chiefship at Kisaru, in Bugahya county. Eriya had served as a

[1] It was, nevertheless, widely believed that the Mukama still continued to appoint favourites from the palace to minor chiefships, and the more progressive constantly criticized him on this ground. In fact, in recent times, such appointments would have been more likely to be to village headmanship rather than to 'parish' chiefship.

'parish' chief for twenty years, during which time he had been transferred seven times. He was a man in late middle age, he was of only limited literacy, and he had no expectation of promotion to a sub-county chiefship.

When one turns to the lowest grade of official chiefs, the village headmen or *batongole*, a somewhat different pattern emerges. I have some information for 45 of them: 16 serving village headmen, 27 'parish' chiefs who had been first appointed at the *batongole* level, and the 2 sub-county chiefs who had risen from the ranks. Five, to begin with, had had *no* former paid employment. Of the rest, the two largest categories were 11 'self-employed' (these included petty traders, artisans, etc.), and 9 'teachers', most of them the lowest grade of mission teachers known as catechists, themselves usually only educated to primary standard, and whose teaching was limited to the small degree of literacy required for baptism. Next came the three categories of employees in private firms, Native Government clerks, and servants in the king's household (4 each). Of the rest, 2 were native government *askaris*, and 3 had held artisans' jobs in the Protectorate Government services.

A typical appointee at this level was Rumondo Muhanga. He was the 'parish' chief of the area in which lay the *kyaro* of Kihoko, where I lived for my first six months in the country, and I got to know him well. His father had been a village headman in a neighbouring 'parish', and when I knew Rumondo he was a man of about fifty. As a boy he attended a Catholic mission school to about standard four (he could not quite remember), and after that he had been a mission teacher (catechist), teaching reading, writing, and scripture. Next he was appointed as overseer on a mission-held property, and in 1932 he was offered, and accepted, a post as village headman. After eighteen years of service at this level he was promoted to a 'parish' chiefship, and he had held this post for about a year when I first met him.

So service as a Bunyoro Native Government clerk was by far the most usual preliminary to appointment as a sub-county or 'parish' chief; 7 out of 13 sub-county chiefs and 9 out of 28 'parish' chiefs had moved directly from clerkships to chiefships. A smaller though still significant number of clerks had been appointed to village headmanships.

The dominance of ex-clerks in the ranks of the chiefs is not surprising. In 1953 there were more than fifty clerks employed at county and sub-county chiefs' headquarters, and the turnover among these men, many of whom were of a fairly low level of literacy, was rapid. As against other candidates for a vacant chiefship, they had the advantage of being well known to the higher chiefs; they worked under their supervision, and were frequently transferred from one chief's headquarters to another's. They were also likely to come into periodic contact with the senior officials of the Mukama's central secretariat, the prime minister (*Katikiro*), the chief justice, and the treasurer, sometimes even with the Mukama himself, both at the Native Government headquarters at Hoima, and at their own chief's headquarters, when these authorities were on tour. Further, these clerks had a day-to-day acquaintance with all of the main departments of a chief's work; hearing and recording cases in the native courts, assessing and collecting tax, publicizing and implementing the various government regulations, and so on. For all these reasons, they were obvious choices for appointment to chiefships at the lower and intermediate levels.

Less need be said of the other categories of employment from which chiefs came. It is, however, worth noting the considerable intake of primary school-teachers or 'catechists' into the lowest rank; these men were at least in some degree literate; they were generally well known in the community and their emoluments as teachers were so low that even the small salary of a village headman (which could be augmented by various minor 'perks') was an incentive to take such a post if one was offered.

The age at which chiefs were first appointed, regardless of the rank at which they entered the service, was remarkably constant at about 34 years. This is consistent with the fact that almost all chiefs had held jobs of other kinds before they were appointed to a chiefship. It is also consistent with the fact that seniority in the territorial chiefship shows little correlation with age; though the village headmen were on the average a little younger than the other grades of chief, most sub-county and 'parish' chiefs were in their middle or late forties, and in fact the average age of the four county chiefs was slightly below the norm. We saw in Chapter 3 that there was nothing gerontocratic about Nyoro

ideas of political authority; political status like other kinds of status was grounded in other factors than age.

We have noted that in the two intermediate grades the intake of new chiefs from outside the service, i.e. not by promotion from the grade next below, was considerable. Of the twenty-five 'parish' chiefs for whom information was available only ten (40 per cent) had been promoted from *batongole* level; all the others were appointed from outside the service. Ten of the twenty-five sub-county chiefs had been appointed from outside; a slightly smaller proportion, but still considerable. The number of men who had succeeded in advancing from a village headmanship to a sub-county chiefship was negligible; of the twenty-five sub-county chiefs serving in 1953 only two had started at the *batongole* level, and none of the four county chiefs had. There was some resentment on the part of the 'parish' chiefs, and of at least some village headmen (though they were on the whole both more poorly educated and less ambitious) of the considerable influx of new sub-county chiefs from outside the service; not unreasonably they saw this as a bar to their own hopes of promotion. It meant, in effect, that most of the 160 or so village headmen were bound to remain at that level throughout their service, and a 'parish' chief's chances of reaching pensionable status as a sub-county chief were hardly greater. In the 1950s the tendency to appoint chiefs from outside the service seemed to be growing, no doubt because better educated candidates were (increasingly) available from outside, than were to be found among the ranks of the *miruka* and *batongole* chiefs. We noted that all but one of the ten sub-county chiefs appointed from outside had had secondary education, while of the fifteen who had been promoted from 'parish' chiefships only three had. Also, the directly appointed sub-county chiefs tended to be a few years younger than the promoted men, their average age in 1953 being 48 as against 51. Of course as far as appointment to 'parish' chiefships was concerned there was no such clear correlation between educational standard and whether a man was appointed from outside or on promotion from a village headmanship; few 'parish' chiefs had been educated beyond primary school.

This state of affairs evidently meant that promotion through the ranks was likely to be slow. The twelve sub-county chiefs

promoted from 'parish' chiefships for whom information was available had averaged thirteen years' service at the lower level before promotion, and a sample of ten 'parish' chiefs promoted from village headmanships had spent, on the average, no less than seventeen years as village headmen before being promoted to *miruka* chiefships. A sub-county chief's prospect of being promoted to a county chiefship was hardly better, since there were only four *masaza*, but at least it was known that county chiefs were only appointed from among the ranks of the sub-county chiefs.

To round off our account of the kinds of men who became chiefs during the last part of the colonial period, something must be said of their religious affiliations. In the 1950s most Banyoro were at least nominal Christians, probably fairly evenly divided between Roman Catholics and Protestants (the latter mostly adherents of the Native Anglican Church, deriving from the Church Missionary Society), with perhaps a slight preponderance of Protestants. There was a small minority of Moslems, and a dwindling number, mostly older people, of 'pagans' (or, more accurately, of adherents of the traditional religion). Among the chiefs these minorities were represented only at the lowest level, two of the village headmen out of a sample of eighteen being 'pagans', and one a Moslem. In view of the near parity of Catholics and Protestants in the general population, it was noteworthy that the proportion of Roman Catholics to Protestants in the ranks of the chiefs decreased very sharply at the higher levels, with the largest gap between the 'parish' chiefs and the sub-county chiefs. Thus of 15 Christian village headmen, 9 were Protestants and 6 Catholics, and of 41 parish chiefs, 26 were Protestants and 15 Roman Catholics; an over-all ratio for these two grades of 6 to 4. But of the 25 sub-county chiefs only 3 were Roman Catholics, and none of the 4 county chiefs was, giving the Catholics a representation at the two higher levels of 1 in 10. Evidently Roman Catholics were at a very marked disadvantage when it came to appointment or promotion to the higher levels of chiefship. This was no doubt partly due to the fact, generally acknowledged, that educational standards in the Church Missionary Society schools were rather higher than those in the Roman Catholic White Fathers' schools (for one thing, not all the White Fathers were native English

speakers). But it also undoubtedly reflected the strong influence
which the Church Missionary Society had had in Bunyoro for
many years; it had always been the 'established' church; both
Mukama Tito Winyi and his predecessor were members of it,
and the famous Kabarega had been converted to it while in
exile in the Seychelles. According to Mrs. Fisher, of fifty-eight
men appointed to chiefships in 1908, 'no less than 52 were
Christian pupils of the senior [C.M.S.] school at Hoima' (p. 190).

Something has already been said of traditional and modern
modes of appointment to chiefly office, and of the degree to
which up to the 1950s territorial chiefship continued to be,
perhaps even more than it had traditionally been, in the
Mukama's gift. Before the reforms contained in the second
Bunyoro Agreement, signed in September 1955, were brought
into effect, and during the period of my fieldwork, the Mukama
felt himself under no moral obligation, as he was under no legal
one, to appoint, promote, and dismiss his chiefs only after
formal consultation with his official advisers.

But of course he did sometimes, probably usually, consult
them, though he was not obliged to follow their advice. There
were recognized procedures for appointment to the various
levels of chiefship. County chiefs were selected by the Mukama
personally, subject only to the approval of the district commissioner, who thus had a right of veto, though he could not
secure the appointment of a man he wanted against the Mukama's wish. Sub-county chiefs were supposed to be nominated
by the county chiefs, and then approved and formally appointed
by the Mukama, and this procedure was often but not invariably
followed. Parish chiefs, likewise, were supposed to be chosen by
the sub-county and county chiefs, though they too were formally
appointed by the Mukama. Many were so chosen, but in the
1950s and earlier the Mukama had appointed a number of them
directly, without consultation with his chiefs, as of course he
was quite free to do under the terms of the 1933 Agreement.
Something was said in Chapter 6 of the considerations which
(and the persons who) might influence him. Village headmen
(*batongole*) were supposed to be chosen, when a vacancy occurred,
by a show of hands on the part of the villagers concerned, at a
meeting called for the purpose and presided over by the 'parish'
chief. If he approved the choice, the new headman was taken to

the sub-county chief and thence to the county chief for formal approval. As we saw, the Protectorate Government was not at all concerned with appointments to the two lower grades of chiefs, though in virtue of his power of veto the district commissioner could instigate dismissal or transfer if he wanted to do so.

I now consider the conditions of service for chiefs. We saw in Chapter 6 that in Bunyoro the notion that a chief should receive a regular official salary was a relatively recent one; up to 1933 chiefs had been remunerated by the cash and goods they received from the peasant occupiers of their official and private estates, supplemented (in the case of the higher grades of chiefs) by a percentage rebate on the poll tax they collected. But after 1933 these resources no longer provided the chiefs with their official means of support, though they still expected occasional gifts of food, beer, and even money from their subjects. These gifts were not (or at least not necessarily) bribes, though they were potentially that; rather they were expressions of the traditional personal interdependence between chiefs and people, and they still implied, at least in principle, the discharge of reciprocal obligations of protection and hospitality by the chiefs. We shall see in the next chapter, however, that in the 1950s these interdependencies, with their associated obligations and expectations, were rapidly breaking down.

In 1953 all official chiefs received monthly salaries. Village headmen received 21 or 22 shillings per month, 'parish' chiefs 32–50 shillings, sub-county chiefs from 75 up to about 125 shillings, and county chiefs from 480 to 580 shillings monthly. All received in addition a temporary cost-of-living allowance of 25 per cent of their salaries. These salaries, especially for the lower chiefs, were quite inadequate to support the standard of living and hospitality expected of chiefs, unless they were considerably supplemented by agriculture, trade, or other means. In fact they were substantially increased in the following year (1954); up to twice the former figures in some cases.[1] But even so the 'parish' chiefs and village headmen remained among the lowest-paid categories of employees in Bunyoro. This naturally

---

[1] Village headmen's salaries were increased to a minimum of 40 shillings, 'parish' chiefs' to a minimum of 58 shillings, and sub-county chiefs' to a minimum of 160 shillings.

affected the regard in which they were held by other Banyoro and especially by their own subjects, some of whom were likely to be much richer than they were. Thus by comparison, in the early 1950s Europeans' domestic servants received 60 shillings or more per month (I paid my own cook 100 shillings, though of course he was informant and friend as well as cook); shop assistants and garage-hands earned 100 shillings or more. Self-employed workers like ironsmiths, carpenters, and shoemakers could earn similar or even greater amounts. Even unskilled labourers could expect wages of 40 shillings a month or over.

County and sub-county chiefs were entitled to pensions on retirement. The two lower grades of chiefs were not, though they might receive cash gratuities after thirty years service, or after ten years if they were over 55 on appointment to their present post. The two upper grades of chiefs were also entitled to free quarters, usually well-built permanent or semi-permanent houses at the chiefdom headquarters. 'Parish' chiefs also had free houses, but these were usually the ordinary rectangular mud-and-wattle thatched dwellings of the type occupied by better-off peasants, though generally a little larger than the average. Village headmen did not receive free housing; the presumption was that they would generally be local people, and would live at home.

The fact, discussed above, that a substantial number of the chiefs in the intermediate ranks came from outside the service had important implications for the kinds of relations which subsisted between chiefs and subjects, especially at the level of the sub-county chiefs. A 'parish' chief, even if he had never been a village headman, lived in and as a member of the local community in a way in which the sub-county chief, with his head-quarters and staff of clerks and policemen, could not. If he did not already know the people of his *muruka* well, he soon came to do so. But a sub-county chief was to some extent insulated in his small official world, and he dealt with the people of his area mostly through his 'parish' chiefs and village headmen.[1] Sub-county chiefs did, of course, tour their areas from time to time

[1] A sub-county chief had one or two clerks under him, and two or three local government policemen-cum-messengers (*askari*). He would also have on his payroll a few labourers for grass-cutting, thatching government buildings, and so on. 'Parish' chiefs and village headmen had no such supporting clerical or executive personnel, officially at least.

and meet their people face-to-face, but they did not live among them as the two lower ranks of chiefs did. This meant that a sub-county chief who had spent some years as a 'parish' chief possessed what his directly appointed and probably better-educated colleague lacked, a first-hand knowledge of the daily task of administration at the grass-roots level.

Contact between the county and sub-county chiefs and the peasant population, inevitably restricted anyway in a hierarchical 'pyramidal' system of territorial administration like Bunyoro's, was further limited by the frequency of transfers at the higher grades. County and sub-county chiefs were much more frequently transferred than 'parish' chiefs and village headmen were. Thus in the course of a twelve-month period during 1952–3, sixteen out of the twenty-five sub-county chiefs were transferred, and after the three years 1949–52 only two sub-county chiefs were in the same sub-counties that they had been in at the beginning of that period. In regard to the county chiefs the pattern was similar, and of course they were even more remote from the ordinary peasant. It seems, then, that a sub-county chief could not expect to stay in the same sub-county for more than about two years, and his stay there might be considerably shorter. Evidently he could not in that time get to know his area intimately, or become closely acquainted with very many of its several thousand inhabitants.

With regard to the two lower grades of chiefs the position was very different. 'Parish' chiefs often stayed in the same *muruka* for from five to ten years, sometimes longer. In fact most transfers appear to have been on promotion to the rank of sub-county chief, and, as we saw, opportunities for such promotions were not frequent. Village headmen were rarely transferred, except on promotion to 'parish' chiefships, for they were almost always appointed in their own villages and, in theory at least, with the agreement of the villagers themselves. Before 1933 they were not transferred at all, for, as we saw in the last chapter, they were in effect indistinguishable from the proprietors of populated *bibanja* and, like them, they drew no salaries, but lived on the commuted tribute which they received from their peasant cultivators.

Some political authority, conceived, like all such authority, as deriving ultimately from the Mukama, was to be found even

below the level of the official chiefs. We saw in Chapter 8 that the proprietors of populated *bibanja* exercised quasi-political rights over their peasant occupiers; but this authority was parallel to rather than subordinate to that of the lowest grade of the official chiefs. There was, however, a category of sub-official but locally recognized subordinates to the village headmen. Not every *mutongole* chief had such an assistant, who was usually known as a 'little' or 'junior' headman (*mukungu muto*), but many did. These men received no salaries, but the headmen might give them a shilling or two from time to time, and a few cents when they carried out such specific tasks as summoning a wanted man from his home. Such an assistant might also settle minor disputes brought to the *mutongole* chief for arbitration, and he could also represent the village headman at meetings called by the 'parish' chief and even by the sub-county chief, if the headman was unable to attend.

The job was not a very rewarding one; indeed, as we noted in Chapter 2, a Runyoro term commonly applied to these unpaid administrative assistants was *ndyamuki*, which means 'What do I get (literally "eat") out of it?' This name was said to date from the 1933 reforms when, as we noted in Chapter 6, some of the minor *bakungu* chiefs were officially recognized and began to receive salaries, while others, probably the majority, were not, and so became both poorer and of lower status than their former colleagues.

But an *ndyamuki* did enjoy certain small privileges. As well as his occasional remuneration by his village headman, he was, like the official chiefs, exempt from participation in communal tasks like road-mending and path-clearing, and he was not required to bring offerings of food or beer (*bitereke*) when a senior chief, the Mukama, or a European officer on tour visited the area. *Ndyamuki* were said, like *kibanja* proprietors, to have a right to a leg of any game animals killed in their areas. Like the lower grades of chiefs, they might also receive from individual peasants occasional small gifts such as a fowl or a few cents, 'to soften their tongues' (*kworobya kalimi*), or 'to close their eyes' (*kwigarra maiso*). These advantages were not substantial, but a certain limited prestige did attach to the position. An *ndyamuki* did possess some authority, however lowly, and he was, in some sense of that very ambiguous term, a *munyoro* or 'chief'.

10

CHIEFS IN A CHANGING SOCIETY

IN the last chapter we saw that there were some important differences between the two upper and the two lower grades of chiefs. This distinction becomes even plainer when we consider their official duties and responsibilities. In the increasingly (but by no means wholly) bureaucratic local government service of the 1950s, both county and sub-county chiefs had to devote more and more of their time to paper-work. They had to keep up a substantial official correspondence on a variety of topics with the authorities both above and below them. Returns relating to the state of tax collection, the planting of food crops, the number of vermin killed, the issue of beer permits, and a number of other administrative matters, had to be prepared and submitted to government headquarters at frequent intervals. Tax collection was a major preoccupation of all chiefs; keeping the registers up to date and collecting the annual dues from an unwilling populace took up a lot of their time.[1] Desperate though rarely successful efforts were made to achieve as complete a collection as possible early in the year, and it was not unusual to see a sub-county or parish chief, complete with table, clerk, and *askari*, established wherever and whenever people were paid money, for example at cotton markets, tobacco-buying posts, and (on pay-days) at Bunyoro's few non-native estates and sawmills. European district commissioners assessed a lower chief's ability largely in terms of his success in bringing in the taxes.

Among the other responsibilities of higher as well as lower chiefs were police work in their areas (mainly the apprehension of criminals, tax defaulters, and other wanted persons), the maintenance of local roads and paths, the enforcing of regulations

---

[1] In 1953 the total tax payable annually by every able-bodied adult man was about 26 shillings, which included certain local rates as well as the Protectorate Government's poll tax.

regarding agriculture, public health, and so on, and the conservation of famine food supplies. But in the 1950s probably the most important concern of the two higher grades of chiefs was with judicial work.[1] As in other territories under British colonial administration, chiefs, as native authorities, presided over courts with specific jurisdictions both in criminal and in civil cases. These courts, established under the Protectorate's Native Authority Ordinance, could not hear cases involving non-Africans (these had to be taken to the European district commissioner's or resident magistrate's court), nor were they empowered to hear cases relating to certain grave crimes like murder, manslaughter, or rape, which were dealt with by the European courts. But a great many offences under the Uganda Laws, as well as cases falling under the head of 'native law and custom', could be and were heard in the native courts, as also were civil suits relating to debt, inheritance, and such matters. Some of the kinds of issues dealt with are discussed in detail below.

In Bunyoro the native court system reflected the hierarchical organization of the local Native Government with which it was identified. There were three grades of native courts. The lowest were the twenty-five sub-county chiefs' courts; most formal court actions began at this level, and for chiefs in the larger and busier sub-counties court work might take up one full day a week, sometimes more. In Bunyoro Monday was the day officially set aside for court work,[2] sometimes Thursday as well, and all the 'parish' chiefs of the sub-county (or their deputies), together with the three or four nominated court assessors, and the village headmen of the areas in which the cases to be heard had arisen, were expected to attend. Sub-county courts were empowered to impose fines of up to 200 shillings, imprisonment up to six months, and to hear civil suits involving money or property up to the value of 200 shillings.

[1] This was no longer so after the 1950s, when chiefs were relieved of their role as judges, the native courts being taken over by a 'professional' native judiciary.
[2] The word for 'Monday' in Runyoro is *Ekiro kya Baraza*, 'Court Day'. *Baraza* is the Kiswahili for any kind of public meeting or discussion. The other days of the week are referred to by the Runyoro numerals (*Ekiro kya Kabiri, kya Kasatu*, etc.), with the exception of Sunday, *Ekiro kya Sabiti* (from 'Sabbath'—of course a numerical indicator too, but not in Runyoro!).

PLATE 7

Typical Nyoro sub-county chief's courthouse. The court is in session

The second grade of Nyoro native courts was the county chief's court; there were four of these, one for each *saza*, and they acted largely, though by no means only, as courts of appeal from the sub-county chiefs' courts. They were empowered to impose fines of up to 300 shillings, one year's imprisonment, and to deal with civil cases involving amounts of up to 500 shillings.

The highest native court was the Bunyoro central court (*Rukurato*), presided over by the chief justice (*Muramuzi*) of the Native Government. It could impose fines up to 500 shillings, sentence to two years' imprisonment, and hear civil cases involving amounts up to 1,000 shillings. This court acted mainly as a court of appeal. Except in some trivial cases, a ladder of appeal existed from the lower courts to the central native court, from it to the district commissioner's appeal court, and thence, via the Provincial Commissioner, to the High Court of the Protectorate. In fact appeals were frequent at all levels: in 1953 the district commissioner complained in his annual report of the 'weakness' of the central *Rukurato* court, and the consequent numerous appeals to him.

All court fees and fines were paid to the Bunyoro Native Government which, in conformity with the usual pattern of indirect rule, had its own treasury and budget, quite separate from those of the Protectorate's provincial administration, though it received assistance from the Central Government in the form of various grants-in-aid and rebates.

Courts were popular in Bunyoro, and as well as the official court members and the parties and witnesses in the case, a considerable number of local people were usually present, sitting and standing about both inside and outside the courthouse. Except in the case of the county chiefs, who had large courthouses of brick or stone with corrugated iron roofs, this building was usually a modest construction of mud and wattle, with thatched roof and open sides. The evidence was recorded by the chief's clerk, who wrote up the record neatly afterwards in Runyoro in the court register. Hearings were usually fairly leisurely, and took place with what appeared to be a marked lack of formality, compared with procedure in Western courts. Though it was sometimes difficult for a foreigner to make out what was going on, through the intermittent argument and

discussion and frequent pauses, there was none the less an underlying order in the proceedings. From time to time the presiding sub-county chief would sharply call the court to order, and there was rarely any doubt as to who was in charge.

Before giving an account of some of the types of cases heard in the native courts, a word more must be said of the kinds of law they administered. Many of the cases they dealt with were penal code offences, or offences under the various Protectorate laws and regulations relating to agriculture, public health, and other matters; the native courts were empowered to deal with these by enabling legislation under the Native Courts Ordinance. But the Native Government could also enact its own laws and by-laws, subject to Protectorate Government approval, and in course of time a considerable body of recorded native law had grown up.

In 1950 an attempt had been made by the Native Government itself to codify all the laws it was empowered to administer, and an official list of all 'Bunyoro Native Government Laws' was available. These fifty or so 'laws', enacted by the Bunyoro Native Government at various times over a period of many years, covered a wide variety of matters. They can be distinguished broadly by reference to whether they formalized traditional—or supposedly traditional—elements of customary law which it was desired to perpetuate, or whether they were European-inspired rules deriving from Protectorate legislation, and reflecting the new demands of the superimposed colonial government. A few of them reflected the Nyoro rulers' own uneasy reactions to current processes of social change, in which traditional and modern values conflicted. A good example is the rule, enacted in the late 1940s, that 'any woman found travelling without a *Rukurato* (native court) road pass shall be liable to a fine of 3 shillings, or to imprisonment for 14 days'. This reflected Banyoro men's concern with the increasing independence of their womenfolk, who by going off on their own either to take paid employment in the towns or to cultivate cotton intensively on the Lake Albert escarpment, could make enough money to secure their freedom, for example, by returning the bridewealth paid for them and so escaping from husbands they disliked. Needless to say the rule proved unenforceable, but male misgivings persisted.

Traditionally based laws related especially to inheritance, marriage, and the custody of children; to the practice and imputation of witchcraft and sorcery;[1] to the maintenance and expression of proper respect for rulers (to insult or 'speak ill' of the traditional 'leaders of the country' was an offence); and to such neighbourly obligations as mutual help and answering alarm calls. More modern, 'imposed' ones were concerned, characteristically, with tax evasion and default; with breach of agricultural regulations (failure to plant and conserve anti-famine food crops, the weeding, and eventual uprooting of cotton and tobacco plants); and with public health, both human (it was an offence, for example, to foul wells or streams from which drinking water was taken, or to transmit venereal disease), and animal (notifiable diseases of domestic animals had to be reported; quarantines had to be observed). Provision was also made in the Nyoro code (as in the Protectorate code) for conviction and punishment for robbery and theft, assault, arson, and excessive drunkenness—all of which were, of course, traditionally disapproved—as well as for opium smoking, gambling, and the use of bad language; in these last offences the influence of the European missionaries was no doubt a significant factor.

A brief look at the kinds of cases dealt with by a few typical native courts will further illustrate this important part of the chiefs' work. As is usual in non-Western courts, no very clear distinction is drawn between criminal and civil proceedings: compensation was usually awarded in cases involving injury to person or property, and penalties were often imposed in issues which most European courts would regard as 'civil'.

A simple analysis of the 491 cases, almost all of them on appeal, heard by the central native court at Hoima during

[1] It is worth noting that under the Protectorate laws it was an offence for a person to 'hold himself out as a witchdoctor, or witchfinder', or to 'pretend to exercise or use any kind of supernatural power, witchcraft, sorcery or enchantment': according to the way of thinking of most Banyoro it was an offence actually to *be* a sorcerer or a witch. Hence the anomaly of courts established under British Protectorate law convicting people in the middle of the twentieth century of being sorcerers. The difficulty was resolved by a 'working misunderstanding'; for ordinary Nyoro peasants the distinction between pretending to be a sorcerer and actually being one was academic so long as sorcerers were caught and punished, however inadequately. (For an account of the role of chiefs in combating sorcery in Bunyoro see Beattie 1963, pp. 46–9.)

the thirteen years from 1939 to 1951, indicates some of the main issues dealt with. The majority of cases, 212 (42 per cent), related to property, including under this head 'civil' claims for repayment of debts as well as charges of robbery and theft. Next came offences against the person, mostly assault, but including also 'witchcraft' cases (*burogo*, strictly sorcery, which Banyoro distinguish from witchcraft) and arson, which is common, since most houses, being made of wood and grass, are highly inflammable. These three categories together made up 32 per cent of the total; witchcraft and arson, taken separately, accounted for 9 per cent and 6 per cent respectively of all offences.

The next major category of cases heard by the central court comprised the 68 offences concerned with marriage and the family, a total of 14 per cent of all cases heard during these years. The largest single sub-category of such offences was adultery (23 cases); the others related to such matters as the return of bridewealth after separation, and the 'ownership', custody, and maintenance of children (Nyoro men often accuse women they have slept with of ascribing to other men the paternity of children they claim to have begotten).[1]

Two of the remaining categories of offences dealt with by this court are worth noting. First, in 39 cases, 8 per cent of the total, the courts were used as a means of disciplining (usually by a fine) subordinate Native Government officials or servants, in some cases chiefs, who had been guilty of negligence or abuse of their office. Second, only 14 cases concerning *bibanja* reached the highest native court during these years, and most of these were about disputed boundaries. This tends to confirm that, as I suggested in Chapter 8, the system as a whole was not resented by most peasants; though a few cases were brought by 'tenants', several of these involved Babito proprietors, whose alleged oppressions were attributed to Bito arrogance as much as to their *kibanja* proprietorship.

Turning now to the county chiefs' courts, my record of cases heard in these is very incomplete. Many were appeal cases from the sub-county chiefs' courts; 18 of the 49 cases heard by the Bugahya county chief's court during 1948 were appeals. It is remarkable that of the 31 cases of first instance heard in that

---

[1] All Banyoro wish to have sons, and so long as their physical paternity can be established, the 'legitimacy' or 'illegitimacy' of their offspring is of little moment.

court during the year a total of no less than 14 were concerned with sorcery. Such cases, which usually involved what were in effect accusations of deliberate homicide, were regarded as too serious for the sub-county chiefs to deal with. But it was believed that they would not receive serious consideration (in Nyoro eyes) in the district commissioner's court, for it was known that he did not believe in sorcery, and so would be unlikely to convict anybody of practising it. The solution was to send such cases to the county chiefs' courts, where they could be, and were, dealt with in terms of the 'working misunderstanding' mentioned above (p. 221 n. 1). Although it was widely felt that the penalties these courts were empowered to inflict on sorcerers were grossly inadequate, they were better than not punishing them at all.

Of the other offences dealt with in 1948 by the Bugahya county chief's court, 6 were offences against property, 5 were offences against the person (assault), and 4 were concerned with marriage and the custody of children.

I turn now to the lowest grade of official courts, the sub-county chiefs' court. An examination of the 54 cases officially heard and recorded by the sub-county chief's court of Kabwoya (Mutaba IV, Bugahya) during the first eight months of 1955 shows that the job of judicially enforcing the many new and irksome regulations regarding planting, hygiene, and so on, was carried out mainly at this level. Thus 20 of these 54 cases (in several of them a number of defendants were tried together) were concerned with breaches of the regulations regarding cotton cultivation, the digging of latrines, and the purchase of licences for beer-making, and a further 4 dealt with tax defaulters. Of the others, cases of assault (15) considerably outnumbered property cases, of which there were 5, all claims for the repayment of debts. Among the other offences dealt with were failure to participate in a communal wild pig hunt, raising a false alarm, and failures in their duties by subordinate officials. No 'witchcraft' cases were heard by this court, for the reason given above. But it is certain that the several sorcery cases taken to the county chief's court had been thoroughly investigated by the sub-county chief first, even though no formal records of the proceedings had been made.

These few examples indicate something of the variety of issues which the two higher grades of chiefs and their courts

were required to deal with in their capacity as judges. But these formal hearings represent only, so to speak, the tip of the iceberg; for as well as hearing cases in court, chiefs at all levels settled many disputes informally. This task fell mainly to the 'parish' chiefs, who had no formal courts or judicial powers, and no clerks to keep records. Most 'parish' chiefs devoted one day a week, usually Wednesday, to the informal hearing of cases. Such a chief would sit with his village headmen or their deputies, and a few other senior members of the community, and only those disputes which he was unable to settle would be taken to the sub-county court. In fact most minor disputes between fellow villagers were dealt with at an even lower level, either by the village headmen or by small groups of kinsfolk and neighbours informally assembled for the purpose.[1]

But the formal court holders often settled cases 'off the record' too. Here is an example. One night a man discovered a neighbour in his goat-house trying to steal one of his goats. He raised the alarm, neighbours came, and the culprit was caught and taken to the sub-county chief's headquarters, which were nearby, and locked up until the morning. At about 10 a.m. the case was heard informally by the chief and a group of neighbours; no record was kept. After discussion, the sub-county chief told the thief to pay 50 shillings, together with two pots of beer, to the complainant. All present agreed with this judgement except the accused, who began to protest. The chief cut him short firmly, saying: 'If you don't like this judgement we will open a formal case against you and you will be sent to prison for twelve years!' Such a sentence by the chief would, of course, have been completely *ultra vires*, but the accused man did not know this. In due course the money was paid, and the beer provided.

I have stressed that contact with the mass of the peasant population took place mainly at the level of two lower grades of chiefs, the 'parish' chiefs and village headmen. This becomes even plainer when we consider the main duties of these lower chiefs. Unlike their superiors, they had no offices and little or no clerical work to do, so they could be, and usually were, constantly on the move in their areas. They spent much of their

---

[1] These informal village tribunals have already been referred to. They are described in Beattie 1957b.

time inspecting people's gardens and fields, supervising the clearing of roads and paths, telling people where and, sometimes, what to cultivate, organizing and often participating in communal pig and baboon hunts, summoning people to attend at court, and carrying out innumerable other minor tasks. They were of and among the people in a way in which the county and sub-county chiefs were not and could not be. It was they who in the last resort represented the government (*bulemi*) to the people, and, through their superiors in the service, the people to the government.

The close association, in social terms, between the lower grades of chiefs and the people was vividly brought home to me when I was living in the village where I first worked, Kihoko. The local village headman and even the 'parish' chief would drop in quite informally to any beer party that might be taking place in any part of his area in which he had business, and he would at once be offered some beer and accepted as a member of the party, without constraint or disturbance, as any other neighbour in good standing would. He might join any family in a meal without formality or fuss. But things were very different when the sub-county chief visited a village. Considerable preparations were made, compounds were swept and paths tidied, and everyone was on his best behaviour. The atmosphere was formal, stiff, somewhat constrained. The marked distinction of status between the two higher and the two lower grades of chiefs was manifest; it was very plain that the former were above, the latter 'of' the ordinary people.[1]

Something must now be said of the system of local councils which had been introduced by the Protectorate Government a few years earlier, with the intention of broadening and 'democratizing' the base of the native administration. The chiefs, down to and including the 'parish' chiefs, were expected to play an important part in the running and popularizing of these councils. There were four grades of them, and in the 1950s they were constituted as follows.

[1] As I have noted elsewhere, there was a trivial but none the less significant index of the difference of status between these grades of chiefs. When I was in Bunyoro all peasants smoked cigarettes with the lighted end inside the mouth, so that no smoke was wasted—I developed a certain proficiency in doing this myself. All village headmen and most 'parish' chiefs, when offered a cigarette, would smoke it in this way. But no county or sub-county chief would dream of doing so; he would smoke it with the lighted end outside, in the European fashion.

At the top there was the district council (*Rukurato*), the chairman of which in 1953 was the Mukama himself. As originally constituted the chairman had been the prime minister (Katikiro), and the Mukama had had no place on the council. In the 1950s there was a good deal of criticism, both by the more enlightened chiefs and by the European administration, of the Mukama's presence on, and domination of, a council whose primary purpose was to tender him advice, and one of the more important intentions of the 1955 Agreement was to remove him from the council and its committees. The other members of the district council were the Katikiro, the chief justice, and the treasurer; all the county and sub-county chiefs; 19 'parish' chiefs, and 14 village headmen, selected from the lower councils; and 10 'popular representatives' (*bakwenda b'abantu*), later increased to 20, similarly elected from the lower councils. The Okwiri (the head of the royal Babito clan) was also a member of the council, together with two nominated Babito. The council met twice yearly, but there was a standing committee which could meet more frequently; there were also a finance committee, an education committee, and an appointments committee. Only this council had the power to enact by-laws; the other regional councils were advisory only.

Each of the four county councils was composed of the county chief, from four to ten sub-county chiefs, and proportionate numbers of 'parish' chiefs and village headmen, together with a number of 'popular representatives', elected by the 'electoral college' method from the sub-chiefs' councils. There were also a somewhat smaller number of directly appointed persons, usually locally important citizens like clergy, school-teachers, or traders, who happened to be in favour with the administration. There were in addition a small number of technical advisers called *bahi amagezi* ('providers of "know-how"'), who were usually local representatives of the various specialist government departments. These councils also met twice a year.

The sub-county councils were constituted on similar lines, under the chairmanship of the sub-county chief. The members were all the 'parish' chiefs in the sub-chiefdom, a proportion of the village headmen, from four to eight 'popular representatives' elected from the 'parish' councils, and a few co-opted unofficial members. These councils too were supposed to meet

twice yearly. Lastly, the lowest grade of councils, the 'parish' councils, consisted of the 'parish' chief and his local village headmen, usually from three to five, together with a small number of people supposed to be elected by popular acclaim, and another three or four local notables nominated by the council. Unlike the higher councils, the 'parish' councils were supposed to meet monthly, but in fact they generally met very much less often.

All the councils kept written records of their meetings, and the lower ones passed on recommendations, through the chief to whom they were advisory, to the council next above them. A representative selection of recommendations from one or two councils at different levels will give a better idea of the main preoccupations of these councils, and so of the chiefs whom they advised, than a more generalized account would do. Naturally the lower councils were chiefly concerned with local matters.

I take first the 'parish' council of Kifumbya, in Bugahya county. Kihoko, where I lived during my first six months in Bunyoro, was a constituent settlement area (*kyaro*) in this 'parish'. Over a period of just under four years (1951–5) the council met ten times—considerably less often than the regulations prescribed. Recommendations minuted during this time related to contemporary economic conditions, local medical and educational services, administrative and taxation matters, and to a concern, widespread throughout Bunyoro in the 1950s, with problems arising from changes in marriage customs and the status of women.

Among the recommendations relating to economic factors were the following: the price of 74 cents per pound paid for home-grown tobacco was too low, and should be increased to 1 shilling; assistance should be provided by the Government in trapping pigs, baboon, and porcupines, and ammunition ought to be obtainable locally for purchase to shoot them with; the price of cloth in the Indian shops at the local trading centre (about six miles distant) should be controlled, 'as they are robbing us'; a postal agency should be opened at the same centre; coffee seedlings for planting should be available at the 'parish' headquarters—not, as now, only at the county headquarters about fifteen miles away.

Recommendations regarding health and medical services affirmed the need for a dispensary at the sub-county

headquarters at Kabwoya (the existing dispensary was oddly situated six miles away in a relatively unpopulated area); requested that patients, especially the poor, should be carried free in the government ambulance; asked for a permanent (female) nurse to be stationed at the dispensary to treat women suffering from venereal diseases (*ndwara z'ensoni*, 'shameful illnesses'); and suggested that householders should not be expected to dig domestic latrines single-handed—co-operative labour should be organized and provided.

As regards education, recommendations were passed advocating free schooling for the children of poor parents; asking that pagan children as well as the baptized should be admitted as pupils; proposing that schooling should be compulsory and defaulting parents punished; complaining that people should not be called upon to contribute free labour (*burungi bw'ensi*, 'for the good of the country') to the building of schools when they were already paying a local education tax; and, rather surprisingly, accepting a 2 shillings annual increase in the same tax.

On matters of local administration, recommendations were passed to the effect that sub-county chiefs should be paid an allowance so that they could entertain visitors at their headquarters (chiefs' failure to entertain on what was supposed to have been the traditional scale was a constant source of complaint); that permanent deputies should be appointed for county chiefs (so that one or other of the sub-county chiefs need not be constantly called to the county headquarters to deputize during the frequent absences on business of the *saza* chief); that officials of both the Native and the Central governments should give notice of their intention to visit 'parishes' and villages on tour (so that the necessary preparations might be made in good time); that a graduated tax (preparations for the introduction of such a tax, to replace the undifferentiated poll tax, were being made at that time) should not be imposed, since 'we are all poor here'; that persons required to attend court as assessors should receive bicycle allowances; and finally (and rather plaintively) that if the 'parish' council's recommendations were turned down by higher authority, the lower council should be told why.

The council's concern, shared by most Nyoro men, with the supposedly increasing immorality and irresponsibility of Nyoro

women, is of interest. During these few years the Kifumbya 'parish' council (all the members were, of course, men) made the following recommendations: rules should be made against prostitution, and a girl who is impregnated by a man should be made to marry him, 'because parents are "eating" a lot of money on account of their daughters just "selling themselves" but not marrying'; divorced women who have repaid their own bridewealth (*bakwezimura*) should not be allowed just to stay at home, but their parents should be compelled to marry them elsewhere, to avoid the dangers of prostitution, disease, infertility, etc.; there should be rules about the return on divorce of marriage gifts, 'we pay goats worth 100 or 150 shillings when we marry, but in case of divorce we only get back ones worth 20 or 30 shillings'.

Clearly some of these recommendations were based on misconceptions about what was practically feasible (the council's rather naïve and obviously masculine views about the preservation of female morality are a case in point), as well as about the 'facts' themselves—thus, for example, transport in the government ambulance was in fact officially free for patients and their families. But they did provide the chiefs, and by way of the higher councils the Protectorate administration, with a useful guide to opinion on matters concerning local government—as on other aspects of everyday life—at the grass-roots level.

Sub-county and county council recommendations can be considered together; virtually all the recommendations made by *saza* councils derived from the lower councils. There follow, in the order in which they were recorded, fifteen recommendations made and minuted by the county chief's council of Bugahya *saza* at its meeting on 29 March 1955.

(1) The Native Government should provide one 'porter' (labourer) for every 'parish', to maintain the *muruka* chief's house.

(2) Chiefs' messengers (*baserikali*) should receive two free suits (of tunic and shorts) per year; at the present time they are generally in rags.

(3) Every school should have a medicine chest for treating the children.

(4) Every 'parish' headquarters should have a copy of the Bunyoro Agreement (of 1933).

(5) Those parts of our country which were taken by the Baganda should be returned to us, because these days things are changing and a new Agreement is proposed, and anyway the Baganda never had any right to these areas.

(6) The form of application for a loan from the Uganda Credit and Savings Bank should be made out in Runyoro.

(7) People should not be allowed to take knives into beer clubs, on pain of punishment.

(8) Beer-sellers should be examined by the doctor, to make sure that they are in good health. Their equipment should also be examined.

(9) The prices at which people are required to sell local foodstuffs to touring officers are now too low; sellers should be allowed to name their own prices.

(10) The wages of labourers employed by the Native Government should be increased, as they have in Protectorate Government departments, to 32 shillings per month.

(11) The hat worn by the Mukama on special occasions should be different from those worn by others, and should be specially made for him.

(12) Members of sub-county chiefs' councils, and members of their courts, should receive cash allowances.

(13) All Native Government officials at and above the rank of village headmen should receive bicycle allowances.

(14) The government should provide a 'tractor' (grader) to improve the road from Kabwoya to Kyangwali, since no labourers can be had for this road (which passes through the uninhabited Bugoma forest).

(15) A piped water supply (from the Wambabya river) should be provided at the cotton store at Biseruka, and wells should be dug at Kabale, so as to keep people cultivating in these areas (most of Bunyoro's cotton is grown in these relatively dry areas near the Lake Albert escarpment).

These minutes give a fair picture of at least some of the preoccupations of chiefs and councils at the intermediate and higher levels. There is a more practical, workmanlike quality about most (though not all) of their recommendations, as compared with those made at 'parish' level. Of course some have come up from the 'parish' councils, for example the request for a 'porter' to maintain the *muruka* chief's house. But the more

impracticable were dropped before they reached the agenda for the county chief's council. Here, too, the preoccupation with the 'Lost Counties', the major political issue in Bunyoro in the 1950s and most articulately voiced at the higher levels, finds expression in the official record.

At the level of the highest of Bunyoro's councils, the district council, many of these now familiar themes recurred, but there was also a growing preoccupation with national, Bunyoro-wide issues. Here, too, the influence of the Mukama, and through him and the Okwiri, of the royal family began to make itself felt. There follow some characteristic recommendations of the district council made during the few years up to and including 1953. They fall conveniently under the three heads of national (Bunyoro) affairs, local administrative matters, and the special interests of the Babito and of the Mukama personally.

Under the first heading came the inevitable request (repeated at most sessions of the Council) that Bunyoro's 'Lost Counties' should be restored. Other recommendations were that the anniversary of the Mukama's accession should be a holiday for Protectorate as well as Native government employees; that the old Nyoro titles of the senior chiefs should be resumed, and the alien Ganda ones, adopted early in the century, discarded (this was done a few years later); that the supervisor of the Native Government's Public Works Department should be an African and not, as he then was, a European; that the Mukama's photograph should be displayed in every sub-county court house; and that the Bunyoro Native Government should be so known, and not, as it sometimes was, as the Bunyoro Local Government. The request was also made on more than one occasion that *mailo* (freehold) land should be permitted in Bunyoro, as it had been in Buganda for more than half a century.

Resolutions on matters of local administration included the following: all chiefs should be provided with official uniforms or robes; special wards should be set aside for chiefs (and perhaps other 'respectable patients') at the hospitals at Hoima and Masindi; salaries should be raised for all grades of chiefs; bicycle allowances should be provided for all council members and court assessors; *miruka* and *batongole* chiefs should be exempt from taxation when they retired.

Turning, finally, to resolutions concerned with the interests and prestige of the Mukama and his Babito kinsmen, it was recommended that a special emblem should be designed for the Mukama's car; he should be provided with first-class accommodation when travelling by rail or ship; a special grant should be made for the further education of the 'crown prince' (John Rukidi); special grants should be made for the education of the children of princes; permanent houses should be built for the Okwiri and Batebe (the king's 'official sister'); the Okwiri and Nyina Omukama (the king's mother) should have increases in salary; new laws should be enacted to 'safeguard' princes and princesses 'in order not to be trespassed upon'; and no court proceedings should be opened against them without authority (exactly what authority the council had in mind was not specified in the record, but it was presumably the Mukama's).[1] There can be no doubt that these recommendations in large part reflected the Mukama's dominance over a council supposed to be advisory to him, even if he did not initiate them himself.

In 1953 it certainly could not be said that the lower councils exercised very much influence on the chiefs whom they were supposed to advise. European administrators frequently commented on their inefficiency, the frivolity of some of their recommendations, and the irregularity of their meetings—some 'parish' councils did not convene for months on end. They complained especially of the apathy with which they were regarded by those whom they were supposed to benefit most, the ordinary people themselves. In 1948 the Provincial Commissioner had written in his annual report: 'Whether on account of their habits of intemperance, or on account of a naturally apathetic and individualistic outlook, the people of Bunyoro have so far displayed little interest in the councils,' and although his diagnosis of the reasons for this lack of interest was somewhat wide of the mark, the position had not greatly changed five years later.

There were several reasons (not those suggested by the Provincial Commissioner) why the council system did not 'catch

---

[1] I owe this selection of *Rukurato* resolutions to the kindness of Professor William Diez, of Rochester University, New York, who was at that time making a study of the working of the local councils in Buganda and Bunyoro.

on' more readily in Bunyoro in the early 1950s. First, although in Bunyoro as in most traditional African states chiefs normally made decisions after consultation with chosen advisers, they did not feel themselves bound by the advice they received, though sometimes they would have been unwise to disregard it. Decision-making was traditionally the rulers' job, not something which could be entrusted to commoners, whether counsellors or not. We noted earlier that before 1953 the Mukama had served as chairman of the standing committee of the district council, thus dominating a committee the *raison d'être* of which was to advise him. This state of affairs was regarded as anomalous by the European administration, and by a small but growing number of more progressive chiefs, but to most Banyoro it was quite acceptable.

Also, where, as in Bunyoro, the traditional division between rulers and ruled was pervasive and ubiquitous, and the making of political decisions was regarded as the proper business of chiefs and emphatically not the concern of ordinary peasants, it was natural that the older chiefs, and most of the ordinary peasants, should regard popular representation in government with very limited enthusiasm. Although the popular representatives on 'parish' councils were supposed to be chosen by the villagers themselves, in fact they were more usually personally nominated by the 'parish' chief or his village headmen. District commissioners often commented on the lack of initiative generally shown by council members, especially by members of the district council; it was asserted that these last only echoed the opinions of the Mukama, who generally spoke first. In the 1950s it was still difficult for any Munyoro to contradict or oppose an opinion expressed by his political superior, especially in public; in hierarchically organized societies like Bunyoro relations with a superior should, as Maquet put it (p. 169), express obedience and dependence rather than 'truth'. It would have been thought quite improper for an inferior to argue with his superior, especially in open court or council. Further, it was widely believed that a chief who showed too great temerity in the district council presided over by the Mukama might find himself passed over for promotion, or even in danger of dismissal. At least up to 1955 this belief may not have been without foundation.

There was another way in which traditional Nyoro ideas of hierarchy and status affected the working of the council system. When I was in Bunyoro there were in the country a number of wealthy, influential, and able men, some of them ex-county and sub-county chiefs of high standing and all still in the prime of life, who might have been expected to have found some place in the councils. In fact, although a few able and ambitious individuals did from time to time acquire council membership, a far greater number did not. This was no doubt partly due to some lack of enthusiasm for public service, but I knew several who would willingly have taken part in the work of the higher councils as unofficial members, had they been asked to do so. That they did not find a place in the system was mainly due, I believe, to the emphasis on the 'electoral college' mode of appointment to the higher councils, whereby most of the unofficial members of these councils were either elected from among the unofficial members of the council next below, or (in a few cases) nominated, in effect, by the Mukama or his chiefs. A well-off business or professional man, or, for example, a retired county chief (of whom, as I said, there were a remarkable number in Bunyoro), would consider it beneath his dignity to serve as an ordinary member of so lowly a body as a 'parish' council, on equal terms with ordinary peasants and village headmen. Also, a busy man might well have found it difficult to afford the time. So unless such a person was nominated at a higher level—and this rarely happened, since powerful and independently minded non-officials were unlikely to be the first choice of either the Mukama or his senior chiefs—he was unlikely to find a place in the system at all.

The structure of the council system was radically altered in 1955 by the new Bunyoro Agreement which, *inter alia*, broadened the basis of representation on the district council, and in particular (as we saw in Chapter 7) provided for the establishment of an appointments committee whose recommendations the Mukama was bound to accept. The democratization of local government in Bunyoro was advancing steadily during the last years of the kingdom. But it was unquestionably true in the 1950s that only a minority of peasant Banyoro had any real desire to participate in political affairs, and I should not be surprised if this were not still to some extent the case even today.

Certainly the opinion was widely held a decade or so ago that the proper people to rule were the rulers; many commoners found it difficult to adapt themselves to a situation in which they were not only permitted but required to express opinions which might contradict those of their political superiors. There is no doubt that the persistence in Bunyoro of values, beliefs, and expectations appropriate to an older order slowed down considerably the development of a viable system of local councils.[1]

Two other themes remain to be considered. The first is the relation of chiefs both to one another and to certain categories of persons who were not chiefs; and the second concerns the ways in which chiefs were regarded, both by other Banyoro and by the British Protectorate's administrators.

We noted earlier that the lower grades of chiefs were often thought to be socially inferior to some of the people who were resident in their areas, and who were thus at least nominally subject to their authority. A village headman of undistinguished family and with only his small salary and unofficial perquisites to live on, might find it difficult to assert his authority, if a conflict arose, against a wealthy *mukama w'ekibanja*, for example, or a Mubito, a business man, or even a clerk or school-teacher. Many proprietors of populated *bibanja*, especially, still felt that they, and not the official chief or village headman, were the proper authorities over their peasant 'tenants'. As we saw in Chapter 8, such a man in any case thought of himself as a kind of chief. Often *bakama b'ebibanja* functioned as intermediaries between the official chiefs and the occupants of their 'estates'. So in many 'parishes' and villages the official chief or headman was by no means the most important or well-known man in the community, as he would have been almost by definition in traditional times. Educated Banyoro have told me that minor chiefs often suffered from an inferiority complex (the term was theirs, not mine), because they were 'despised' and looked down upon by their more distinguished subjects.

This was evidently not the case, at least to anything like the same extent, in the case of the two higher grades of chiefs. Almost all of them had been educated to secondary standard,

---

[1] For an interesting and perceptive (if not always wholly accurate) account of the different development under the British administration of local government institutions in three Uganda districts, one of them Bunyoro, see Burke.

and most had had 'professional' experience in white-collar jobs before they had become chiefs. But the chiefly service was a single political body, and despite the differences between them there was a good deal of solidarity between the higher and lower ranks; especially against 'outsiders'. When their authority was challenged, chiefs of all ranks tended to present a common front. Adverse criticism of chiefs by laymen was discouraged, and complaints of bribery or oppression by them were heard with scant sympathy for the complainant. This is not to say that relations between the lower chiefs and the people in their areas were hostile; on the contrary, as we have seen, they were for the most part relaxed and friendly. But lower chiefs' sense of inferiority in some contexts sometimes tended to make them rather sensitive to criticism by laymen, especially by those whose slight educational advantage might imply a claim to 'superiority', and when conflict did arise they would look to their official superiors for support.

Two cases heard in sub-county chiefs' courts during my stay in Bunyoro will illustrate this point. In 1950 a mission teacher brought a case against a village headman, alleging that he had accepted a bribe of 50 shillings to drop a prosecution. The court dismissed the case on the ground that there was no evidence that the money handed over was a bribe (equally, no evidence was adduced to show that it could have been anything else). The court then charged the teacher with 'slandering' the village headman, and imposed a fine of 100 shillings, or three months in gaol. The question whether or not the charge of bribery had been made in good faith was not discussed; the important thing was to teach the defendant that it was none of his business to criticize the village headman. 'He had assumed authority to which he had no right' (*akagenderra okweha obusobozi*), the record states, and 'he had stuck his nose into matters that were none of his business' (*nayetaha omu mulimo ogutaligwe*). In the second case, heard at about the same time, a mission catechist was thrown into gaol for having been 'rude' to a native court in which he was a witness. He subsequently and unsuccessfully, brought a case against the sub-county chief for false imprisonment.

Turning now to the relationship *between* chiefs, in the 1950s these still exhibited a number of aspects characteristic of the

'patrimonial' and personalized traditional system, rather than of the bureaucratic 'civil service' administration to which the Bunyoro Native Government was at that time seen by some (for example by Hailey) as approximating. When a senior chief visited one of his subordinate chiefs he was formally received, and would expect to receive gifts in cash or kind, or both, from his host. I was told that when a county chief formally visited one of his sub-county chiefs, especially (though not only) on the latter's first appointment, he might receive a present of a goat, or at least of meat worth up to 10 shillings or so, and in addition a cash gift of 20 or 30 shillings. Similar prestations were said to take place when a sub-county chief formally visited one of his 'parish' chiefs, the gifts being proportionately smaller, perhaps consisting of a chicken or a few shillings. As we noted earlier in this chapter, on the occasion of such visits a general impression of excitement and tension was very marked. A special meal would be prepared, houses and compounds brushed and tidied, and everyone would wear his best clothes.

No such gifts, or fuss, would be made when a 'parish' chief visited one of his village headmen. For these two categories of officials were in daily contact with the people and with one another, and generally their relationship was quite informal. Here, as we saw, the division between the two upper grades of chiefs, with their offices, courts, and clerical staffs, and the two lower grades, who lived among the people, attended beer parties and other local events, and were well known to everyone, was clearly manifested. For Nyoro peasants, the county and sub-county chiefs represented the superimposed power of 'government' (*bulemi*), as opposed to the local community, in a way, or at least to a degree, in which the 'parish' chiefs and village headmen, who were neighbours and probably kinsmen as well, did not.

How, in general, were chiefs regarded, and what was expected of them? Naturally the qualities demanded by their European superiors differed in important respects from those looked for by most of their Nyoro subjects. In Bunyoro, as elsewhere in colonial Africa, chiefs were faced with the virtually insoluble problem of attempting to conform at one and the same time to two incompatible sets of standards. European expectations can be briefly listed. They reflected, in particular, the 'universalistic'

values of modern bureaucratic government; naturally chiefs were expected not to show favour, but to apply the law without regard to personal ties of kinship or friendship. They were expected, also, to show a proper spirit of respect and co-operation with their European superiors.

While I was in Bunyoro, the then chief justice (*muramuzi*) of the Native Government, a Munyoro of considerable dignity and distinction, was required by the European district commissioner to hear in his court a case in which a lower chief (who happened to be a relative of the chief justice) was charged with concealing the whereabouts of a wanted criminal. This affair was something of a *cause célèbre*; the wanted man was an ex-game-scout who had murdered a policeman sent to arrest him, and who had recently been captured after a year's 'Robin Hood' existence, shooting game with a stolen gun and ammunition, and selling it cheaply to the people. The *muramuzi* duly heard the case against the chief, but although he found him guilty, the offence did not seem to him a particularly heinous one, and he sentenced him only to a small fine. The district commissioner, incensed at what he thought was a totally inadequate sentence, ordered the chief justice to retry the case. He did so, and this time acquitted the accused. Thereupon, it is said, the district commissioner (who could hardly have failed to regard this as a deliberate affront to himself) gave the chief justice the option of either resigning (he had anyway almost reached retiring age) or being dismissed. He resigned.

Great importance was also attached by the Protectorate administration to efficiency in the collection of poll tax, court fees, and other dues, to the expeditious hearing of court cases, and to promptness in dealing with correspondence. High standards of honesty were expected, and irregularities in the handling of cash often led to dismissals. Drunkenness was also seriously regarded. A bright, agreeable manner with Europeans was expected; a surly and withdrawn demeanour was adversely commented on. A sub-county chief who was widely criticized by his subordinates and subjects for his jumpiness, lack of dignity, and tendency to angry abuse,[1] was reported on by a European officer on tour as being 'full of energy'; 'a good chief

---

[1] Banyoro have a word, *ndabukya*, for such clever, quick, irritable people, with a tendency to throw their weight about.

with lots of drive and character'. Conversely, it was said of a chief of good family, a Mubito, locally popular but less assimilated to Western norms, that he was 'indolent, and drinks too heavily'. Other categories of European approbation were 'reliable and loyal', 'firm', and 'full of progressive ideas'.[1]

Many of the expectations held by traditionally minded Banyoro naturally differed considerably from those implied in European judgements. For them, chiefs of all ranks were entitled to respect and obedience because they were 'the Mukama's spears' (*macumu g'Omukama*), deriving their authority from him. 'There must be chiefs, for otherwise how could the Mukama rule his country?', I was told. And naturally the higher a chief's rank the greater his prestige and ritual status (*mahano*), and the greater the respect due to him. Achieved qualities of intelligence and ability were important, but in themselves they did not make a chief; only the king's favour could do that. And although in the 1950s criticism of the chiefs was growing rapidly among the educated, most peasants at least still showed them marked respect.[2]

The following are some of the qualities looked for in chiefs by most Banyoro. Ideally, especially in the higher ranks, they should be men of good family. Though there was and apparently always had been a good deal of social mobility in Bunyoro, the notion of a ruling class was certainly explicit, centred on but not restricted to the Bito royal line. A chief should be dignified and calm, and he should show 'politeness' (*makune*, a highly valued quality in Bunyoro) towards inferiors as well as superiors. He should not shout and rant at his subordinates, as Europeans sometimes did. He should know his people and visit among them constantly; however efficient he was at office and court work,

---

[1] The continued popularity of some of the largest *kibanja* proprietors was no doubt at least partly due to the fact that although they were, as we saw, themselves, in traditional terms, a kind of 'chief,' they were not, as the official chiefs were, required to conform to Western ideas of efficiency and political morality.

[2] At the same time that I was engaged in field-work in Bunyoro an investigation was being carried out in Buganda to determine the order in which different categories of people would rank as 'important persons'. It was very clear from this investigation that the less educated sections of the community ranked the chiefs and other officials of the Kabaka's government as among the 'most important', while the better educated tended to rank local politicians, business and professional men, and other persons of 'achieved' qualification, at the top of the scale. Though there were fewer persons of these latter categories in Bunyoro, popular attitudes would certainly have divided on similar lines.

a chief who rarely left his headquarters was not popular. A strong chief was respected, but he should not be 'fierce'; Banyoro often criticized chiefs who punished a first offender by fine or imprisonment instead of merely warning him. Village headmen and 'parish' chiefs, like the *bakama b'ebibanja*, were still expected to protect their people against the exactions and demands—many of which seemed to them unreasonable—of the superimposed 'government'. Finally, chiefs should be generous; like the Mukama they should provide feasts and beer drinks for their people from time to time, and they should give help in food or money to anyone in need.

During the last years of the Protectorate it would have been difficult if not impossible for Nyoro chiefs to have satisfied all of the often conflicting demands of their European masters and of their Nyoro subjects. I have mentioned some of the criticisms of the chiefs made by European administrators; those made by Banyoro themselves are even more revealing. They too reflected the dual standard now being required of chiefs. Older, more traditionally minded and less-educated Banyoro criticized them for failing to conform to traditional patterns; the younger and better educated criticized them on exactly opposite grounds, for failing to conform to modern standards of democratic leadership, as they understood them. But the issues were not always as clear-cut as this; though traditional and modern standards usually conflicted, they sometimes coincided.

The emphasis on a chief being, ideally, of 'good family' has been noted. It was a common complaint in the 1950s that senior chiefs were not members of aristocratic Bito or Huma families with a tradition of ruling, as (it was supposed) they used to be. Though it may be doubted if a majority of the chiefs ever were such, the criticism is significant. I was often told that these days anybody could become a chief; most senior chiefs were merely commoners (*bairu*) who had risen to their high positions either through the Mukama's personal patronage, or by the Europeans' favour. Both traditionalists and progressives agreed that it was wrong that appointment to chiefship should depend solely on the Mukama's personal favour. Certainly a chief could not be a chief without this favour, at least until the 1955 Agreement altered the basis of chiefly appointment. But unless he could also claim good family (in the traditionalists' view), or was qualified

by training and ability (in the progressives' view), he ought not to have been given a chiefship, certainly not at the county or sub-county level. Older men often referred scornfully to the modern chiefs as mere 'porters' or manual labourers (*bapagazi*). They meant that they were simply paid employees, interested only in their salaries, 'perks', and prospects of promotion, not in their people. One informant said: 'long ago chiefs trusted and depended on their peasants, for their living came directly from them: now they do not care about them, for their money comes from the government, not from the people.' Banyoro who reflected on the present state of their country (and many did) were well aware of the extent to which the traditional bond between chiefs and people depended upon the constant passage of goods and services between them.

So criticisms of what chiefs did, or failed to do, as well as criticisms of what they were, varied according to the status and values of the critic. A common complaint, also made as we have seen of the Mukama, was that chiefs no longer entertained and feasted (*kwinura*) their people as they had done in former times, although they still expected the traditional gifts of produce (*bitereke*) from their subjects when they were on tour. Those who complained did not always realize that the limited amount of produce reluctantly supplied to the chiefs in this way was quite insufficient to enable them to provide feasts of beer and meat for the people on what was supposed to have been the tradi-tional scale, and it was certainly impossible for them to do it on their salaries. As one chief told me, 'When they [the peasants] have paid their taxes, they do not feel under any further obliga-tion to us'.

County and sub-county chiefs were also criticized on the grounds that they no longer stayed long enough in one place to get to know their people; we saw above that this was largely true. Also, the many European-imposed regulations which the chiefs were required to enforce, relating to such matters as the provision and depth of pit-latrines, the design of houses and kitchens, the kinds and quality of crops to be planted, were resented by most peasants (as indeed they commonly were by the lower chiefs who were required to enforce them). Often, people said, these irksome rules and regulations were harshly enforced, without previous discussion or explanation.

It was also constantly said that the higher chiefs of the present generation were weak and sycophantic in relation to the powers above them (the Mukama and the British administration), compared with their predecessors of even twenty or thirty years earlier. This was often attributed by the more sophisticated to the wide personal powers of appointment, promotion, and dismissal conferred on the Mukama by the 1933 Agreement. Strong and independently minded chiefs had, it was said, gradually been weeded out and replaced by weaker and more compliant personalities. Certainly, as we noted before, in the 1930s and 1940s a number of well-known and highly respected county chiefs had either resigned or been dismissed while still in the prime of life, and this was generally (though usually covertly) attributed to the Mukama's personal dislike of them.[1]

I remarked above that on the whole chiefs maintained solidary relations among themselves as against outsiders, and that, at least at the 'grass roots' level, represented by the 'parish' chiefs and village headmen, their relations with the ordinary people were good. But inter-chief as well as chief–subject relations were often said to have deteriorated since traditional times. An informant wrote: 'Nowadays *saza* chiefs do not get on with their sub-chiefs, nor with their subjects. And *gombolola* chiefs do not get on with their *miruka* chiefs, nor with their subjects. And *miruka* chiefs do not get on with their subjects, *batongole* chiefs do not get on with their subjects, and *bibanja* owners do not get on with the people who live on their *bibanja*.'

Two points may be noted about this brief text. First, only in the case of the two higher ranks of chiefs is reference made to their 'getting on' with the chiefs next subordinate to them, as well as with their subjects; in the case of the 'parish' chiefs (as, of course, in that of the village headmen, who had no official subordinates), reference is made only to their relationship with their subjects. This illustrates the point, already made, that it

---

[1] Of course the European administration was not immune from criticism either. An elderly official in the Native Government wrote: 'After the last war [1939–45] the Government took away all the older administrative officers, who were good men and liked us Banyoro, and replaced them by new ones who do not like us, and treat us unkindly.' He continued, 'Europeans who speak up for Africans and who admit that Europeans have sometimes done bad things are sent back to their own country, or are even got rid of by poisoning.' Statements of this kind were common.

is at the lower grades of chiefship that relations with the ordinary people are all-important. When one considers the role of the *muruka* chief, it is his relations with the people in his area, rather than his relations with his two or three subordinate village headmen, that come to mind. The second point worth noting here is the classifying, in the last sentence of the text, of the owners of populated *bibanja* with chiefs; as we saw in Chapter 8, for most Banyoro in the 1950s a *mukama w'ekibanja was* a kind of 'chief'; hardly less so than his salaried and official contemporary.

The conflicts that this informant, perhaps rather exaggeratedly, referred to, like the other strains implied by the criticisms we have been considering, evidently reflect the stage of transition which the Nyoro polity, like many others in colonial Africa, was at that time undergoing. A traditional mode of government, structured 'patrimonially', in Max Weber's terms, in which political links were also personal ones, was changing (and I dare say the process still continues) into a modern, 'civil-service' type of administration, in which bureaucratic norms were at least ideally paramount, and in which it was no longer possible for chiefs (who were anyhow now becoming something of an anachronism) to know all, or even a substantial number, of their subjects individually. In Bunyoro, as elsewhere, changes in the formal structure of political institutions had in many instances outpaced corresponding changes in attitudes and values. Consequently many Banyoro entertained expectations in regard to their chiefs (as many chiefs did in regard to their subjects) which in the nature of the situation as it then existed could no longer be satisfied.

To conclude, then, chiefs in Bunyoro, like chiefs in many other parts of colonial Africa, were required to conform to two separate and often incompatible sets of standards. One of these was appropriate to a state of affairs which had long since ceased to exist in its original form; the other was appropriate to a modern bureaucratic type of administration which, although sometimes superficially adhered to, had not yet really taken root. The system was no longer the traditional one, nor was it the impersonal, modern civil service which it was sometimes thought to be. As we have seen, it contained elements of both systems, and at the same time elements incompatible with either. So

inevitably the chiefs were subject to criticism from one point of view or the other; sometimes from both points of view at once. On the one hand, they were respected as 'the Mukama's spears'; on the other they were despised because they were inferior in wealth, education, and social standing to many who were not chiefs. On the one hand they were admired if they were educated, enterprising, efficient, and sober; on the other they were distrusted because they did not mix more with their people and provide them with constant feasts and beer drinks. On the one hand they were required to adhere to the universalistic and specific norms of bureaucratic administration; on the other they were expected to acknowledge the particularistic and diffuse obligations of the traditional polity, as far as relations with kinsmen, friends, and neighbours were concerned. The dilemma was, in effect, insoluble, and tribute should be paid to those many hard-working and devoted *banyoro*, at all levels, who lived with it and, on the whole, coped with it so well.

11

CONCLUSION: BUNYORO AND BUGANDA[1]

IN this book I have sought to describe a political process, or rather a combination of processes, rather than a political structure as such. Evidently an equilibrium model of balanced opposition would have been quite inappropriate to Bunyoro, at least during the past century, and probably at all stages in its history. Certainly both the Nyoro political system and the ways in which it was regarded have undergone continuing and radical change under the pressure of Western contact. And, as we have seen, change did not take place evenly on all fronts; in Bunyoro as elsewhere the traditional and the modern have often coexisted uncomfortably, and in earlier chapters I have described some of the conflicts to which this state of affairs gave rise. As has recently been pointed out, political anthropology can no longer concern itself mainly with 'cyclical' or 'repetitive' processes; increasingly it must deal with processes of radical development and change.[2] It must, that is, be historical.

But even a changing system must be seen as structured at any point in time, if it is to be called a system at all, and I have also necessarily given some account of the system of more or less institutionalized relationships, and the values associated with them, which constituted the *Obukama bwa Bunyoro–Kitara* both when I studied it in the 1950s and in those earlier periods for which adequate evidence is available. It may be useful to conclude with an attempt to place the kingdom of Bunyoro, as it has been described in this book, in the comparative context

[1] For helpful comment on and criticism of the comparison set out in the following pages I am grateful to the members of a graduate seminar in the Department of Anthropology and Sociology, University of Manchester, where it was first proposed, and especially to Dr. Martin Southwold, whose informed critical comments on my representation of traditional Buganda have been particularly valuable.

[2] See, for example, Swartz, Turner, and Tuden, p. 8.

which the ethnography of at least one neighbouring kingdom provides. So in this chapter I compare Bunyoro with the adjoining state of Buganda. This attempt conforms at least in some part with Schapera's excellent injunction that the most useful comparisons are those based on intensive regional study, embracing all the peoples in a specific area (Schapera 1953, p. 359).

In Chapter 6 I gave some account of the traditional Nyoro state, and explained that it was seen, at least by Banyoro, as the successor kingdom to the great Cwezi empire of Kitara, which is supposed to have extended, in the fourteenth or fifteenth century, over the greater part of present-day Uganda. Accordingly Banyoro saw their relationship with neighbouring kingdoms, especially with the adjacent ones of Toro and Buganda, as similar to that between parent and child, and indeed we saw that Toro's breakaway from the parent kingdom was only ratified in European times. But Buganda's supposed derivation from Bunyoro is validated only by a myth which is not shared by Baganda, who prefer a different version, establishing Ganda origins as distinct and as of at least equal antiquity with Bunyoro's. We shall see that there are indeed significant structural differences, as well as important similarities, between the two kingdoms.

Naturally the Toro kingdom reproduced all the essential features of the Nyoro one from which it seceded. As regards Ankole, effective political links with that country are recorded only in the traditional histories of the two kingdoms, and they were mostly hostile. It seems that during the eighteenth century Bunyoro lost considerable areas to the southern kingdom (in earlier times a part, like all the surrounding countries, of the great Cwezi empire), as well as to Buganda. In traditional times, Ankole was even more loosely structured politically than Bunyoro; its rulers were pastoral Bahima and not Babito, and as is well known their kingdom showed a sharp division between the ruling Hima minority and the agricultural Bairu, who are said to have outnumbered their pastoral masters by about nine to one.[1] Though the Nkore and Nyoro kingdoms resemble one another in some respects, the division between pastoralists and

[1] For a brief account of Nkore (Ankole) history see Morris 1962, also Morris 1964, pp. 1–10.

agriculturalists was never so strongly stressed in Bito-governed Bunyoro, even though notions of Huma-based prestige survive in attenuated form to the present day. The distinction was scarcely found at all in Buganda, where Bahima were simply 'cattle-men', usually aliens, employed by rich and powerful Ganda princes and chiefs.

Of greatest interest in the present context, then, is a comparison of the Nyoro state with Buganda, the only neighbouring kingdom (except Toro) with which it shared an extensive land frontier, and with which it has for centuries sustained continuing relations, though mostly hostile ones.[1] It is remarkable that the two kingdoms differed so much in both culture and social organization. Indeed, although in recent generations Buganda has been by far the most powerful of the four kingdoms, it has always been the 'odd man out'. Both in language and in certain other aspects of its culture such as its clan and kinship systems, Bunyoro is a good deal closer to Ankole, even to the small kingdoms of north-western Tanzania, than it is to its closest neighbour.

The central topic of this chapter is to be the structural differences between the polities of the two kingdoms, but it will be useful to begin by noting some important underlying dissimilarities in their physical environments, ecology, and cultures. Whether, and if so to what extent, any of these dissimilarities can be correlated with the differences which I call 'structural', will be considered later in this chapter. Somewhat arbitrarily, eight such underlying differences can be identified.

First, although much of Bunyoro resembles much of Buganda in topography and climate, there are considerable regions of Bunyoro, especially in the 'Lost Counties' area, which are higher, drier, and less fertile; these were formerly largely given over to grazing. Most of Buganda, especially near Lake Victoria, has a much higher rainfall and is considerably more fertile.

With this is associated, secondly, a major difference in basic food crops. The traditional staple of Bunyoro is finger-millet

---

[1] It should be remembered, though, that traditional warfare was usually local and sporadic rather than 'total', and did not preclude other kinds of social relationships: in fact there has always been a good deal of communication between the two kingdoms. Roscoe, for example, reports that salt and hoes, in particular, were imported by Buganda from the western kingdom (1911, p. 5).

(*eleusine*), called *buro* in Runyoro, a crop characteristic of rather drier zones. On the other hand, Buganda's typical food is *matoke*, made from cooked plantains of a number of varieties; plantains do best in a relatively moist climate. Planting and maintaining a grove of plantains requires much less time and labour than does the cultivation of an annual crop of millet: a plantain garden needs little attention, and continues to bear for many years. It also occupies a good deal less space than a millet field and has a far greater yield per acre.

Third, there are the even greater differences between a pastoral and an agricultural way of life. I suggested in Chapter 2 (p. 14 n. 1) that Bunyoro's traditional commitment to pastoralism has been much exaggerated, especially by Roscoe, but there is no doubt that even in the 1950s pastoralism was the Nyoro ideal. The cattle-herding Bahuma were an acknowledged aristocracy, and even today the Nyoro language contains many idiomatic references to cattle and to the values associated with them.[1] Buganda lacks any such pastoral tradition. Certainly, as we have noted, some Baganda chiefs and other important people owned herds of cattle, and they employed pastoral Bahima to take care of them. But in Buganda the Bahima were not an upper class. They were simply professional herdsmen from Ankole or elsewhere, employed as servants, not respected as superiors. Roscoe reports that even so 'the Bahima were inclined to regard their masters as their inferiors' (Roscoe 1911, p. 417), but it appears that this sentiment was reciprocated, Baganda themselves despising their 'Bayima' servants (personal communication from M. Southwold).

Fourth, and associated with the two foregoing, there was undoubtedly a very great difference between the two kingdoms in density of population. Of course there is now no means of knowing precisely what this difference was in traditional times; it has certainly been considerable since the turn of the century.[2]

---

[1] Here is an example taken from the context of marriage. Although bridewealth has for many years been paid in cash, not cattle, it is still called *mukaga*, 'six' (i.e. six head of cattle). In the course of the marriage ceremonies a small cash payment (*z'enjunju*, 'for the blows') may still be demanded by the bride's representative to recompense him for the energy he must expend in beating the bridewealth cattle (were there any) as he drives them home. See Beattie 1958*a*, p. 8.

[2] In 1902 Sir Harry Johnston estimated the population of Buganda as something over 1,000,000 (though he thought that it had been as much as four times larger a generation earlier, in Mutesa's time), that of Bunyoro as 'not exceeding 110,000'

Evidently Bunyoro's combination of millet cultivation with pastoralism in at least some areas must always have implied a very much more dispersed population than Buganda's concentration on plantain cultivation. The obvious implications of this major difference between the two kingdoms from the point of view of political centralization and control are considered below.

Turning now to specifically cultural differences between the two peoples, there was, fifthly, a marked difference in language. Runyoro and Luganda are indeed closely related, but a Munyoro can more easily converse with a man from Ankole or even a Muhaya from north-western Tanzania, than he can with a Muganda. I myself found little difficulty in understanding Kikerewe, spoken on the island of Ukerewe in southern Lake Victoria (which represents the extreme south-eastern tip of what may be called the Nyoro-speaking crescent), but I never acquired more than a smattering of Luganda. Roscoe's work in Bunyoro was not done through Runyoro, his ignorance of which is plain from his book *The Bakitara*, but through Luganda. Baganda working in Bunyoro have to learn the language, though they do not find this difficult.[1]

Sixth, the clan systems of the two countries were quite different. According to Roscoe (1911, pp. 138–40) there were thirty-six Ganda clans,[2] named after animal species, or, less often, after plants or other things which their members held in special regard. Particular areas, or 'estates' as Roscoe called them, were traditionally associated with these clans, and through local clan councils members often acted corporately. The clan system in Bunyoro, and among the other interlacustrine Bantu peoples, was very different. There are 150 or more clans (*nganda*) in Bunyoro, and their members are widely dispersed throughout the country and beyond. They have no enduring associations with particular territories, and they never

---

(1902, vol. ii, pp. 591, 640). In 1959 (the year of the most recent census) Buganda's population density per land square mile was 114, Bunyoro's (excluding the unpopulated Murchison Falls National Park) 32·4 (*Uganda Census 1959: African Population*, Nairobi, 1961).

[1] A Muganda priest wrote to me, after being posted for about two months in Bunyoro: 'I can now understand Lunyoro; it is still however difficult for me to express myself properly.'

[2] Fallers upgrades this total to 40 (p. 71); Southwold to 'about 50' (p. 85).

act corporately above the level of the local lineage group. Although the members of each clan respect a certain animal or plant species, or some other object, clans are not named after their 'totems'. I have argued that Nyoro clans are properly regarded as categories rather than 'groups'.[1]

Connected with the above difference, seventh, are some dissimilarities in the kinship terminology itself. The most important of these relate to the greater stress laid in Bunyoro (terminologically if not in actual behaviour) on unilineality. Thus Bunyoro has a straightforward Omaha-type cross-cousin terminology, Buganda has not.[2] These differences in terminology, combined with linguistic differences and with the differences in the type and significance of clan organization, have meant that the familiar idiom of clanship and kinship was not ready to hand as a means of facilitating quick and easy relationships between members of the two kingdoms. Of course such relationships were sometimes established, but not, by Banyoro, so extensively or readily as with neighbouring Batoro or Banyankole, with whom they share both language and kinship terminology.

The eighth difference to be mentioned here, none the less important in that it is one of degree, is that distinctions of hereditary status appear to have been more strongly stressed in Bunyoro than in Buganda. In neither kingdom was there anything like the clear-cut division into pastoral aristocrats and agricultural peasants described for Ankole and some other southern kingdoms, but in Bunyoro there was at least the tradition of a Huma aristocracy, and the ruling Babito clan, at least those of its members who could claim actual agnatic relationship with a ruling Mukama, claimed and were accorded high status. Of course there were hereditary distinctions of status in Buganda too, but in the absence both of a royal clan (see below) and of

---

[1] Beattie 1957a, pp. 319–25.

[2] There are, however, suggestions of some underlying similarities in terminology. Thus the Luganda term for 'mother's brother', *kojja*, of which the ethnography offers no translation, might conceivably be derived from some such form as *nyoko musajja*, '(your) mother man', or, more loosely, 'male mother', and the term for 'father's sister', *ssenga*, might likewise be associated with the term *ise*, 'father', and *'nkati'* (or *'-kazi'*), 'woman'. These suggestions arose in discussion with the Revd. P. Kalanda, himself a Muganda, but I should add that Dr. M. Southwold is sceptical of them. Also, there is no suggestion in contemporary Buganda of an Omaha-type cross-cousin terminology, such as is found in Bunyoro.

a hereditary class of cattle-herding aristocrats, such distinctions seem to have been both less ubiquitous and less strongly emphasized.

These, then, are some of the more important background differences between the two kingdoms, both ecological and in terms of their separate cultures. I turn now to the main theme of this chapter, the differences between them which are expressly political. The crucial distinction, which all the other differences either express or reflect, is that Buganda had evolved a very much more centralized form of government than Bunyoro. I mean by this simply that in Buganda political power was more firmly concentrated at a single centre than was the case in Bunyoro. The distinction is thus one of degree; evidently the traditional Nyoro state was much more centralized than, for example, the kingdom of the Nilotic Shilluk, whose king 'reigns but does not govern'.[1] But it is of central importance none the less, and we shall see that it is associated with important differences in kind between the political institutions of the two kingdoms. Historically regarded, this reflects the fact that while the Nyoro kingdom seems in traditional times to have been very widely extended, though (as we saw in Chapter 4) much diminished in recent centuries, the Ganda kingdom, although it had expanded as Bunyoro contracted, was still relatively small and compact when the Europeans first arrived there just over a century ago.[2]

Differences in political organization between the two kingdoms may conveniently be considered under four main heads. First, they differed with regard to the means and degree of communication possible within them. Second, there were differences in the origins, statuses, and internal organization of the royal lines themselves. Third, the ways in which and the conditions under which the king's powers were exercised differed. And fourth, there were differences in the manner and degree in

---

[1] Evans-Pritchard 1962, p. 74. The great earthworks at Bigo in Mubende, the traditional heart of the ancient Kitara empire, which were constructed about the fourteenth or fifteenth century, argue a comparatively high level of central control, at least temporarily, at that period. See Posnansky, p. 5.

[2] Of course Buganda's high level of centralization as compared with neighbouring kingdoms has been stressed by historians. See, for example, Oliver 1963, p. 189: 'during the years of its obscurity Buganda has been slowly evolving a much more homogeneous and centralized form of society than Bunyoro was ever to achieve.'

which the king's central authority was associated with traditional ritual beliefs and practices. In all of these four contexts Buganda's higher level of centralization, and Bunyoro's more dispersed type of political organization, are more or less clearly expressed.

The very different quality of communication which it was possible to maintain in the two kingdoms is evidently related to the greater compactness of the Ganda state. Early visitors to Buganda describe the well-planned and carefully maintained system of roads, or rather broad footpaths, which radiated from the capital to all corners of the kingdom.[1] The importance of these relatively rapid means of communication in what Audrey Richards has called a 'pedestrian state', especially one whose terrain, where uncultivated, is covered with dense vegetation and contains innumerable papyrus swamps and streams, is evident. They enabled the king and his officials at the capital to maintain close political contact even with outlying parts of the kingdom, all of which could easily be reached by runner within a day or two.

Also relevant in this connection is the use of canoe transport made by the Baganda rulers.[2] Before the period of rapid Ganda expansion westwards in the nineteenth century most Baganda lived not very far distant from Lake Victoria or one of its inlets, and of course many of the Kabaka's subjects inhabited the offshore Ssese Islands. There are graphic accounts in the literature of the great fleet of war canoes which was at the Kabaka's disposal, and it is probable that canoe transport, as well as being of military significance, was also of considerable importance as a means of political communication between the capital, which although frequently shifted was usually sited fairly close to the lake, and outlying areas of the country along the lake shore, as well as the islands.[3]

There was nothing like these means of rapid communication in Bunyoro. According to Roscoe, 'there were no roads opening

[1] Speke says of the roads on his first entry into Buganda in February 1862 that they were 'as broad as our coach-roads, cut through the long grasses, straight over the hills and down through the woods in the dells—a strange contrast to the wretched tracks in all the adjacent countries' (p. 274). See also Grant, p. 209; Johnston 1902, vol. i, p. 85; and Roscoe 1911, p. 4.

[2] My attention was drawn to the importance of this by a member of the graduate seminar at Manchester University referred to on p. 245 n. 1 above.

[3] See Stanley, pp. 305–6. See also Roscoe 1911, p. 385, where he reports that the island chiefs had to 'maintain a number of canoes ready for state service'.

up the country, and no attempt had been made to connect the country residences of chiefs with the capital' (1923, p. 73). Little use was made of canoes on the arid and sparsely populated coastline of Lake Albert, except by a few small and isolated fishing communities. It is clear that Baganda possessed, and maintained, the physical means to achieve a very much more centralized administration than was possible in Bunyoro.

This had important military implications. Traditionally both countries depended for their armies on a 'militia', summoned in emergency from all parts of the kingdom. The development in both states during the second half of the nineteenth century of something like a standing army was an innovation, due to a combination of factors, of which the growing availability of muzzle-loading guns and the increasing wealth (through their monopoly of trade) of the rulers themselves were no doubt among the most important.[1] But up to the close of the century, the bulk of the armies raised in both Buganda and Bunyoro were spearmen levied from all parts of the two kingdoms. And evidently troops could be assembled more quickly and in larger numbers, either for attack or defence, in densely populated Buganda with its ample communication network, than was possible in the neighbouring kingdom.[2]

More fundamentally, the distinction between the two kingdoms in terms of compactness and ease of travel within them implied that political authority throughout Buganda possessed what may be described as a more homogeneous quality than was possible in Bunyoro. In principle, and it seems in large measure in fact, chiefs—and subjects—in all areas of Buganda were equally subject to the Kabaka's central power; subordinate authorities held their delegated powers under similar conditions. Fallers (p. 73) has stressed that the more or less rigid hierarchy of modern times, at least below the level of the ten great *ssaza* chiefs, is a recent innovation, but the system of territorial administration, with its ranked ordering of superior and inferior, may be said to have been at least incipiently hierarchical. Even

---

[1] Kabarega's 'standing army' of *Barusura* was referred to in Chapter 6. For some discussion of the conditions for the growth of professional armies see Andrzejewski, especially chap. ii. For a reference to the conditions of military service in traditional Buganda see Fallers 1964, p. 83.

[2] We noted in Chapter 4 that armies of up to 20,000 Baganda were mobilized in the 1890s for the invasion of Bunyoro under British direction.

though, as Fallers says, the system in pre-European times was very much more 'ragged' than the modern one, its more centralized organization and excellent communications enabled the Kabaka 'to maintain active control over a territory one-quarter the size of England without written communication and with no means of travel on land beyond the human foot' (Fallers, p. 105). Under British influence the system readily becomes the 'neat pyramidal structure' familiar to us from the literature, sharing some (though of course not all) of the qualities of a modern bureaucracy.

It might be said that the Ganda state had, as it were, sharp edges: one was either in it or outside it. Though it is said that the Kabaka was recognized as 'overlord' by the neighbouring small states to the east and south (in present-day Busoga and Buhaya), these statelets were not themselves part of Buganda, but were rather tributary states, paying tribute to the greater kingdom as the price of preserving their internal autonomy. The ground of their subjection was force or the threat of it; no validation was claimed for it in myth or traditional history.

The position in Bunyoro was different, though no doubt the difference can be exaggerated. The more widely dispersed Nyoro state was very much less evenly administered; although in theory the Mukama's power was absolute, in day-to-day matters his authority declined as one approached the peripheral areas of the kingdom. Bunyoro too had lesser and in some respects dependent polities beyond its borders (so far as these can be precisely specified). But the relationship of these neighbouring peoples with the Mukama was not simply one of tribute payment on threat of conquest, as appears to have been the case for Buganda's eastern and southern neighbours. It was rather one of freely acknowledged and ceremonially expressed interdependency. We noted in Chapter 2 that gifts were given to the Mukama by Lango and Acholi chiefs, who acknowledged the Nyoro king's supremacy while at the same time preserving effective independence, and in return for these expressions of respect these lesser rulers were granted the Mukama's formal acknowledgement of their local authority, and received regalia of office from him. Bunyoro's Nilotic neighbours to the north thought of themselves, and were thought of by Banyoro, as 'mothers' brothers' to the ruling Bito dynasty, for Rukidi

Mpuga's mother Nyatworo was a Nilotic Mukidi. Thus the relationship between the Nyoro kingdom and its Nilotic satellites was not simply one of political dominance; it was conceived also in kinship terms, and it is to be noted that in the idiom of Nyoro kinship, sisters' sons are said to 'rule' their mothers' brothers.[1]

In fact, on the northern and north-eastern borders of traditional Bunyoro it would have been difficult to say where the Nyoro state ended, and where separate but in some degree dependent polities began: indeed in the context of broadening and varying shades of influence the question might have been meaningless. As boundaries hardened during the British period some of Bunyoro's Nilotic 'dependants' were incorporated in the reduced kingdom (the Chopi or Jopalwoo of the Kibanda county of Bunyoro are still Nilotic speakers); others were included in the separate administrative districts of Acholi and Lango. The Victoria Nile, and not any traditional division in language, culture, or political allegiance, became the formal northern boundary of the attenuated Nyoro state.

I turn now to the second major field of differences between the two states, those relating to the royal lineages themselves. Here four points are of particular importance.

The first is that the origins of the royal lines are differently conceived in the two kingdoms. As we saw, the Bito dynasty in Bunyoro derives both in myth and, as is now apparent, in fact from a take-over by intrusive Nilotic-speakers from north of the Nile. Thus the Bito rulers, and the Bito clan to which they belong, regard themselves and are regarded by others as *sui generis*, separate and distinct from the numerous other clans which make up the Nyoro people.[2] Bunyoro tradition ascribes to the Ganda royal line a (literally) twin origin with its own, Kimera, the third Kabaka in Roscoe's list (Roscoe 1911, p. 231), being represented in the Nyoro version as the younger twin brother of Rukidi Mpuga, and the first Kabaka, not the third. Roscoe represents the first Ganda king, Kintu, as having come from outside, and as having been 'of a different stock from the

[1] Beattie 1958a, p. 19.
[2] This statement needs to be qualified by the observation that non-royal Babito, 'just Babito', are for practical purposes regarded scarcely differently from other people. Even so, a slight *cachet* attaches to them as Babito, and unlike all the other Nyoro clans the Bito clan is not exogamous. See pp. 95–8 above.

aborigines', whom he at once began to subdue and amalgamate (1911, p. 186). Thus the accounts Roscoe received are not basically incompatible with the Nyoro version, which indeed is the one generally accepted throughout the northern inter-lacustrine area.[1] But it has been argued by the distinguished Ganda historian Sir A. Kagwa and, following him, by Fallers, that the Ganda royal line emerged not by intrusion from else-where, by conquest or otherwise, but as *primus inter pares*, as one among a number of patrilineal descent groups originally of roughly equal status (Fallers, p. 76). According to Fallers, this 'tradition of past equality', at least in the central core area of the kingdom, meant that early Kabakas had to treat the clans and their heads with some circumspection. Although it is plain that the power of the Kabaka grew steadily at the expense of that of the clan heads or *bataka*, Ganda clans have certainly formed at times a focus of opposition to the king's central power. But there is no evidence that this opposition ever formed a real threat to the kingship.

In both Bunyoro and Buganda the clans were bound to the kingship through numerous ritual, ceremonial, and domestic offices in the palace (as well as through 'marriages' of their women by the king). These offices were vested in patrilineal clans or lineages. But in Buganda the Kabaka's ultimate—and in Faller's view hard-won—dominance over the clans (we shall see below that he is not himself a member of a distinctive royal clan) is expressed in his title of *Ssabataka*, 'chief of all *bataka* or clan heads'. There is no equivalent title in the case of the Nyoro king, although in Bunyoro as in Buganda accession to positions of authority within the clans (e.g. to lineage headship) as well as outside them had to be validated by the Mukama or by his deputy appointed for the occasion. The more numerous and dispersed Nyoro clans (with the exception of the royal Bito clan) seem never to have had anything like the political importance of the Ganda ones. So the structure of the Nyoro clan system did not involve the strengthening and explicit assertion of the central power of the state in contradistinction to the clans, as seems to have occurred, at least in some degree, in Buganda.

The second important difference between the two royal lines is that while in Bunyoro there was, as we have seen, a large and

[1] See, for example, Oliver 1963, pp. 184–5.

widely distributed royal clan (or perhaps congeries of clans), with the bushbuck (*ngabi*) as its 'totem' or avoidance object, in Buganda there was no 'royal' clan at all. There was, of course, a royal lineage, and succession was always in the male line, but princes took the clan names and avoidances of their mothers, and according to Roscoe the 'totems' of the royal line (the lion, the leopard, and the eagle), which might perhaps better be called 'emblems', were rarely mentioned (1911, pp. 128, 187). This had the very important consequence that in Buganda the growth of a powerful clan of 'royals', sharing a common name, a common avoidance object, and the concept of common patrilineal descent with the king, and demanding in consequence special privileges and powers, was discouraged, if not altogether prevented. After two or three generations a Ganda 'peasant prince' tended to become absorbed in the commoner clan of his mother, and he ceased to command any special authority or distinction.

In Bunyoro, as we saw in Chapter 5, the position was very different. All Babito who could claim known genealogical connection, however remote, with a reigning Mukama regarded themselves and were regarded as a special class, entitled by birth to powers and privileges not accorded to ordinary people. Only those whose fathers had actually reigned were eligible to succeed to the throne (in fact there were usually a great number of these as many Bakama were remarkably philoprogenitive), but the others, especially those whose genealogical links with the Mukama were close, were held in scarcely less regard, and some held high political positions in the kingdom.

Thus we may say that, structurally regarded, the problem of containing possible revolt by dissident princes was dealt with (not, it must be said, very effectively in either case, as we shall see below) by two diametrically opposed means. In Bunyoro, where Bito princes (and princesses) expected as of right a measure of political authority—we saw in Chapter 5 that Babito seem always to have been fairly well represented among the territorial chiefs and palace officials—the danger was countered by, as it were, 'placating' them with the grant of limited political power. In Buganda, consistently with its very much higher concentration of power at the centre, the princes were rigorously and explicitly excluded from any share at all in political

authority. Roscoe reports that from the reign of Kabaka Semakokiro (the twenty-seventh Ganda king, nine kings and six generations back from the recently deposed Mutesa II) onward, this exclusion took the drastic form of putting princes to death as soon as a new king had secured the succession by begetting sons of his own (1911, pp. 188–9). Southwold justly doubts whether such a practice could rightly be described, then or later, as 'customary', though undoubtedly Semakokiro and some later kings have on occasion had potential rivals—including, in Semakokiro's case, his own sons—either imprisoned or put to death (Southwold, pp. 114–17). Even the Ganda 'peasant princes', who presumably constituted no direct danger to the succession (though no doubt as persons of prestige and influence they might have formed focuses of opposition to an unpopular Kabaka), appear to have been firmly excluded from any contact with chiefship. Roscoe even goes so far as to say that no prince was allowed to visit or attach himself to any chief, lest that chief should support his guest's claim to the kabakaship.[1] In fact, as was noted above, revolts by dissident princes have been a feature of the traditional histories of both kingdoms (though commoner in Buganda than in Bunyoro), but the very different means of dealing with the danger in the two kingdoms clearly reflects the very much greater power held by the ruler of the more strongly centralized of the two.

Consistent with the large political role allowed to Nyoro princes (as contrasted to the lack of any political role permitted to Ganda ones), is the third major dissimilarity to be considered here in the internal organization of the two royal lines, that is, the very different degree of importance attached in each kingdom to the official head of the princes. In both countries this official (*Okwiri* in Bunyoro, *Kiwewa* in Buganda) was the previous king's eldest son, as such himself debarred from the royal succession. But Bunyoro's Okwiri appears to have been a very much more important figure than Buganda's Kiwewa. In view of the princes' high political status in the former kingdom, and their total exclusion from positions of influence in the latter, this is what we should expect. As we saw in Chapter 5, in matters concerning the Babito the Okwiri took precedence over the Mukama himself, with whom he dealt directly, and he was given

[1] Roscoe 1911, p. 188. See also Fallers, p. 69, and Southwold, p. 86.

a special 'estate' (that is, a territorial chiefship) in the Mwenge
area of the kingdom (Roscoe 1923, pp. 172–3). Individual Nyoro
princes had no privileged access to the Mukama; their complaints and disputes were taken to the Okwiri, who could settle
them without reference to the king, and usually did so.

In Buganda, according to Roscoe's account, the Kiwewa was
a figure of very much less importance. Although Roscoe states
that he was responsible for the conduct of his brother 'princes of
the drum', his responsibility was not directly to the Kabaka, but
to the commoner chief *Kasuju*, who was in charge of all the
princes (1911, p. 188). The head of the peasant princes, also
called Kiwewa, was, according to this account, an even less
important figure, directly responsible to another commoner
chief called *Ssabalangira* ('head of the princes'), who was in turn
responsible to Kasuju. Although, as princes, both Kiwewas
would have had land given to them for their support, Roscoe
makes no mention of any special 'estate' held by either of them
in virtue of his office, as he does in his account of Okwiri in *The
Bakitara*. Thus, if Roscoe's account is correct, the lesser political
importance of the Ganda princes would seem to have been
clearly reflected in the lower status ascribed to their heads.[1]

The different statuses ascribed to the heads of the princesses
in the two kingdoms expresses a comparable distinction. In
Bunyoro *Kalyota*, the head of the princesses, held high political
office, and assumed a special relationship with the Mukama—
though she was not, as Roscoe thought, his 'queen', in the sense
of being his consort and the mother of his children. In Buganda
the role of the king's official sister (*Lubuga*, also called the 'queen'
by Roscoe [1911, p. 84]), and that of the head of the princesses,
were kept distinct, the latter, *Nasolo*, possessing no such exalted
status.

The fourth difference relating to the royal lineages themselves was in the customary mode of succession to the kingship
in the two states. In Buganda, as Southwold has convincingly
shown, 'a brother was preferred to a son', and although brother-
to-brother succession was characteristic only of his 'second

---

[1] It should be said that at any rate in recent times Ssabalangira, the 'head of the
princes', was himself a peasant prince and not a commoner, and that the office
of 'head of the peasant princes' (Roscoe's second 'Kiwewa') seems not to have
existed (personal communication from M. Southwold).

period' (i.e. from the fifteenth to the twenty-seventh Kabaka inclusive), this mode of succession represented the Ganda ideal: fraternal succession was also the preferred mode in everyday life (pp. 104 ff.). As Southwold shows, although fraternal succession provided for a succession of strong and mature kings, it also implied a constant danger of rebellion, and some of the stronger kings of his 'third period' preferred to follow the example of the first of them, Semakokiro, and secure their own sons' succession by killing or confining their brother princes.[1]

In Bunyoro it is clear that filial, not fraternal, succession was the preferred norm, as it is also in commoner succession; for kings as for ordinary people one's proper heir is one's son, preferably a younger one (Beattie 1957a, p. 328). Of Bunyoro's twenty-three Bito kings from Rukidi to Kabarega, eighteen succeeded their fathers. Of the five exceptions, one, Oyo, succeeded his deceased twin brother, who had left no son to succeed him, and the other four succeeded by rebelling against their brothers.[2] This marked difference in the pattern of succession is evidently consistent with the centralization of political power in the hands of the Ganda king and the exclusion of the princes from any share in it (so that a prince's only hope of power was to gain the kabakaship), and the wider distribution of such power in the less centralized Nyoro polity, where princes enjoyed recognized status, and were often appointed to positions of political authority. But the king's brothers were never regarded as preferred successors to the Nyoro throne. In Bunyoro, for kings and commoners alike, youth was not a bar to inheritance. Of course this gave rise to its own problems, and there are many Nyoro stories of elder brothers who, as guardians, converted their younger brothers' patrimony to their own use. It seems also to have meant, in particular, that Nyoro kings were on the whole more dependent on the guidance of their official advisers than the Ganda Kabakas were. The story of

[1] In the end this led, paradoxically, to the weakening of the kingship at the expense of the commoner chiefs, for young kings, lacking in strength and experience, were bound to be dominated by their senior advisers, in particular by the Katikiro (see Southwold, pp. 120–1).

[2] These were the only Bito kings to achieve kingship by rebellion. Two of them rebelled against a *younger* brother, and possibly the others did so as well; information is lacking. See K. W. 1936, pp. 77, 81; 1937a, pp. 54, 59, 62.

Isaza and the zebra hide will be recalled in this connection: it is right that the young should rule, but they neglect the counsel of their elders at their peril.

Turning now to the third main context in which there were important structural differences between the two polities, the conditions under which, and the manner in which, the king's power was actually exercised differed significantly in each of them. Here there are three themes; the traditional nine-year limit on the Nyoro king's reign, the king's role in appointing subordinate authorities, and the difference in the degree of despotism shown by the rulers of the two kingdoms.

In Chapter 3 I gave an account of the rite called *njeru*, said to have been performed in traditional times after a king had ruled for nine years (it will be recalled that nine is an auspicious number for Banyoro). In the course of the ritual the king is supposed formally and publicly to relinquish power: though he could continue to reign, he should henceforward abstain from war, and he should hand over effective governmental powers to his ministers and chiefs. This rule does not seem to have been very often, or very rigorously, observed in practice. K. W., however, explicitly states that four Bito kings carried out the rite of *njeru* 'in order to bring peace to the country', though it does not appear from his account that all of them did so after the specified term of nine years.[1] But whether or not the ritual was ever carried out, in part or in whole, it is certainly quite explicit in Nyoro tradition,[2] and whatever its other significances it plainly implied that the Mukama's powers were traditionally conceived as subject to temporal limitation, a limitation imposed, in at least one instance, by the will of his chiefs and people. No corresponding rite is described for Buganda (to Baganda such an arrangement would have appeared absurd) or, indeed, for any of the other interlacustrine kingdoms.

The second difference between the two kingdoms to be considered under this head is the degree to which the king was personally involved in the appointment to or delegation of political authority throughout the realm (in both kingdoms it

---

[1] As was noted in Chapter 5, the four kings were the fifth, sixth, and eighth of the dynasty (Winyi I, Olimi I, and Winyi II), and the eighteenth, Duhaga I.

[2] It is described also in Fisher, pp. 130–2, and Bikunya, pp. 52–4. Fisher, whose text was based on a manuscript prepared by the kings of Bunyoro and Toro, reports that the first two Bito kings died after reigning for nine years.

could be said, at least ideally, that all authority 'belonged to' the king, so all appointments were in a sense 'delegations' by the ruler). In Buganda every chief and every heir to land, in fact everyone who succeeded to a position of political authority, however subordinate, had to be presented personally to the Kabaka (Richards 1964, p. 362). In Bunyoro this was not so: we saw in Chapter 6 that only the higher ranks of chiefs were required to attend personally at the palace when appointed, to 'drink milk' with the king (or to accept coffee-beans at his hands). In the case of lower authorities the Mukama would send a deputy or representative (*mukwenda*) to install the person appointed to office. This representative did not have to be anyone of great importance. Usually he was a dependant from the palace on whom the king wished to bestow a small favour, for the *mukwenda* would expect to receive a gift from the person he installed. No doubt this difference between the two kingdoms in part reflected the greater compactness and denser population of the Ganda kingdom, and its better communications, but it also clearly expressed in concrete terms the Kabaka's traditional personal concern with and power over all appointments to positions of authority in the kingdom, a power which Kabaka Mutesa II retained until the violent termination of his reign in 1966.

Thirdly, although it is evident that the degree of despotism exercised by traditional African rulers is not precisely measurable (and in any case despotic behaviour by a ruler is not a necessary consequence of a high degree of centralization of power in his hands—though all other things being equal, the greater his monopoly of power the more likely he is to abuse it), the writings of the early European visitors to the interlacustrine kingdoms suggest a far higher degree of ceremonial, formality, and arbitrary cruelty in the Ganda capital than in the Nyoro one. The Ganda palace was, of course, much larger and more elaborate than the Nyoro one.[1] There is nothing in the literature to suggest that in Bunyoro in Kamurasi's and Kabarega's time there was anything like the elaborate ceremonial described for

---

[1] See, for example, the plans of the two capitals and royal enclosures at the end of Roscoe 1911 (between pp. 516–17) and between pp. 86–7 of Roscoe 1923. See also Speke, p. 526, for a reference to the dirty and farmyard-like character of the Nyoro capital.

Mutesa's court by Speke and Grant (Speke, chap. xi; Grant, chap. x). Emin Pasha wrote of Kabarega, about twenty years after Speke's and Grant's visit, that he 'does not appear to care to be bound by ceremony—the exact opposite to Mtésa, the conceited ruler of Ugánda' (p. 62). The accounts in the literature of the daily and arbitrary slaughter of wives and subjects by Mutesa and his successor may have been exaggerated, though the eye-witness accounts of Speke and Grant can hardly have been wholly fabricated. Although no doubt cruelties took place at the Nyoro capital too, they do not seem to have been so constant and conspicuous a feature of daily life as they were in Buganda. Speke (p. 525) describes Kamurasi as 'of a mild disposition compared with Mtésa', and Emin, writing of Kamurasi's successor Kabarega, says that 'a sentence of death is but seldom decreed by the king, for, as Kabréga very justly observed to me, "a dead man pays no taxes"' (1888, p. 89). Such prudent considerations would have been of much less weight in more densely populated Buganda.

No doubt the rulers of both kingdoms sometimes acted despotically; it would be remarkable if they had not. But it seems plain that the size and elaborateness of the Kabaka's court, and the constant arbitrary executions by which he exhibited his life-and-death powers over his subjects, far exceeded anything found in Bunyoro or the other neighbouring countries. Even if this was not a direct consequence of the greater centralization of power in the ruler's hands in the Ganda kingdom, it is evidently entirely compatible with it.

Of the traditional contexts in which the structure of the two kingdoms differed, I consider here, fourthly and lastly, the different ways in which, and extent to which, the kingship was concerned with traditional religious beliefs and practices in the two countries. In neither kingdom was religion of central importance to the kingship; religious belief did not constitute its *raison d'être* as it did in some traditional African kingdoms. Both Buganda and Bunyoro were basically secular monarchies; Roscoe was mistaken in describing the Mukama of Bunyoro as 'the great high priest of the nation', and the Kabaka of Buganda was (if that be possible) even less so. Both rulers had their priests, but they themselves played no priestly role on behalf of their people in relation to the spirit world. Both were indeed

required to participate in a good deal of royal ritual, associated especially with the coronation and with certain annual 'refresher' ceremonies; and from the ethnographic evidence it is plain that more of the Nyoro Mukama's time was taken up in daily ceremonies 'for the good of the country' (mostly associated with cattle) than was the custom in Buganda. In Chapter 5 I developed the theme that much of Bunyoro's royal ritual may be understood as an expression, in symbolic terms, of the Mukama's central authority and power; that much less ceremonial (as opposed to etiquette or 'ceremoniousness')[1] appears to have characterized the Ganda court would seem at least to be consistent with the Kabaka's more thorough and unambiguous grasp of central secular power in his kingdom.

Nevertheless the traditional forms of the spirit mediumship cult, which constituted the religion of the people of both countries in pre-European times, do appear to have reflected a rather closer association between kingship and cult in Buganda than in Bunyoro. Though this relationship in Buganda may be exaggerated (rulers in both countries have not hesitated to suppress cult priests who offended them), the cult of the ghosts of dead kings seems to have been of at least some importance in Buganda. According to Roscoe, 'the ghosts of kings were placed on an equality with the gods, and received the same honour and worship' (1911, p. 283). Roscoe even claimed that the worship of the national gods was under 'the immediate control of the king' (p. 273), but this probably means little more than that the priests of the cults, like everybody else in the kingdom, were directly subject to his power. Fallers remarks that apart from the royal accession and refresher ceremonies, 'the particular structure of Ganda society received little ritual support' (p. 101), but he goes on to say that 'perhaps the most prominent religious specialists were the persons attached to the two types of national religious centre—the *masiro* (tombs) of dead kings and the *biggwa* (temples) of the major gods' (p. 102). As 'national religious centres' the royal tombs were presided over by the 'official sisters' and a number of widows of the deceased Kabaka concerned (or rather by the lineage successors of these persons), and associated with each of them were mediums to transmit the former Kabaka's advice and warnings

---

[1] My attention was drawn to this useful distinction by Dr. M. Southwold.

to his reigning descendants, who were expected to visit the ancestral tombs for this purpose from time to time. It is, then, reasonable to suppose that the cult of the ghosts of dead kings commanded some public interest and importance in traditional Buganda, and that the explicit association of the cult with the ruling dynasty, despite the occasional conflict between them, served at least to some extent to sustain the central and dominant role of the kingship.

In Bunyoro the kingship was, as we have seen, associated with a great deal of ritual, probably more so than the Ganda kingship, but so far as can be ascertained it was little, if at all, assimilated to or even associated with the mediumship cult; certainly it was not so to the same degree as in Buganda. In fact Babito men were expressly debarred from participation in the cult. The tombs of former Nyoro kings (*magasani*) were indeed shrines of national importance, but there is no evidence that they were ever important centres of cult activity, though feasts were held at them from time to time, and, according to Roscoe, a man was chosen each year to represent the dead king and subsequently strangled there (1923, pp. 126–7). The only reference in the ethnography to the ghost of a dead king being prayed to or otherwise approached by a living Mukama is to that of Nyarwa, the tenth Bito king, who was murdered by his brother Chwa I. Chwa and his descendants feared the ghost of the murdered Mukama, and have sought ever since to conciliate it by periodic sacrifice.[1]

In Bunyoro the traditional mediumship cult centred on the Bacwezi hero-gods, who are identified both with certain natural phenomena and with the short-lived and quasi-mythical dynasty supposed to have arrived and vanished mysteriously before the Bito appeared. There is nothing like a national cult of the ghosts of deceased Bakama of the reigning Bito dynasty comparable with that described for the Baganda. The Bito rulers were, of course, central, even semi-divine, figures, and they derived some of their prestige from their mythical link with their marvellous Cwezi predecessors. But they were not Cwezi; their uncouth

---

[1] K. W. 1936, p. 81. Unlike most ghosts, which are associated with the underworld, Nyarwa was said to have ascended into heaven (*akatemba omwiguru*, 'he ascended on high'). Roscoe (1923, p. 211) misquotes and mistranslates the text of a prayer to Nyarwa, apparently without realizing that Nyarwa was a deceased Bito king.

Nilotic origins were not forgotten. Nor were they, in Nyoro thought, the only powerful influence in the kingdom. Apart from the still-powerful spirits of the long-departed Cwezi, the Bahuma pastoralists continued to be thought of as a class (even though they had long since ceased to exist as such in Bunyoro) of superior status to the Babito, whom, as we noted in Chapter 2, they regarded as mere 'peasants' (*bairu*).[1] In these respects, again, although in both kingdoms the traditional religious cults were in some degree seen as standing in opposition to the kingship, they seem to have been even less systematically assimilated to it, at least conceptually, in Bunyoro than in Buganda.

It may be useful now to summarize the foregoing comparisons, bearing in mind that, as I have said, not all the differences listed are equally radical or important, and that some of them are differences in degree or emphasis rather than in kind. I began by listing, as a basis for the structural comparison advanced, eight 'background' differences, the first four ecological and demographic (climate and terrain, staple crops, extent of and regard for pastoralism, and population density); the second four cultural (language, clan systems, kinship terminology, concern with hereditary status). Then, taking the degree of political centralization as the crucial distinction between the two states, I considered differences in political structure and organization under four heads. First, I described Buganda's better communications, and indicated their political and military importance, as compared with Bunyoro's. Second, I discussed differences in the internal organization of the two ruling lines, with particular regard to ideas about their origins, the implications of Buganda's lack of, and Bunyoro's possession of, a royal 'clan', attitudes towards and treatment of royal agnates, and the modes of succession to kingship. Third, I considered the ways in which the royal power was exercised, and discussed the restrictions on it implied by the Nyoro rite of *njeru* (of which there was no Ganda counterpart), the larger part played by the Ganda king in appointments to office, and the higher degree of autocratic despotism which seems to have characterized the Ganda court. And finally, I discussed the different degree in which the kingship was integrated with traditional ritual and religious institutions in the two kingdoms.

[1] Nyakatura, p. 65.

What conclusions, if any, may be drawn from this comparison? The central and underlying theme throughout this chapter has been the higher degree of centralization in the Ganda kingdom, and most of the structural differences which I have described can be seen as expressions, or aspects, of this fundamental distinction. But why should the traditional Ganda state have been so much more centralized than the Nyoro one? The question does not admit of a simple answer. Relevant to it are likely to be a variety of historical events, the emergence of strong or clever leaders at certain times and places, the success or failure of individual invasions, battles and struggles for power, the different incidence of such factors as famine and disease. Evidence about such events as these is for the most part inaccessible to us, and likely to remain so. But even if the physical, ecological, and demographic factors discussed early in this chapter cannot be regarded as sufficient causes of the greater centralization of the Ganda state, some of them may certainly be held to have contributed to it. Buganda's small area and relatively dense population, once they became facts, together with the development of means of rapid communication by both land and water which they made possible, certainly facilitated a more central type of government. A pastoral way of life, followed in at least some parts of traditional Bunyoro, would have been incompatible with a degree of central control comparable with what could be achieved among the denser and more sedentary population of Buganda. The cultivation of plantains as a staple, anyway the work of women rather than men, gave Ganda men much more leisure than the demands of stock-keeping or millet cultivation could provide for Banyoro, and so facilitated a much wider participation in war, politics, and court affairs.

I do not think that we can go much further than this. But to see things in context is at least in some measure to understand them, and a comparison of the two kingdoms against their ecological and (so far as it can be ascertained) historical backgrounds, even at the 'outline' level which is all that has been attempted here, may enable us to understand each of them a little better. That, at least, has been the limited aim of this chapter.

Like so many other kingships, the *Obukama bwa Bunyoro-Kitara* has had its day. No doubt when executive authority has moved from the person of the sovereign to a variety of other decision-making officials and bodies in some form of civil service, as it is bound to do in a modern democratic state, kingship, and with it traditional chiefship, must become an anachronism, retained (if it is retained at all) for reasons that are sentimental, or at least symbolic, rather than utilitarian. But symbols may have practical importance too. There is no doubt that the importance of the Nyoro kingship was steadily declining during the middle years of this century (as that of the Ganda kingship was also, until its dramatic revival after the Kabaka's exile and return in the 1950s). But it was still held in sufficient esteem, especially after its reform in terms of the 1955 Agreement, to have made the case for its retention as a symbol and focus of local Nyoro unity, at any rate for a time, at least arguable. In the 1950s the ordinary Nyoro was first and foremost a Munyoro; he had little intellectual or emotional concern with Uganda nationhood as such (though he had at that time a real fear of Ganda domination in an independent Uganda). The Uganda Protectorate was after all a European invention, and loyalty to the new national state, for which there was no prototype in traditional political thought, could not quickly or easily replace loyalty to a traditional kingdom, which gave the majority of its members a sense of identity and 'belonging' unavailable elsewhere. It might be, and has been, argued that at the time of Uganda's Independence the powerful local loyalties associated with the four interlacustrine Bantu states could, had circumstances been different, have continued to constitute a powerful source of social and political stability, out of which a sense of wider, national identity might gradually have emerged. But however this may be, the experiment was not tried; Buganda, in bringing destruction upon itself brought it also on its three neighbours, and Mr. Obote's Order of 8 September 1967 became inevitable.

Of course, the processes of rapid social and political change which were taking place in Bunyoro in the 1950s and before, some of which I have described in this book, have not ceased since Independence. The people whose institutions we have been considering are no longer members of the Nyoro State,

but of the Republic of Uganda. But I think it is likely that enough of their characteristic institutions, beliefs, and values still survive—rapidly changing though they may be—to enable them to make, as Banyoro, their own distinctive contributions to the new state.

GLOSSARY OF RUNYORO WORDS
USED IN TEXT[1]

BUKAMA, O-. The Nyoro kingship, also the Nyoro kingdom.

BUKUNGU, O-. Village headmanship, or the area administered by a village headman (MUKUNGU); same as BUTONGOLE.

BULEMI, O-. Government: the substantive form of the verb LEMA.

BURO, O-. Finger millet (eleusine), the staple grain.

BUSURU, O-. Payment formerly made by peasants to the proprietors of the land they lived on.

BUTONGOLE, O-. Same as BUKUNGU.

GOMBOLOLA. Sub-county (from Luganda).

KA, E- (pl. MAKA, A-). Home, household; residential family group.

KALYOTA. The king's 'official sister'.

KATIKIRO. The king's chief minister (from Luganda).

KIBANJA, E- (pl. BIBANJA, E-). An estate in land, often containing peasant occupants.

KIKALI, E-. The king's enclosure.

KONDO, E- (pl. MAKONDO, A-). Crown worn by king and specially favoured senior chiefs (ABAJWARA KONDO).

INURA, OKU-. To give a feast for dependants, as king or chiefs for people.

LEMA, OKU-. To rule, govern; to be too hard for or too much for.

TINA, OKU-. To fear, respect.

KWIRI, O-. The head of the Babito; the king's eldest brother.

KYARO, E-. A settled area, neighbourhood.

MAHANO, A- (sing. IHANO). Something wonderful, out of the ordinary; dangerous ritual quality or power.

MAKUNE, A-. Politeness; good manners.

MPAKO, E-. Honorific personal name or title, of Nilotic origin.

MUBITO, O- (pl. BABITO, A-). Member of royal clan.

MUBITOKATI, O- (pl. BABITOKATI, A-). Woman of royal clan.

MUCWEZI, O- (pl. BACWEZI, A-). (1) Member of dynasty of ancient rulers; (2) spirit associated with that dynasty, object of the MBANDWA spirit mediumship cult; (3) member of the BACWEZI clan.

[1] I follow M. B. Davis (1938) in listing nouns under their prefixes, giving the initial vowel after the word; verbs (which all have the same prefix, OKU-) are listed alphabetically according to their roots.

MUGEMA, O-. Chief having custody of the royal tombs.

MUGONGO, O-. Raised and usually populated area of land between streams and swamps.

MUHUMA, O- (pl. BAHUMA, A-). A person claiming pastoral descent; a cattle-herder.

MUJAGUZI, O-. King's head regalia man.

MUJWEKI, O- (pl. BAJWEKI, A-). 'One who dresses another'; custodians of king's crowns and apparel.

MUKAMA W'EKIBANJA, O- (pl. BAKAMA B'EBIBANJA, A-). Proprietor of an estate in land, usually with peasant occupants.

MUKETO, O-. The king's treasurer.

MUKUNGU, O- (pl. BAKUNGU, A-). Formerly a great chief, equivalent to county chief; in recent times village headman, same as MUTONGOLE.

MULEMI, O-. Ruler, chief: from verb LEMA.

MUNYAMIRWA, O- (pl. BANYAMIRWA, A-). Palace official.

MUNYORO, O- (pl. BANYORO, A-). (1) A member of the Nyoro people; (2) a chief or other eminent person.

MURAMUZI, O-. The king's chief judge.

MUSEKURA, O- (pl. BASEKURA, A-). Informal adviser to the king.

MUSIGIRE, O-. Deputy.

MUTEMBUZI, O- (pl. BATEMBUZI, A-). Member of Bunyoro's first dynasty of rulers.

MUTONGOLE, O- (pl. BATONGOLE, A-). Village headman; same as MUKUNGU.

MUZIRO, O- (pl. MIZIRO, E-). Object of ritual respect and avoidance.

MWIHWA, O- (pl. BAIHWA, A-). Child of a woman of one's clan; 'sister's son'.

NGOMA, E-. Drum; the Nyoro kingship.

NYINA OMUKAMA. The king's mother.

NYINEKA. The head of a household.

NZIGU, E-. Blood vengeance.

RUGANDA, O- (pl. NGANDA, E-). Clan; aggregate of putative agnates, whether these constitute a group or not.

RUKURATO, O- (pl. NKURATO, E-). Council, court.

SAZA (or ISAZA) (pl. MASAZA, A-). County.

BIBLIOGRAPHY

ANDRZEJEWSKI, S., 1954. *Military organization and society*, Routledge & Kegan Paul, London.

ASHE, R. P., 1894. *Chronicles of Uganda*, Hodder and Stoughton, London.

BAKER, S., 1867. *The Albert N'yanza, great basin of the Nile and explorations of the Nile sources*, vol. 2, Macmillan, London.

—— 1874. *Ismailia*, vol. 2, Macmillan, London.

BEATTIE, J. H. M., 1954a. 'The *Kibanja* system of land tenure in Bunyoro, Uganda', *Journal of African Administration*, 6. 1. 18–28.

—— 1954b. 'A further note on the *Kibanja* system of land tenure in Bunyoro', ibid. 6. 4. 178–85.

—— 1957a. 'Nyoro kinship', *Africa*, xxvii. 4. 317–39.

—— 1957b. 'Informal judicial activity in Bunyoro', *Journal of African Administration*, ix. 4. 188–95.

—— 1958a. 'Nyoro marriage and affinity', *Africa*, xxviii. 1. 1–22.

—— 1958b. 'The blood pact in Bunyoro', *African Studies*, 17. 4. 198–203.

—— 1959. 'Rituals of Nyoro kingship', *Africa*, xxix. 2. 134–44.

—— 1960a. *Bunyoro: an African kingdom*, Holt, New York.

—— 1960b. 'The Nyoro', Chapter 6 in RICHARDS, A. I. (ed.), *East African chiefs*, Faber (for the East African Institute of Social Research), London.

—— 1960c. 'On the Nyoro concept of '*mahano*', *African Studies*, 19. 3. 145–50.

—— 1961a. 'Democratization in Bunyoro', *Civilisations*, 11. 1. 8–18.

—— 1961b. 'Group aspects of the Nyoro spirit mediumship cult', *Rhodes–Livingstone Journal*, 30. 11–38.

—— 1961c. 'Nyoro mortuary rites', *Uganda Journal*, 25. 2. 171–83.

—— 1963. 'Sorcery in Bunyoro', in MIDDLETON, J., and WINTER, E. H. (eds.), *Witchcraft and sorcery in East Africa*, Routledge & Kegan Paul, London, pp. 27–55.

—— 1964a. 'Bunyoro: an African feudality?', *Journal of African History*, 5. 1. 25–35. (Republished in DALTON, G. (ed.), *Tribal and peasant economies*, Natural History Press, New York, 1967, pp. 80–101.)

—— 1964b. 'Rainmaking in Bunyoro', *Man*, 64. 179. 140–1.

—— 1965. *Understanding an African kingdom: Bunyoro*, Holt, Rinehart and Winston, New York.

—— 1968. 'Aspects of Nyoro symbolism', *Africa*, xxxviii. 4. 413–42.

—— 1969. 'Spirit mediumship in Bunyoro', in BEATTIE, J., and MIDDLETON, J. (eds.), *Spirit mediumship and society in Africa*, Routledge & Kegan Paul, London, pp. 159–70.

BIKUNYA, P., 1927. *Ky' Abakama ba Bunyoro*, Sheldon Press, London.

BLOCH, M., 1961. *Feudal society* (trans. L. A. Manyon), Routledge & Kegan Paul, London.

BURKE, F. G., 1964. *Local government and politics in Uganda*, Syracuse University Press, Syracuse, N.Y.

CASATI, G., 1891. *Ten years in Equatoria and the return with Emin Pasha* (trans. Mrs. J. R. Clay), vol. ii, Warne, London & New York.

COLVILE, H., 1895. *The land of the Nile springs*, Arnold, London.

CRAZZOLARA, J. P., 1937. 'The Lwoo people', *Uganda Journal*, 5. 1. 1–21.

—— 1950. *The Lwoo, Part I, Lwoo migrations*, Missioni Africane, Verona.

CZEKANOWSKI, J., 1917. *Wissenschaftliche Ergebnisse der Deutschen Zentral-Afrika Expedition 1907–1908, vol. vi/i: Forschungen im Nil-Congo Zwischengebiet*, Klinkhardt and Biermann, Leipzig.

DAVIS, M. B., 1938. *A Lunyoro–Lunyankole–English and English–Lunyoro–Lunyankole dictionary*, Uganda Bookshop, Kampala; S.P.C.K., London.

DUNBAR, A. R., 1965. *A history of Bunyoro–Kitara* (East African Studies, 19), O.U.P., Nairobi, for East African Institute of Social Research.

EMIN PASHA (EDUARD SCHNITZER), 1888. *Emin Pasha in Central Africa, being a collection of his letters and journals*, ed. and annotated by G. Schweinfurth, F. Ratzel, R. W. Felkin, and G. Hartlaub, Philip, London.

—— 1916–21. *Die Tagebücher von Emin Pascha*, ed. Dr. Franz Stuhlmann, vols. i, ii, iii, iv, and vi, Georg Westermann, Braunschweig.

EVANS-PRITCHARD, E. E., 1962. 'The divine kingship of the Shilluk of the Nilotic Sudan' (The Frazer Lecture, 1948), chap. 4 in EVANS-PRITCHARD, E. E., *Essays in social anthropology*, Faber and Faber, London, pp. 66–86.

FALLERS, L. A., 1964. 'Social stratification in traditional Buganda', chap. 2 in FALLERS, L. A. (ed.), *The king's men*, O.U.P., London, for East African Institute of Social Research, pp. 64–116.

—— (ed.), 1964. *The king's men*, O.U.P., London, for East African Institute of Social Research.

FISHER, A. B., 1911. *Twilight tales of the black Baganda*, Marshall, London.

FRAZER, Sir J., 1911. *The dying god (The golden bough*, 3rd edn., part iii), Macmillan, London.

GANSHOF, F. L., 1952. *Feudalism* (trans. P. Grierson), Longmans Green, London.

GESSI PASHA, R., 1892. *Seven years in the Soudan* (trans. Wolffsohn and Woodward), Sampson Low, Marston, London.

GIRLING, F. K., 1960. *The Acholi of Uganda*, H.M.S.O., London.

GOODY, J., 1963. 'Feudalism in Africa?', *Journal of African History*, 4. 1. 1–18.

GORJU, J., 1920. *Entre le Victoria, l'Albert, et l'Édouard: Ethnographie de la partie anglaise du vicariat de l'Uganda*, Imprimeries Oberthür, Rennes.

GRANT, J. A., 1864. *A walk across Africa*, Blackwood, Edinburgh and London.

HAILEY, Lord, 1946. Introduction to MEEK, C. K., *Land law and custom in the colonies*, O.U.P., London.

—— 1950. *Native administration in the British African territories: Part I, East Africa; Uganda, Kenya, Tanganyika*, H.M.S.O., London.

—— 1957. *An African survey* (revised edn., 1956), O.U.P., London.

JOHNSTON, H., 1902. *The Uganda Protectorate*, Hutchinson, London.

K. W., 1935. 'The kings of Bunyoro–Kitara', *Uganda Journal*, 3. 2. 155–60.

—— 1936. 'The kings of Bunyoro–Kitara, Part II', ibid. 4. 1. 75–83.

—— 1937a. 'The kings of Bunyoro–Kitara, Part III', ibid. 5. 2. 53–69.

K. W., 1937*b*. 'The procedure in accession to the throne of a nominated King in the kingdom of Bunyoro–Kitara', *Uganda Journal*, 4. 4. 289–99.

KAGWA, Sir A., 1934. (First published in Luganda, 1905) *The customs of the Baganda* (trans. E. B. Kalibala and ed. M. Mandelbaum Edel), Columbia University Press, New York.

KARUBANGA, H. K., 1949. *Bukya nibwira*, Eagle Press, Nairobi.

KATYANKU, L., and BULERA, S., 1950. *Obwomezi bw'Omukama Duhaga II*, Eagle Press, Nairobi.

LUGARD, F. D., 1892. *British East Africa and Uganda: a historical record compiled from Captain Lugard's and other reports*, Chapman and Hall, London.

—— 1893. *The rise of our East African empire*, Blackwood, Edinburgh and London.

—— *c.* 1900. *The story of the Uganda Protectorate*, Horace Marshall, London.

MACIVER, R. M., 1947. *The web of government*, Macmillan, New York.

—— and PAGE, C. H., 1950. *Society: an introductory analysis*, Macmillan, London (English edn.).

MAQUET, J. J., 1961. *The premise of inequality in Ruanda*, O.U.P., London for International African Institute.

MAUSS, M., 1954. *The gift* (trans. by I. Cunnison), Cohen and West, London.

MEEK, C. K., 1946. *Land law and custom in the colonies*, O.U.P., London.

MOLSON, Lord. See under UGANDA.

MORRIS, H. F., 1962. *A history of Ankole*, East African Literature Bureau, Kampala.

—— 1964. *The heroic recitations of the Bahima of Ankole* (Oxford Library of African Literature), Clarendon Press, Oxford.

MURDOCK, G. P., 1959. *Africa, its peoples and their culture history*, McGraw-Hill, New York.

NEEDHAM, R., 1967. 'Right and left in Nyoro symbolic classification', *Africa*, xxxvii. 3. 425–52.

NSIMBE, M. B., 1968. *Omweso: a game people play in Uganda*, Occasional Paper no. 6, African Studies Center, University of California, Los Angeles.

NYAKATURA, J., 1947. *Abakama ba Bunyoro Kitara*, St. Justin, P.Q., Canada.

OBERG, K., 1940. 'The Ankole', in FORTES, M., and EVANS-PRITCHARD, E. E. (eds), *African political systems*, O.U.P., London, for International African Institute, pp. 121–62.

OGOT, B. A., 1967. *History of the Southern Luo, vol. i, migration and settlement*, East African Publishing House, Nairobi.

OLIVER, R., 1953. 'A question about the Bachwezi', *Uganda Journal*, 17. 2. 135–7.

—— 1955. 'The traditional histories of Buganda, Bunyoro and Nkole', *Journal of the Royal Anthropological Institute*, 85. 111–17.

—— 1963. 'Discernible developments in the interior, *c.* 1500–1840', chap. 6 in OLIVER, R., and MATHEW, G. (eds.), *History of East Africa*, vol. i, Clarendon Press, Oxford.

POSNANSKY, M., 1966. 'Kingship, archaeology and historical myth', *Uganda Journal*, 30. 1. 1–12.

POSTLETHWAITE, J., 1947. *I look back*, Boardman, London.

RADCLIFFE-BROWN, A. R., 1940. Preface to FORTES, M., and EVANS-PRITCHARD, E. E. (eds.), *African political systems*, O.U.P., London, for International African Institute, xi–xxi.
—— 1952. *Structure and function in primitive society*, Cohen and West, London.
RICHARDS, A. I., 1964. Epilogue to FALLERS, L. A. (ed.), *The king's men*, O.U.P., London, for East African Institute of Social Research, 357–94.
—— 1966. *The changing structure of a Ganda village*, East African Studies no. 24. East African Publishing House (East African Institute Press), Nairobi.
ROBERTS, A. D., 1962. 'The Lost Counties of Bunyoro', *Uganda Journal*, 26. 2. 194–9.
ROSCOE, J., 1911. *The Baganda*, Macmillan, London.
—— 1922. *The soul of Central Africa*, Cassell, London.
—— 1923. *The Bakitara or Banyoro*, C.U.P., Cambridge.
RUBIE, J. G., and THOMAS, H. B. See under UGANDA PROTECTORATE.
SCHAPERA, I., 1953. 'Some comments on comparative method in social anthropology', *American Anthropologist*, 55. 3. 353–62.
SELIGMAN, C. G., 1934. *Egypt and negro Africa: a study in divine kingship* (The Frazer Lecture, 1933), Routledge, London.
SOUTHALL, A. W., 1953. *Alur society*, Heffer, Cambridge.
SOUTHWOLD, M., 1966. 'Succession to the throne in Buganda' in GOODY, J. (ed.), *Succession to high office*, Cambridge Paper in Social Anthropology no. 4, C.U.P. for the Department of Archaeology and Anthropology, pp. 82–126.
SPEKE, J. H., 1863. *Journal of the discovery of the source of the Nile*, Blackwood, Edinburgh.
STANLEY, H. M., 1878. *Through the dark continent* (2 vols.), Sampson Low, Marston, Searle and Rivington, London.
SWARTZ, M. J., TURNER, V. W., and TUDEN, A. (eds.), 1966. *Political anthropology*, Aldine Press, Chicago.
THRUSTON, A. B., 1900. *African incidents*, Murray, London.
UGANDA: *Report of a Commission of Privy Counsellors on a dispute between Buganda and Bunyoro* (the 'Molson Report'), 1962, H.M.S.O., London.
UGANDA PROTECTORATE, 1932. *Enquiry into land tenure and the Kibanja system in Bunyoro, 1931*, Report of the Committee (the 'Rubie and Thomas Report'), Entebbe, Uganda.
WILSON, L. T., and FELKIN, R., 1882. *Uganda and the Egyptian Soudan*, vol. i, Sampson Low, Marston, Searle and Rivington, London.
WOOD, J. G., 1868. *The natural history of man, being an account of the manners and customs of the uncivilized races of men: Africa*, Routledge, London.
WRIGLEY, C. C., 1958. 'Some thoughts on the Bachwezi', *Uganda Journal*, 22. 1. 11–17.

INDEX

ЛЕНИНГРАД

CATHOLIC THEOLOGICAL UNION

3 0311 00136 1109

WITHDRAWN

DT 433.245 .N92 B42 1971
Beattie, John.
The Nyoro state

DEMCO

W9-CWV-012

The Catholic
Theological Union
LIBRARY
Chicago, Ill.